Mailing Lists

There are many Internet mailing lists dedicated to discussions about Linux. For more information, you can send an e-mail message to majordomo@vger.rutgers.edu with only the word lists in the body.

ftp Sites

You will find files about Linux on all of these anonymous ftp sites:

Site	Directory	Contents
sunsite.unc.edu	/pub/Linux	Source of up-to-date Linux kernels and many other Linux files; also store-house of the Linux Documentation Project manuals
tsx-11.mit.edu	/pub/linux	A general repository of programs and files about Linux
ftp.cdrom.com	/pub/linux	Home of Slackware Linux

World Wide Web Pages

The following World Wide Web pages deal with Linux or Linux-related software:

http://sunsite.unc.edu/mdw	The best jumping off point for information about Linux
http://www.xfree86.org	The home page of the XFree86 Project, the people who ported the X Window system to Linux

The Complete Linux Kit

Compiled by
Daniel A. Tauber

SYBEX®

San Francisco • Paris • Düsseldorf • Soest

Acquisitions Manager: Kristine Plachy

Developmental Editor: Gary Masters

Editor: Kris Vanberg-Wolff

Technical Editor: Gary Foster

Book Designer: Suzanne Albertson

Technical Artist: Cuong Le

Desktop Publisher: Lynell Decker

Screen Graphics Manager: Aldo X. Bermudez

Production Assistant: Rhonda Holmes

Indexer: Ted Laux

Cover Designer: Joanna Kim Gladden

Library of Congress Card Number: 94-74628

ISBN: 0-7821-1669-8

Manufactured in the United States of America

10 9 8 7 6 5 4

Warranty

SYBEX warrants the enclosed CD to be free of physical defects for a period of ninety (90) days after purchase. If you discover a defect in the CD during this warranty period, you can obtain a replacement CD at no charge by sending the defective CD, postage prepaid, with proof of purchase to:

SYBEX Inc.
Customer Service Department
2021 Challenger Drive
Alameda, CA 94501
(800) 227-2346
Fax: (510) 523-2373

After the 90-day period, you can obtain a replacement CD by sending us the defective CD, proof of purchase, and a check or money order for $10, payable to SYBEX.

Disclaimer

SYBEX makes no warranty or representation, either express or implied, with respect to this medium or its contents, its quality, performance, merchantability, or fitness for a particular purpose. In no event will SYBEX, its distributors, or dealers be liable for direct, indirect, special, incidental, or consequential damages arising out of the use of or inability to use the medium or its contents even if advised of the possibility of such damage.

The exclusion of implied warranties is not permitted by some states. Therefore, the above exclusion may not apply to you. This warranty provides you with specific legal rights; there may be other rights that you may have that vary from state to state.

To Linus B. Torvalds and all the others who have worked to make a free operating system a reality.

ACKNOWLEDGMENTS

I would like to acknowledge the people who have contributed to creating Linux: Linus B. Torvalds for writing Linux itself; Matt Welsh for writing the *Linux Installation and Getting Started* manual, which is included here with his permission as Book II, and for coordinating the Linux Documentation Project; and Patrick Volkerding, for assembling and maintaining Slackware Linux.

At Sybex, thanks go to Dr. R.S. Langer and Gary Masters, who championed this project; Kris Vanberg-Wolff for quietly and persistently editing the manuscript; and Gary Foster for reviewing the manuscript for technical accuracy. Thanks also to Barbara Gordon, Chris Meredith, Kristine Plachy, Janet Boone, and Celeste Grinage for their many contributions at Sybex; and to the production team of Rhonda Holmes and Lynell Decker, who made this book a physical reality.

Aaron Kushner introduced me to Linux, and Erik Ingenito convinced me it was a real operating system. They certainly deserve some credit for the existence of this book.

My family—Margaret Tauber, Ron and Frances Tauber, and Jessica and Martin Grant—remain a source of support and encouragement for which I am always grateful. Finally, my thanks to Brenda Kienan, companion and colleague, who first suggested I write a book, then co-authored seven, and then assisted with this one.

CONTENTS AT A GLANCE

TABLE OF CONTENTS

INTRODUCTION

What you have in your hands is something new in the world of computers. While many people have dreamed of a free, full-featured operating system for a long time, it took Linus B. Torvalds, along with hundreds of other operating system developers from all over the world, to make the idea a reality in the form of Linux. Linux is new in the sense that it was not developed by a commercial organization for profit; it was developed so that it would be available to anyone who wanted to use and improve it for distribution to others who could use and improve it. Linux is a Unix clone—a completely workable, robust operating system like Unix—but one that you can use on your PC.

To get Linux, you must usually download it from the Internet—a process that can take days—or buy it on a CD from mail-order sources that don't include a book with the software.

As a longtime Linux fan and user, I wanted to provide a CD-ROM/book package that would bring together the best Linux options in an easy-to-install format. In this kit, you will find:

- A CD-ROM containing Slackware Linux and its source code
- Detailed instructions on installing Slackware Linux, including information on the X Window system and the DOS Emulator (Book I)
- Matt Welsh's *Linux Installation and Getting Started* manual (Book II)

What's on the CD-ROM

The CD-ROM that comes with this kit contains Slackware Linux— the most full-featured and easy-to-install distribution of Linux around. It includes X Window, the GNU C Compiler, communications programs, TCP/IP networking software, and more. In addition to Slackware Linux, you will find its source code, a DOS Emulator that lets you run DOS applications under Linux, a full set of manuals about Linux produced by the Linux Documentation Project, and many other helpful HOWTO files. There are thousands of files on the CD-ROM—you'll find everything you need to make the most of Linux.

How This Book Is Organized

This book is divided into two sections. Book I was written by me, Dan Tauber, and includes detailed instructions for installing Slackware Linux. Book II was written by Matt Welsh and contains information about Linux and Unix in general.

What's in Book I

The detailed instructions in Book I will help you get Slackware Linux quickly installed to an *existing* DOS drive. The real bonus here is that you don't have to go through the usually required, time-consuming process of repartitioning your hard drive. Book I also includes information that will help you install and use the X Window system and DOS Emulator that come on the CD.

What's in Book II

Book II contains Matt Welsh's *Linux Installation and Getting Started* manual. Here you will find all the information you need to start using any form of Linux, including Slackware. Whether you are a Unix newbie or an experienced guru, you will find useful information in Book II.

Who You Are

In preparing this kit, I had to make some assumptions about who you are and what you know. Generally, I assumed that you already have some experience using a computer, and that you know the basics of using MS-DOS—how to format a disk and copy a file, for example. While some of you may already be familiar with Unix, such knowledge is not necessary. Book I includes all the information you'll need to install Slackware Linux from the CD-ROM, and Book II provides a valuable overview of Unix and how it applies to Slackware Linux.

Conventions Used in This Book

Throughout this book a consistent set of typographical conventions have been used to help you understand the information presented. *Italic* is used both to present terms that may be new to the reader and to provide emphasis. Anything that you are instructed to type appears in a special font, `like this`. This same font is used for commands, usernames, and filenames.

Some information is set aside from the regular text in the form of Notes, Tips, and Warnings.

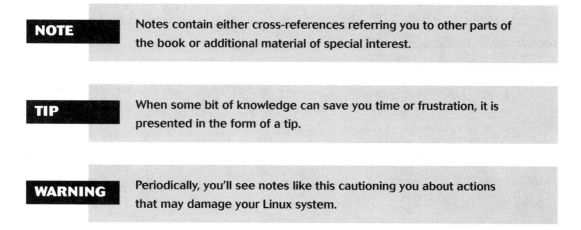

NOTE Notes contain either cross-references referring you to other parts of the book or additional material of special interest.

TIP When some bit of knowledge can save you time or frustration, it is presented in the form of a tip.

WARNING Periodically, you'll see notes like this cautioning you about actions that may damage your Linux system.

Linux Installation and Getting Started, which is included as Book II, uses some additional conventions. See the preface to Book II for a description of these.

Time to Get Started

Get ready, get set, let's go. As you turn the pages that follow and install the CD, you will learn how to turn your 386-based computer into a Unix workstation.

BOOK I

Getting Going with
Slackware Linux

Daniel A. Tauber

What is Linux?

- What's So Great About Linux?

- Where Linux Came From

- Where Slackware Comes In

- Slackware Linux Compared to Other Unix Operating Systems

What's So Great About Linux?

Don't let the name confuse you—Linux is, by any measure, the same as Unix. It is, however, the first full-featured, Unix-compatible, 32-bit operating system available for a 386, 486, or Pentium-based computer that is free *and* easy to install. Once you have installed Linux on your computer, you'll have access to everything you expect from a Unix workstation.

You will find Slackware Linux, which is included on the CD-ROM that comes with this book, ready for a whole suite of tasks. You will also find that Slackware Linux provides a perfect way for you to learn about Unix and Unix system administration. With Slackware Linux, you will be able to run MS-DOS programs from Linux using the DOS Emulator included on the CD-ROM. You'll also find many games to keep you amused. And, since we include the full source code for Slackware Linux on the CD-ROM, you can actually *see* how the operating system works. The braver souls among you can even venture into making improvements to Linux and see how your improvements work.

As you become more comfortable with the basic features of Slackware Linux, you can start exploring any of the more specialized pieces of software that come with the package. Slackware Linux includes software that allows you to do all sorts of things, from connecting to the Internet to developing software to desktop publishing.

Slackware Linux includes all the communications and Internet tools that are common on any Unix workstation—everything from TCP/IP to UUCP, and all the programs you use with them. It also comes with e-mail programs that allow you to send and receive electronic mail, and includes software that brings Usenet news directly to your computer.

The software development tools that come with Slackware Linux are excellent. You'll have the choice of working with C, C++, Objective C, Lisp, or SmallTalk. By installing Slackware Linux on a PC at your home, you can start developing software that you can easily move over to other Unix machines.

Slackware Linux also includes X Window Version 11 Release 6, which is the standard windowing system for Unix workstations. X Window allows you to see many programs running at the same time—each in a separate window. Slackware Linux's X Window package comes with many X Window applications, ranging from paint programs and fractal generators to games.

I have also provided on the CD-ROM a version of TEX, one of the most powerful and flexible typesetting packages available. While TEX does not give you the ease of use of a WYSIWYG (What-You-See-Is-What-You-Get) word processor, it does give you all the power you need to lay out and produce complicated book-length documents. Once Slackware Linux is on your machine, you are ready to start using TEX.

In Book I, I will show you how to install Slackware Linux on your PC from the enclosed CD-ROM. By the time you are done with this book, you will have a ready-to-use Unix machine on your desk.

Where Linux Came From

NOTE See Chapter 7 for information about Internet resources for Linux, including Usenet newsgroups dedicated to the discussion of Linux.

Linux started as a learning project for Linus Torvalds while he was an undergraduate student at the University of Helsinki. He had been working with another operating system distributed with source code—but not freely—called Minix. According to a Usenet message he later posted announcing his work, he started Linux 'just as a hobby'. What started as a hobby has turned into one of the most robust operating systems available.

The original goal of Linux was not to provide a full operating system, but rather to produce the kernel of an operating system. As the usefulness of Linux grew, so did the number of people helping Linus write it. People with specific skills in certain areas of the kernel took over those parts. Currently, Linus coordinates a team of hundreds of programmers from around the world, all volunteering their time to help make Linux a reality.

A Brief History of Free Software

You may find the idea of a free operating system funny at first—even hard to believe. Freeware has always played an important role in the computer science community. Long before commercial companies started creating and distributing software, most software was given away in source code. The point of giving away source code was twofold: first, it allowed the programs to be distributed and used on many computers; second, it allowed other programmers to learn from the programs.

Linux fulfills both of these points. Since the full source code to Linux (and all the software that makes up Slackware Linux) is freely available, you can use it to learn about operating systems. In addition, having the source code available has made a number of *ports* (translations of Linux to other computers besides the 386 PC) possible. At the moment, Linus is working on a version of Linux for the DEC Alpha computer, and other people are working on versions for the Motorola 68030 and PowerPC computers.

Many of the freely available programs that come with Slackware Linux are the result of the Free Software Foundation's GNU project. The GNU Project— which stands for GNU's Not Unix—was started when Richard Stallman decided to write a free operating system. What started as one man's vision has turned into an international project with many people participating in writing the pieces of software that are needed to create a free operating system. The eventual goal of the Free Software Foundation's GNU project is to build a free operating system much like Linux. Even though the Free Software Foundation's GNU Project is working on a different operating system than Linux— known as *The Hurd*—much of their work has helped Linux. For example, the Linux kernel is compiled with the C compiler written by the Free Software Foundation.

Another source for many pieces of Slackware Linux is the University of California at Berkeley. U. C. Berkeley has been involved in developing variations on Unix for many years. Recently, they have started to freely distribute their version of Unix for the 386 with source code under the name FreeBSD. Some of the source code from FreeBSD has made its way into Slackware Linux.

Where Slackware Comes In

1

Linux itself is only a *kernel*—or the heart—of a Unix-like operating system. It knows how to read and write to disk drives, allocate memory, and do other very basic manipulations of your computer's hardware. Many of the pieces of the operating system that you interact with, such as the login program you see when you first start a Linux session and the shell that allows you to type commands for the computer to execute, are external programs. Programs like these are not part of the Linux kernel. So, to turn Linux into a full-featured operating system, complete with all the extra programs you need, Linux needs to be bundled with lots of other software. A number of groups have started to build distributions based on the Linux kernel. Slackware is the most popular and easiest to use of these Linux distributions.

Slackware takes the Linux kernel and builds a full operating system around it. It includes thousands of programs, including the GNU C compiler, MIT's X Window windowing system, the emacs text editor, games, network utilities, and much, much more.

Slackware Linux Compared to Other Unix Operating Systems

The Slackware Linux installation process is as easy, if not more so, as that of any other commercial version of Unix. Instead of spending days getting Unix up and running on your machine, you'll have a working system in half an hour. Once you have Slackware Linux installed on your machine, you can start developing software using all of the software development tools that accompany Slackware. You can also start accessing the Internet, whether via a dial-up connection with the SLIP/PPP software that comes with Slackware, or with the included ethernet drivers. In short, Slackware Linux allows you to do everything that you can do with any other version of Unix.

CHAPTER

2

Prepping Your Machine for Slackware Linux

- What You Need

- Prepping Your Hard Disk

- Creating the Boot and Root Diskettes

Slackware Linux is a powerful operating system based on Unix. As with other forms of Unix, you must do some preparatory work before you can start installing it. In this chapter, I'll show you how to check your disk drive to see if it's ready for Slackware Linux, and how to create the two floppy diskettes needed to start the installation process from files provided on the CD-ROM.

> **NOTE** You can install Slackware Linux either to an existing DOS drive or to an empty partition on your hard disk. In this book, we'll show you how to install Slackware Linux to an existing DOS drive without erasing the data already stored on the drive. Without the hassle of repartitioning your hard disk, you'll have Slackware Linux up and running in no time. You'll find notes throughout this book with specific information about creating a partition dedicated to just Slackware Linux.

One oddity in preparing your machine for Slackware Linux is that you must be working from DOS. While this may sound funny at first, it actually makes a lot of sense. Before you install Slackware Linux, you need to run a number of programs to make sure that your hard drive is ready. In order to run these programs, you need to be running an operating system, and since I can safely assume that you already have MS-DOS installed on your computer, I'll use that as the operating system.

What You Need

When determining whether your hardware is supported by Slackware Linux, keep in mind that Linux was developed primarily on inexpensive IBM PC clone computers. This means that the more common a particular piece of hardware is, the more likely it is that you will find it supported by Linux. You will find a summary of supported hardware on the inside front cover of this book. See Chapter 1 of Book II for more detailed information. In general, your computer should include:

- a 386SX or better CPU
- at least 4 MB of RAM

- an IDE hard disk and controller, with at least 20 MB of available storage
- a CD-ROM drive

NOTE While Slackware Linux supports other types of hard disks and controllers besides IDE, in this book we focus on getting Slackware Linux up and running with an IDE hard disk and controller. You'll find notes throughout the book with information about using Slackware Linux with a SCSI disk drive, although we do not cover the subject in depth.

For a Minimal System

For a minimal working system, you'll want to have a 386SX or 386DX CPU, 4 MB of RAM, and 20 MB of free disk space. 20 MB of disk space is just enough to install the bare minimum of what Slackware Linux has to offer. You will soon find yourself wanting more space so you can use some of the extra goodies that come on the CD-ROM.

For a Useful System

While the minimal system described above will allow you to get Slackware Linux up and running and to get a basic feel for the system, it will not allow you to install and use any of the many "extras" that come with Slackware Linux. If you want to start really using Slackware Linux, you will find that you need a 386 or better CPU with 8 MB of RAM and at least 100 MB of disk space.

If You Want to Run X Window

One of the most popular programs that you can run with Linux is MIT's X Window windowing system. The Slackware Linux CD-ROM that comes with this book includes X window version 11 release 6. If you want to run X Window on your computer, you will need additional memory. X Window itself can fit nicely, along with the rest of Linux, onto a 100 MB drive with a minimum of 8 MB of RAM, but you will find that the system runs much faster if you have at least 16 MB of RAM.

Prepping Your Hard Disk

The first step in installing Slackware Linux is to verify that your hard disk is ready to hold the software. In this section, I'll show you how to verify that the DOS file system used by both DOS and Linux to keep track of your files is error free.

Checking Your DOS Drive

Unfortunately, the data used to keep track of files on a DOS disk tends to get corrupted fairly often. This can happen any time the computer is either turned off or crashes. Usually, this does not have a noticeable effect on DOS programs, but Slackware Linux is made up of many thousands of files, and errors in the file system can wreak havoc. Here we will show you how to check your DOS drives and repair any errors. You will also find out how much free storage space you have on your hard disk.

With DOS 6.0 or Newer

Starting with DOS 6.0, Microsoft introduced SCANDISK, a program that scans your hard disk for errors. Using SCANDISK, you can identify and fix any problems with the way information is stored on the disk. In order to use SCANDISK to check the status of the C: drive, do the following:

1. From the MS-DOS command line, type scandisk c: and then press ↵. SCANDISK will start running and will display information on the screen, as shown in Figure 2.1. If you are planning on installing Slackware Linux to a drive other than C:, substitute that drive letter for C: above.

   SCANDISK checks your disk for a whole host of possible errors. If it finds any errors while it is checking your hard disk, it will display a message on screen like the one shown in Figure 2.2 , and give you the option of fixing the error. You should elect to have SCANDISK fix any errors that it finds, and continue.

2. Once SCANDISK is finished checking the DOS file system for errors, it will ask if you want to check the physical media for errors. You should elect to do this by pressing Alt-Y.

FIGURE 2.1:

As it checks your disk drive for errors, SCANDISK keeps you informed by displaying messages on screen.

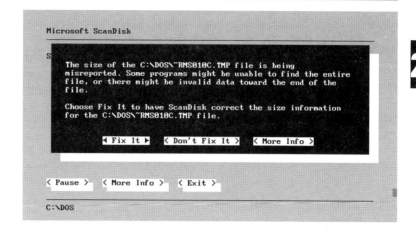

SCANDISK will now check for any physical errors on the hard disk. If it encounters any, you should tell it to mark the sector as bad so it will not be used to hold Slackware Linux.

With DOS Prior to Version 6.0

In versions prior to DOS 6.0, Microsoft included CHKDSK, a program that verifies the DOS file system. While it will not verify the physical aspects of the hard drive, it will still locate and fix any errors in the DOS file system.

FIGURE 2.2:

SCANDISK can fix errors that it finds in the DOS file system.

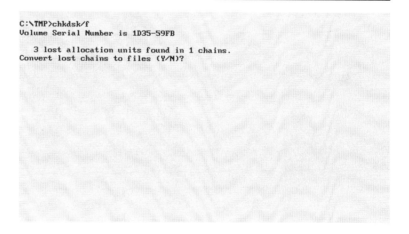

To use CHKDSK to check the drive onto which you are planning to install Slackware Linux, follow these steps:

1. From the MS-DOS prompt, type chkdsk c:/f. This will load CHKDSK and tell it to fix any errors that it finds on the C: drive. If you are planning on installing Slackware Linux to a drive other than C:, substitute the other drive for C: above. CHKDSK will display status messages on screen as it checks the drive.

2. When CHKDSK is done, it will display information about the amount of free space available on the drive. You should verify that you have enough space on the drive to install Slackware Linux (see above for details—you will want at least 15 MB for a very minimal system, and 100 MB or more for a full-featured system).

3. If CHKDSK found any errors while it was checking the file system, it will ask you if you want to write the fixes to disk. Type Y and press ↵ to write the changes that will fix the file system. You can see the results of running CHKDSK on a diskette in Figure 2.3.

You now have verified and fixed, if necessary, the file system on the drive that will hold Slackware Linux.

FIGURE 2.3:

It is a good idea to have CHKDSK find and repair errors in the DOS file system before you install Slackware Linux to the drive

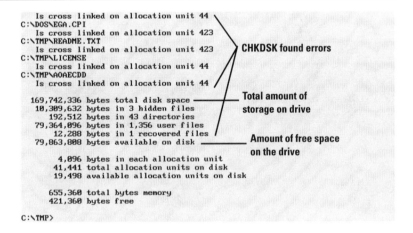

Creating the Boot and Root Diskettes

2

The program that installs Slackware Linux on your computer actually runs under Linux. So, you need to run Linux in order to install Slackware Linux. To get around this, when we first install Slackware Linux we start the computer with a special pair of diskettes that hold copies of the Linux and Slackware Linux installation software.

You can create these two diskettes using the CD-ROM that accompanies this book. We have included *disk images*—or disk files that contain copies of these two diskettes—on the CD-ROM, along with a program that will copy these disk images onto a floppy. You will need two high-density floppy diskettes that fit in your A: drive—either 5¼"or 3½"—the size doesn't matter. These are the diskettes onto which you will copy the boot and root disk images.

Creating the Boot Disk

The boot disk holds a copy of the Linux kernel. The CD-ROM that comes with this book includes disk images of boot disks for a number of common computers, so you will have to choose the correct one for your computer. All of the boot disk images for 5¼" 1.2 MB disks are located on the CD-ROM in the \bootdsks.12 directory. Similarly, the boot disk images for 3½" 1.44 MB disks are located in \bootdsks.144.

If you have an IDE hard disk and a standard SCSI CD-ROM, you should use the boot disk image stored in the file scsi. This is the kernel image that will most likely work with your computer. If you have a non-SCSI CD-ROM, find its name in the non-SCSI CD-ROM column in the following list and pick the appropriate kernel image file from the second column.

Non-SCSI CD-ROM	File
Sony CDU31 or CDU33a	cdu31a
Sony CDU531 or CDU535	cdu535

Non-SCSI CD-ROM	File
Mitsumi	`mitsumi`
NEC 260	`nec260`
Sound Blaster Pro or Panasonic	`sbpcd`

In the following instructions, we will assume that you want to use the boot disk image stored in the file `scsi`. If you are using a boot disk stored in a different file, just substitute the name of the new image file as we go.

TIP

You will find some additional boot disk image files in the `\bootdsks.12` and `\bootdsks.144` directories. These are for machines that have special hardware such as SCSI hard disk controllers or network cards. The file README contains information about each of these boot disk images.

We are going to make these disks from MS-DOS, so you should be at an MS-DOS prompt. I'm assuming that your CD-ROM player works under MS-DOS and has been properly configured. If you need help getting MS-DOS to work with your CD-ROM player, you should refer to the documentation that came with either your computer or your CD-ROM drive.

1. From the MS-DOS prompt, make your CD-ROM drive current. For example, if your CD-ROM is your G: drive, type g: and then press ⏎ at the DOS prompt. The DOS prompt will change to reflect the current drive.

2. Now change into the directory that holds the boot disk images. If you have a 5¼" 1.2 MB boot drive, type cd `\bootdsks.12` and then press ⏎. If you have a 3½" 1.44 MB boot disk, type cd `\bootdsks.144` and then press ⏎.

3. You are now ready to write the boot disk image to a floppy disk. Place a blank, formatted floppy disk into your computer's A: drive and type `\ rawrite` and then press ⏎. The Raw Write program will load and ask you for the name of the source file.

4. Type `scsi`. If you found a better boot disk image to use from the table above, replace `scsi` with the name of the new boot disk file, and press ↵.

5. Raw Write will now prompt you to enter the drive to which you want to write the disk image. Type `a:` and then press ↵ to tell Raw Write to copy the contents of the image file onto the A: drive.

2

Raw Write will now start copying the contents of the disk image file onto the floppy disk. When it is finished you will be returned to the DOS prompt.

We now have a boot disk that will load the Linux kernel onto your computer. In the next section, we'll create the root disk.

Creating the Root Disk

The root disk contains the Slackware Linux installation program. Creating the root disk is very similar to creating the book disk except that you do not have as many choices as to which disk image to use. The disk images for the root disk are stored on the CD-ROM in the directories `\rootdsks.12` and `\rootdsdks.144`. The `\rootdsks.12` directory contains root disk images for 5¼" 1.2 MB floppy disk drives, while the `\rootdsks.144` directory contains root disk images for 3½" 1.44 MB floppy disk drives. To create the root disk, follow the steps below.

TIP You will find disk images for other Slackware Linux installation files along with the disk image we use for our installation. These other files are used when you are installing Slackware Linux to its own partition—not to a DOS drive. The README file in the root disk directory contains additional information about these other root disk images.

1. The current directory should still be located on the CD-ROM. If it is not, change to the CD-ROM by entering the CD-ROM's drive letter followed by a colon, and then press ↵. For example, if your CD-ROM drive is your G: drive, type `g:` and then press ↵.

2. Now change into the directory that holds the root disk images. If you have a 5¼" 1.2 MB boot disk, enter `cd \rootdsks.12` and then press ↵. If you have a 3½" 1.44 MB boot disk, enter `cd \rootdsks.144` and then press ↵.

3. You are now ready to create the root disk. Place a floppy disk into your computer's A: drive. Type \rawrite and then press ⏎.

4. Type umsds144 if you have a 3½" A: drive, or umsds12.gz if you have a 5¼" A: drive, and then press ⏎. The Raw Write program will transfer the root disk image to your floppy disk.

You now have both the boot and root disk ready, and can start up your computer under Slackware Linux.

> **TIP**
>
> The root disk we just created includes a special version of the Slackware Linux installation program designed to install Slackware Linux onto an existing DOS drive. It is also possible to install Slackware Linux onto a drive dedicated just to Linux by using the root disk based on the color144 or color12 disk image file. You can read more about installing Slackware Linux to its own partition in Chapter 2 of Book II.

You're Ready to Rumble

Now that you have verified that the drive onto which you are going to install Slackware is free of errors, and you've created a pair of Slackware Linux diskettes, you are ready to install Slackware Linux.

CHAPTER

THREE

Installing Slackware Linux

- Deciding Which Disk Sets and Packages to Install

- Installing Slackware Linux from the CD-ROM, from Floppies, or from Your Hard Disk

3

Now that you have prepared your hard disk to hold Slackware Linux and created the pair of diskettes used to start the installation process, you are ready to install Linux onto your computer. Since Slackware Linux is so big and includes so many packages, I'll spend some time telling you what is included and how to select what you need to install. Actually installing Slackware Linux should not take more than 15 minutes. Once Slackware Linux is installed, you will be ready to start exploring all the features and possibilities that it makes available to you.

Deciding Which Disk Sets and Packages to Install

TIP   Book I discusses how to install Slackware Linux on an existing DOS partition—without erasing any of your current data. You can also install Slackware Linux to a partition dedicated just to Linux (See Chapter 2 of Book II). Installing Slackware Linux to a dedicated partition is a more involved process, but the end result is a faster Linux system.

Before you actually start installing Slackware Linux it is a good idea to figure out which of the many components you will want. Slackware Linux is made up of a number of disk sets—seventeen in all. Each of the disk sets contain related packages. For example, the development disk set contains packages related to software development, such as the C compiler package. You do not need to install all of the disk sets—or even all of the packages in any one of the disk sets. Some of the packages are required just to get Slackware Linux up and running on your computer. Other packages contain useful programs such as the C compiler or e-mail software. Some other packages contain software you will never need. The following table lists all of the disk sets.

NOTE Don't let the term "disk set" confuse you. It's a holdover from when Slackware was distributed only on diskette. Each of these "disk sets" are broken down into a series of "disks," which are stored in a separate directory on the CD-ROM. All of the disks and disk sets we talk about in Book I are included on the CD-ROM.

Disk Set	Contents
A	Base system—required to run Linux
AP	Applications and other useful files
D	Software development tools
E	GNU emacs—a powerful text editor
F	A collection of FAQs (Frequently Asked Questions) and other documentation about Linux
I	Documentation for GNU software readable by the GNU info program
N	Support for TCP/IP networking, e-mail, and Usenet news
OOP	GNU Smalltalk and support files
Q	Alpha kernel sources and binary images
TCL	The Tcl/Tk programming environment and related files
X	All the files you need to install and use X Window

Disk Set	Contents
XAP	Applications that run under X Window
XD	X Window server development tools and support files
XV	Xview 3.2 Release 5 and Open Look window manager, both for X Window
IV	Interviews libraries and applications
Y	Games such as Doom and Tetris
T	The $\TeX$ and $\LaTeX$ typesetting systems

Each of the above disk sets are further broken down into a series of packages. You should not necessarily install all of the packages in a given disk set. Some disk sets, such as A—the base system—include conflicting packages, or two packages that do the same thing in different ways.

When you install Slackware Linux, I recommend that you start with the contents of the A and AP disk sets first. After installing these, you will have a bare minimum Linux system. If you want to be able to compile programs on your machine, you should install the appropriate packages on the D disk set. If you are interested in running X Window, you should also install the X and XAP disk sets, as these contain X Window and its applications.

NOTE   Chapter 5 discusses installing and configuring X Window in detail. (See also Chapter 5 of Book II for a more general discussion of X Window.)

The Most Important Choice:
Choosing the Correct Kernel

On the A disk set you will find two different Linux kernels. You must install one—and only one—of these kernels in order to have a functioning Slackware Linux system. The kernel you choose is dependent on the hardware in your computer. Each of the kernels in the A disk set has been built to run on a different hardware setup. Though Slackware Linux includes kernels for a wide range of hardware configurations, if your particular hardware configuration is not addressed by one of the kernels on the CD, then you will need to have someone else *build*—or compile—a new kernel for you. The CDROM-HOWTO file in the CD's /HOWTO directory contains information about building a new kernel. In order to build a new Linux kernel, you must have Linux already installed and running on a machine—this is why you need a friend who already has Linux up and running to build the kernel for you. The actual process of creating the kernel is beyond the scope of this book. To find out more about compiling the Linux kernel, read the Linux Kernel HOWTO.

While you are installing Slackware Linux onto your computer you will be asked whether you want to install certain packages. As a rule of thumb, except for the A and AP disk sets, you should not install a package that you are unfamiliar with. If you install all of the packages from all of the disk sets, you will end up with a giant Slackware Linux system, requiring over 100 MB of disk space—something most of us do not have. The rest of this section describes the contents of each disk set in more detail.

A   The A disk set contains the most basic parts of Slackware Linux. You must install the packages marked as "required" on the A disk set in order to run Linux on your computer. On this set you will find the Linux kernel and programs that are very fundamental to its operation. As you install it, you will find that most of the packages are required, so you do not have a choice about whether to install them.

AP   On the AP disk set you will find applications and other useful files. While you can get a Slackware Linux system to boot up by only installing the A disk set, you will want many of the programs that are offered on the AP disk set as well. By installing the AP disk set you will have access to useful features such as the on-line manual pages and the common Unix file utilities.

D   On the D disk set, you will find packages required to develop and compile software on your machine. Even if you are not planning on doing software development on your computer, you'll find many of the packages in this disk set useful. Many Unix programs are distributed as "source code." In order to use these programs on your Slackware Linux machine, you need the proper compiler. If you are planning on doing any software development, note that you will need to install the Linux kernel source code from this disk set. The kernel source code includes files needed when compiling other programs.

E   The E disk set contains emacs—probably the most powerful and complex text editor ever written. If you are already familiar with emacs from working on other Unix machines, you will want to install this disk set. If not, you may want to try using some other editors before jumping into using emacs—it has a very steep learning curve. You will find other text editors on the AP disk set.

F   On the F disk set, you will find Frequently Asked Questions (FAQs) and other documentation for Slackware Linux. We highly recommend that you install the contents of this disk set, as the FAQs provide answers to many questions about the rest of your Slackware Linux system. Once you have installed the F disk set, you will find these files in the /usr/doc/faq directory.

I   The I disk set contains documentation for the GNU software that makes up a large part of Slackware Linux. The documentation included on this disk set is in a format readable by the info program. To access this set of documentation, use the info command.

N   On the N disk set, you will find all the software you need to access the Internet including software for both TCP/IP and UUCP networking. The TCP/IP software works whether your computer is on an ethernet network with a dedicated connection to the Internet, or is connected via phone lines using SLIP (Serial Link Internet Protocol) or PPP (Point-to-Point Protocol). This disk set also includes a very ingenious package called term that allows you to create an Internet connection between your machine and a machine attached to the Internet. By using term, you do not need to have a SLIP or PPP account to attach your computer to the Internet. You can dial into any other Unix machine on the Internet and create the connection needed. The UUCP software included allows your computer to dial up another computer that is attached to the Internet in order to transfer mail and other files. This disk set also contains e-mail software, Usenet news server software, and Usenet newsreader software.

3

OOP   On the OOP disk set, you will find a copy of GNU Smalltalk, along with support files and add-in libraries. Smalltalk is a very popular object-oriented programming language. You only need to install this disk set if you want to write a computer program in Smalltalk.

Q   The Q disk set contains alpha (untested) versions of the Linux kernel. While you may find it fun to look at some of these versions of the Linux kernel, you can always retrieve much more updated versions of the kernel from the Internet. (See Chapter 8 of Book I for information about getting new versions of the kernel from the Internet.)

TCL   T is a scripting language for writing simple Unix programs. Tcl is ideal for writing short programs that do not require all the power that a full computer language gives you. Also on this set is Tk, an extension to Tcl, which allows you to write simple X Window programs.

X   The X disk set contains XFree86 3.1.1, a version of MIT's X Window Version 11 Release 6 windowing system tailored for Slackware Linux. X Window is a windowing system for Unix workstations, much like Microsoft Windows or Macintosh. (See Chapter 8 of Book I for information about installing, configuring, and using X Window.)

XAP   The XAP disk set contains a collection of applications that run under X Window. You will find many useful programs, ranging from Seyon—a very good terminal program that allows you to call other computers with a modem—to games and graphics software. In order to use the programs on this disk set you must have X Window installed and properly configured on your computer.

XD   The XD disk set contains the tools required to create new X Window servers. You only need to install these disk sets if you plan on writing a new X Window server or modifying any of the X Window servers that come with Slackware Linux.

The X Window server is the part of the X Window system that controls the screen. X Window servers are very complicated pieces of software, and writing or modifying one is not covered in this book. To develop X Window servers on your computer, you'll need to install the X and D disk sets in addition to this disk set.

XV　　The XV disk set contains Xviews 3.2 Release 5. Xviews is a library of X Window code that some X Window applications require. This disk set also includes the Open Look window manager for X Window. You only need to install files from this disk set if you either want to run X Window Applications that require Xviews, or wish to use the Open Look window manager. In order to use the contents of the XV disk set, you must have X Window installed and configured (X Window is located on the X disk set).

IV　　On the IV disk set, you will find Interviews, a set of X Window libraries and programs written by Sun Microsystems. You only need to install software from this disk set if you either want to use Interviews applications (very unlikely) or wish to use the applications that come with Interviews. You need to have X Window installed and configured in order to use the contents of the IV disk set.

y　　The Y disk set contains several games. Many of these are text-based games such as Tetris. (The XAP disk set includes games for X Window.)

T　　On the T disk set, you will find TeX and LaTeX. TeX is a typesetting system developed by Professor Donald Knuth at Stanford University. LaTeX is a macro package developed by Leslie Lamport that simplifies using TeX. Both are very powerful—and complicated—systems. Many books have been written on TeX and LaTeX alone.

Installing Slackware Linux

The easiest way to install Slackware Linux is from the CD-ROM that comes with this book. As long as Slackware Linux supports the CD-ROM in your computer, you should use this method. It is possible, however, to install Slackware from either your hard disk or from floppy diskettes. See "Installing From Your Hard Disk" or "Installing From Floppy Disks" below for instructions on copying the necessary parts of the CD-ROM to either your hard disk or to floppies before you start installing.

Installing from the CD-ROM

I have told you what disk sets make up Slackware Linux and now you are ready to start the installation process. The rest of this process is rather simple—you'll decide which packages you wish to install on your computer, and then wait as they are copied from the CD-ROM to your hard disk. A word of warning, however. Slackware Linux is as full-featured an operating system as you can get. It is not uncommon to have to install the software two or three times before you get things to your liking. That is not to say that you will not have a working system after your first installation, but don't get discouraged. Slackware Linux is well worth any extra time you must spend reinstalling it a few times to get everything right. Get out the two floppy diskettes that you created in the last chapter—the boot disk and the root disk. You will now use these two diskettes to start up your computer and the Slackware Linux `setup` program.

1. Start with your computer turned off. Place the boot disk that you created in the last chapter into your Computer's A: drive, and then turn on the machine. You should see the BIOS information screen you see every time that you start up your computer. Then, after a few seconds, you should see the message

   `Loading Linux...`

   displayed on the screen. This message tells you that the Linux kernel is loading into your computer's memory from the boot disk.

2. As the Linux kernel loads, it will display messages on screen. After a few seconds, you will be prompted to enter information about the hardware in your computer with the line

   `boot:`

   At this point, just press ↵ to continue the booting process. If needed, you can now enter additional information for the kernel to use.

TIP At the boot prompt you can enter information that Slackware Linux uses to run on your computer. To find out about the parameters you can enter here, see the various HOWTO documents located in the CD's /HOWTO directory.

3. More messages will appear on screen as different parts of the kernel continue to load. After a while, you will see another message on screen asking you to switch diskettes. This message is telling you that it is time to place the root disk that you made in the last chapter into the disk drive. Remove the boot disk from your A: drive and insert the root disk. Press ↵ to continue.

4. Linux will start the last stage of installation. The following message will appear asking you if you want to set up a swap file.

```
Slackware Linux UMSDOS install disk v. 2.1.0.

Hello, and welcome to Linux. Unless have more than 4 megabytes of
RAM, you'll need a swap file to install. This should be created on
the DOS partition that you plan to install on.

Device    Boot Begin Start End  Blocks  Id  System
/dev/hda1   *     1     1  600  182381   6  DOS 16-bit>=32M
/dev/hda2         601  601 682   24909   4  DOS 16-bit<32M

Use which device (such as /dev/hda1, or ENTER to skip)?
```

If you only have 4 MB of RAM in your computer, you should set up a swap file by typing the device to which you are installing Slackware Linux and pressing ↵. (For more information on how devices correspond to DOS drive letters, see the table below.) If you do not need to create a swap file, just press the ↵ key to continue. When the root disk is finished loading, you will see the following login prompt

```
slackware Login:
```

This prompt tells you that Linux is now running on your computer and is waiting for you to log in.

5. Type root and then press ↵. This will log you in to the system as root—the superuser. The root user on any Unix computer has full access to the computer. You must be logged in as root in order to install Slackware Linux.

6. Now that you are logged in to the system, you will see the prompt

   #

   This tells you that the system is waiting for you to enter a command. You should now type setup and then press ↵ to continue the setup process.

The Slackware Linux setup program will appear as shown here.

```
        Slackware Linux setup (UMSDOS version FD-2.2.0)

Welcome to Slackware Linux setup.
Select an option below using the UP/DOWN keys and SPACE or ENTER.
Alternate keys may also be used: '+', '-', and TAB.

HELP        Read the Slackware setup HELP file
KEYMAP      Remap your keyboard if you're not using a US one
QUICK       Choose quick or verbose install mode [now: VERBOSE]
MAKE TAGS   Experts may customize tagfiles to preselect packages
ADDSWAP     Set up your swap partition(s)
TARGET      Configure a DOS partition to accept Linux
SOURCE      Select source media
DISK SETS   Decide which disk sets you wish to install
INSTALL     Install selected disk sets
CONFIGURE   Reconfigure your Linux system
EXIT        Exit Slackware Linux setup
```

You will use this program to install the rest of Slackware Linux on your computer.

Before you continue with the process of installing Slackware Linux, you should become familiar with how you use the setup program. Use the ↑ and ↓ keys to move the highlight around the screen, and the ↵ key to make selections. Yes/No questions will appear near the bottom of the screen. Use the + and - keys to change your answer to these questions. Most of the Yes/No questions actually have three answers: Yes, No, and Quit. Selecting Quit stops the program before Slackware Linux is fully installed on your computer.

7. The first thing we need to do in the setup program is to select the drive to which we are installing Slackware Linux. Use the ↓ key to highlight the word Target, and then press ↵.

TIP If you only have a single hard disk in your computer, and that hard disk only contains one partition, you can skip ahead to step 10. You do not need to specify where you want to install Slackware Linux, since you have no choice.

The Slackware Linux setup program will display a list of disk drives in your computer. Disk drives are displayed as they appear in Linux—as device names. The device names are made up of two characters—hd for IDE hard drives or sd for SCSI hard drives—followed by a letter—a for the first hard disk drive or b for the second hard disk drive—followed by the partition number. Some common device names and corresponding drives are displayed in the table below.

Device name	DOS drive
/dev/sda1	First partition on the first SCSI hard disk. This usually corresponds to DOS's C: drive.
/dev/hda2	Second partition on the first IDE hard disk. This usually corresponds to DOS's D: drive on a single-drive system.
/dev/hdb1	First partition on the second IDE hard disk. This corresponds to DOS's D: drive on a two-drive system.
/dev/hdb2	Second partition on the second IDE hard disk. This usually corresponds to DOS's E: or F: drive on a two-drive system.

Device name	DOS drive
/dev/sda1	First partition on the first SCSI hard disk. This usually corresponds to DOS's C: drive.
/dev/sda2	Second partition on the first SCSI hard disk. This usually corresponds to DOS's D: drive on a single-drive system.
/dev/sdb1	First partition on the second SCSI hard disk. This corresponds to DOS's D: drive on a two-drive system.
/dev/sdb2	Second partition on the second SCSI hard disk. This usually corresponds to DOS's E: or F: drive on a two-drive system.

8. If you have more than one hard disk in your computer, or you have a single hard disk that contains more than one partition, you will need to type in the partition onto which you wish to install Slackware Linux, and then press ↵. For example, if you have an IDE hard disk drive and wish to install Slackware Linux onto the first partition of the first drive (referred to as the C: drive in DOS) type /dev/hda1 and then press ↵.

9. The setup program will now display the DOS and OS/2 Partition setup dialog box. Note that this only appears if you have more than one hard disk in your computer, or more than one partition on your single hard disk.

    This is where you can pick other DOS or OS/2 partitions that you want to be visible when you are running Slackware Linux. Since we are focused on getting Slackware Linux up and running right now, press ↵ to skip this step. A dialog box will appear asking if you want to continue installing Slackware Linux. Select Yes with the arrow keys and press the Tab key to highlight No, and then press ↵ to continue.

10. You are now presented with a choice of source media for Slackware Linux—this is where you tell the setup program where you are installing from.

```
1 Install from the target DOS partition
2 Install from a different partition
3 Install from floppy disk
4 Install via NFS
5 Install from CD-ROM
```

If you are installing from the CD included with this book, type 5 and then press ↵. You are now presented with a dialog box allowing you to choose which of the disk sets you want to install.

NOTE   At this point, you may be presented with some additional dialog boxes in which you must select your CD-ROM drive. These dialog boxes vary depending on the type of CD-ROM you have.

TIP   If the setup program starts displaying error messages on screen, it is because Slackware Linux cannot read from your CD-ROM player. If this is the case, see the sections below about copying disk sets from the CD-ROM to either your hard disk or floppy disk. Then redo the installation as described here, except, in step 10 above, select either Install from the target DOS partition or Install from floppy disks as the source media. You should now be able to continue installing Slackware Linux. If you are installing from floppy disk, you will be prompted from time to time to change the disk in the disk drive.

11. Select the disk sets by highlighting the set name using the arrow keys and pressing the space bar. Once a disk set is selected, an "X" will appear next to its name. You must install the A disk set—this contains the fundamental parts of Slackware Linux that you must have on your computer. You should

3

also select to install the AP disk set, as this contains many programs common on Unix workstations. The N disk set is required if your computer is on a network and you wish to access the network from your machine. The D disk set contains the complete Linux development system—everything from a C compiler to libraries and debuggers. Select the D disk set if you will be compiling software on your machine. Both the F and I disk sets provide additional documentation about Slackware Linux and different programs that are included with it.

TIP
It is best to install only the A and AP disk sets the first time you install Slackware Linux. Installing these two disk sets will give you all of the basic functionality of a Unix workstation. You can always add more software later using Slackware Linux's `setup` command.

12. Once you have finished selecting the disk sets you wish to install, press ⏎ to continue. The `setup` program should display a dialog box asking if you wish to use Prompting mode. Prompting mode is the mode in which the `setup` program asks you if you want to install each package individually. You should use the arrow keys to highlight Normal and then press ⏎.

The `setup` program will now start copying files from the CD-ROM onto your hard disk. As it starts to copy each package, it will display a dialog box describing the package and asking if you wish to install it. You can use the + and - keys to toggle your replies between Yes, No, and Quit. Selecting Yes for any package will cause the `setup` program to install the package. Selecting No tells the `setup` program not to install the package. Selecting Quit will end the `setup` program and return you to the first menu.

13. As the `setup` program displays each package that is included in the disk sets you elect to install, choose the ones you want by verifying that the box near the bottom of the window says Yes, and pressing ⏎. Skip packages by using the + key to change Yes to No, and pressing ⏎. Some of the packages are required for Slackware Linux to operate. You will not be given a choice whether to install these. The `setup` program will install them automatically.

WARNING   While you are installing the A disk set, you will be given two choices for a kernel. The first one only includes drivers for an IDE hard disk controller—not for a SCSI controller. If you have a SCSI CD-ROM you should not pick this kernel. You should pick the second kernel you are offered, which includes drivers for both IDE and SCSI devices.

14. Once you are done installing the disk sets selected in step 11, you are given a chance to create a boot disk. You need to create this boot disk in order to start up Slackware Linux, so select Yes in the dialog box by pressing ↵. Place a formatted high-density floppy disk in your A: drive, and press ↵ a second time. The setup program will create the boot disk.

15. After you have created the boot disk, the setup program may display more dialog boxes asking if you want to set up additional software packages that you have installed. The dialog boxes that appear will depend on which packages you elected to install earlier. In general, it is good to have the setup program configure the packages that you have installed. It is easier to later modify the configuration files that are created at this point than to create new configuration files from scratch.

TIP   The number of dialog boxes and the information the Setup program asks you for at this time is dependent on what you decided to install. If you are just installing software from the A and AP disk sets, as we recommend for a first-time installation, you will only be prompted with the dialog boxes about creating a boot disk.

Installing from the Hard Disk

If you cannot install Slackware Linux from your CD-ROM drive, you can install it by first copying the contents of the disk sets you wish to install from the CD to your hard disk. You can then install them just as fast as if you were installing from the

3

CD. Once you have Slackware Linux copied to your hard disk, you can follow the directions for installing from the CD. When you get to step 10, select option 1: Install from the target DOS partition. This tells the setup program to read the Slackware Linux disk sets from the same hard disk you are installing to. This can take up a lot of space on your hard disk, since you need both the installed Slackware Linux and the Slackware Linux disk sets on your hard disk at the same time. Once you have installed Slackware Linux in this manner, you can remove the extra copy. See "Copying Slackware Linux Disk Sets to Your Hard Disk," below for instructions on how to copy the contents of the CD-ROM to your hard disk.

NOTE You only need to copy Slackware Linux disk sets from the CD to your hard disk if your CD-ROM drive is not supported by Slackware Linux and you wish to do an installation from your hard disk.

Copying Slackware Linux Disk Sets to Your Hard Disk

You can install Slackware Linux from your computer's hard disk as well as from the CD. Before you install from the hard disk, you must copy the contents of the disk sets you wish to install from the CD to your computer.

You have two options—you can either copy the entire Slackware Linux distribution to your hard disk, or only the disk sets that you plan to install. Copying the entire distribution is quicker and easier than just copying the required disk sets, but it also takes more space.

To copy all of the Slackware Linux disks to your hard drive, follow these instructions:

1. From the DOS prompt, type xcopy d:\slakware /s c:\slakware and then press ↵. XCOPY will load and display the following message.

        Does slakware specify a file name
        or directory name on the target
        (F = file, D = directory)?

2. Now type d and then press ↵ to indicate that you are copying a directory and not a file.

3. XCOPY will now copy the files, displaying the name of each file as it is copied. When it is done, the DOS prompt will reappear on screen.

You have just copied the entire Slackware Linux distribution to your hard disk, and can now install Slackware Linux from your hard disk instead of from the CD-ROM.

If you do not have the storage space on your hard disk to hold the entire Slackware Linux distribution, you can copy only the disk sets you wish to install. To do this, follow these instructions:

1. With DOS up and running on your computer, type c: to change to your hard disk. If you want to copy the disk sets to a drive other than C:, such as D:, then change to that drive instead.

2. Type mkdir \slakware and then press ↵ to create the directory that will hold the Slackware Linux disk sets. After the directory is created, a command prompt will appear on screen.

3. Now type cd \slakware and then press ↵ to change to the directory you just created to hold the Slackware Linux disk sets. After pressing ↵ , the command prompt should appear, this time reflecting this directory.

4. With the CD in the CD-ROM drive, type xcopy d:\slakware\a /s a1 and then press ↵. A message will appear asking if the target is a directory. (Note, if you access your CD-ROM drive from DOS with a drive letter other than D:, you should use that letter.

5. Type Y and then press ↵ to indicate that the target you are copying to is a directory and not a file.

The contents of the A1 disk will now be copied to your hard disk. Repeat steps 4 and 5, replacing the filename with the names of each of the diskettes you wish to copy. The A disk set contains the disks A1, A2, A3, and A4. The AP disk set contains AP1, AP2, AP3, AP4, and AP5. Use the table below to determine the number of disks in each of the disk sets.

Disk Set	Number of Disks
A	4
AP	5
D	10
E	5
F	2
I	2
N	4
OOP	1
Q	4
T	10
TCL	?
Y	3
X	14
XAP	3
XD	3
XV	3
IV	1

Once you have copied the disk sets you wish to install to your hard disk, you can specify the hard disk as the source during installation. You do this in the dialog box where you tell the Setup program to install from the CD-ROM drive.

Installing from Floppy Disks

Installing Slackware Linux from diskettes is the most time-intensive method you can use. Once you have copied the parts of Linux you wish to install from the CD to the floppy, you can then use the floppies to install Slackware Linux. While this method is more time-consuming than installing from a copy of the disk sets on your hard disk, it requires a lot less hard disk space. When you install Slackware Linux from a copy of the disk sets on your hard disk, you need twice the amount of hard disk storage, both for the Slackware Linux disk sets and for the installed Slackware Linux. Once you have Slackware Linux copied to a set of floppy disks, you can follow the directions for installing from the CD. When you get to step 10, select option 5: Install from floppy disk. You can then go ahead and finish installing Slackware Linux. As you install Slackware Linux you will be prompted to switch floppy disks from time to time. See "Copying Slackware Linux Disk Sets to Floppy Disks" below for instructions.

NOTE   You only need to create Slackware Linux diskettes if your CD-ROM drive is not supported by Linux and you choose not to install from your hard disk.

Copying Slackware Linux Disk Sets to Floppy Disks

To install Slackware Linux from floppy diskettes, you first need to copy onto floppies the contents of the disk sets you wish to install. This can take a large number of blank diskettes. Check the table in "Copying Slackware Linux Disk Sets to Your Hard Disk" above to find out how many diskettes each of the disk sets requires, and determine the total number of blank diskettes you need before continuing. The diskettes should be blank and high-density.

Once you know how many diskettes you will need, follow these instructions. We assume that your CD-ROM drive appears as the D: drive from DOS.

3

1. From the DOS prompt, change to your CD-ROM drive by typing `d:` and then press ↵.

2. Type `cd \slakware` and then press ↵ to make the directory on the CD-ROM that contains the Slackware disk sets current. The prompt should now reflect this directory.

3. Place a blank, formatted, high-density disk in your computer's A: drive.

4. Now type `copy a1\*.* a:` and then press ↵. DOS will copy the contents of disk number 1 of the A disk set to the floppy disk. When it is done coping, the prompt will return.

5. When DOS is finished copying files to the disk, remove the disk from the drive. You now have the Slackware disk on floppy disk.

6. Repeat steps 3 through 5 for each of the Slackware disks you wish to copy to floppy disk.

You now have a copy of the disk sets.

You're Ready to Go

Congratulations! If all went well, you have Slackware Linux installed and running on your computer. You are now ready to take a quick tour around the system. In the next chapter, we will show you how to boot up your new Slackware Linux system and create a user account. Once you have created a user account, you may also want to turn to Chapter 3 in Book II for a Linux tutorial.

CHAPTER

FOUR

Booting Slackware Linux

4

- Booting with the Boot Disk

- Some Initial Housekeeping

- Logging In with Your New Account

- Quitting Slackware Linux

Booting with the Boot Disk

Now that you have Slackware Linux installed on your computer, you're ready to boot it up and start using Linux. To boot up Linux on your machine, you will use the boot disk labelled "Slackware Linux Boot" that we created at the end of the last chapter—right after we finished installing Slackware Linux to the computer. Do not use the installation boot disk that we made in Chapter 2 to boot up the Slackware Linux installation program.

1. With your computer turned off, insert the boot disk into your computer's A: drive and then turn on your machine.

2. You will first see the normal BIOS information screen that you see every time you start up your computer. After a few seconds, you should start to see messages on screen as Linux loads.

3. Once the system is up and running, you will see the following login prompt

   ```
   Welcome to Linux 1.2.3

   darkstar login:
   ```

What If Your Machine Doesn't Start?

A whole host of problems can prevent your machine from starting up correctly. The most common problem you will encounter is trying to boot the system with a kernel that does not support your hard disk. Remember, if you have an IDE hard disk controller, you will need to boot a kernel that includes IDE support. Likewise, if you are using a SCSI hard disk controller, your kernel will need to have SCSI support. You should have chosen which kernel to install in Chapter 3. If you selected the wrong kernel, you will need to reinstall Slackware Linux, this time picking the correct kernel.

Accessing the CD-ROM from DOS

The CD-ROM that comes with this book includes lots of Linux documentation. You can access this documentation straight from DOS. One caveat when accessing the CD-ROM from DOS—DOS cannot display some of the filenames used on the CD. This is because Linux supports long filenames, while DOS has rather strict limits on the length of, and what characters can appear in, filenames.

The directory that contains the most documentation is the HOWTO directory. In this directory, you will find all of the Linux HOWTO documents—short, detailed articles about using Linux. These are all stored in regular text files, so you can use any DOS or Windows word processor or text editor to view and print them.

4

Some Initial Housekeeping

Now that you have Slackware Linux installed on your computer, you are ready to configure your machine for daily use. Don't worry, this work is not as hard as you may think—in fact, it's easy compared to the initial installation.

Logging In as Root

You should be looking at the following login prompt on your screen

```
Welcome to Linux 1.2.3
darkstar login:
```

This means that your machine is waiting for you to identify yourself as a user. Since you have not yet created an account for your use, we will log in with the special username root. This is a special user also referred to as the superuser. Many of the tasks you need to do to configure and maintain your Linux system can only be accomplished while logged in as root.

> **TIP**
> You can also become the root user after you have logged in with a different username by using the su command. When you issue this command, the system will respond by asking you for the root password. Once you have entered this password, you will have full access to the system just as if you logged in with the name root.

1. At the login prompt now on screen, type root and press ↵. Slackware Linux will not ask you for a password since we have not assigned one to the root account yet. After you have logged in, you will see the following command prompt

   #

That's all there is to it. You are now logged into the system as the superuser.

Changing the Root Password

Remember, root is a special user who has full access to the system. When you—or someone else—is logged into your machine as the root user, they are free to read and delete any file in the system, regardless of the file's owner or purpose. Leaving your system without a root password is just asking for trouble. Even if you are the only person who uses the system, you still want to set up a root password so you won't accidentally log in as root and cause damage to your Linux system.

To change the root password, follow these steps:

1. At the command prompt

   #

   type passwd and then press ↵. The system will respond by displaying

   ```
   Enter new passwd:
   ```

NOTE If a password had already been assigned to the root user, you would first be prompted to enter the old password. This is an added security step to ensure that the person changing the password knows the original password. Note, too, that you can use the password command to change the password of other users besides `root`. The `passwd` command changes the password of whatever user you are currently logged in as when you issue the command.

2. Now type a password to assign to the root user and then press ↵. The following message will appear

```
Reenter password:
```

3. Reenter the same password that you entered in step 2. The `passwd` command makes you enter the password two times to prevent typos. Don't forget your password...it's a real pain to change the root password once it's forgotten.

WARNING When you assign a password to the root user, don't forget it. You may want to write it down and store in a safe place. Don't leave it sitting next to your computer for anyone to see.

Creating a User Account

Now that we are finished setting the root password, we are ready to create a user account. This is the account that you will use while doing most of your work with Linux. Information about each user on your system is kept in the file `/etc/passwd`. Luckily, Slackware Linux comes with a program called `adduser` that makes adding users to this file quick and easy. To create the user account, you should still be logged in as `root` and looking at the following command prompt

```
#
```

Follow these steps to create a user account for your own use:

1. Type `adduser` and then press ↵. You will see the following message.

```
Adding a new user. The user name should not exceed 8 characters
in length, or you many run into problems later.

Enter login name for new account (^C to quit):
```

2. Now type in the username for this new account. First names always make good usernames, so you may want to enter your first name and then press ↵. For example, I would enter dan and then press ↵. When you press ↵, you'll see

```
Editing information for new user [dan]
Full Name:
```

3. Slackware Linux keeps track of a number of pieces of information about each user, including his or her name. You should now enter your full name. For example, I would enter Dan Tauber and then press ↵. Once you press ↵, you will see the line

```
GID [100]:
```

4. So far, this is the oddest looking question to which you'll need to respond. Linux and Unix both put users into groups. Users in the same group can easily share files. The default group for each new user is called "users." At this prompt, you enter the number of the group to which this new user should belong. The number 100 is always associated with the group "users," so you should just press ↵ at this point to accept this group. Once you press ↵, you will see

```
Checking for an available UID after 500
501
First unused uid is 501

UID [501]:
```

TIP   Information about groups is kept in the file /etc/group. You can add new groups to this file using the groupadd command. To do this, just type groupadd *group* at the shell prompt. This will add the group you name in *group* to the /etc/group file. You can read more about groups in Chapter 4 of Book II.

5. Like groups, usernames are also associated with numbers. The `adduser` command just found the lowest user number that it could use—in our case 501—and is suggesting that we use it for this new user. Unless you are fond of a particular number, you should always accept the user number that the command wants to use by pressing ↵. When you press ↵, you will see

```
Home Directory [/home/dan]:
```

6. The `adduser` command is now asking you where the home directory of this new user should be located. Each user on your system will have a *home directory*—a place to store files. Slackware Linux comes set up with each user's home directory as a subdirectory in the /home directory. You should just press ↵ again at this point to accept the default home directory. When you press ↵, you will see

```
Shell [/bin/bash]:
```

7. You are now telling Slackware Linux which program to use when this user logs into the system. The shell is the program that accepts input from the keyboard and runs commands. It is equivalent to the program `command.com` in DOS. `bash` is the default shell for Slackware Linux and you should go ahead and press ↵ now to accept this shell. You will see

```
Password [dan]:
```

8. The `adduser` command is now asking you to enter a password that will be used with this new account. You should type in a password and then press ↵. You will need to remember this password when you use the account. If you are not concerned about security, you may want to make the password to this account the same as the password you assigned to the root account earlier in this chapter. Once you have entered the password and pressed ↵, you will see

```
Information for new user [dan]:
Home directory: [/home/dan] Shell: [/bin/bash]
Password: [happy] uid: [501] gid: [100]

Is this correct? [y/N]:
```

WARNING If your machine is connected to a network, or you are concerned about security, you should not use the same password for both your user account and the root account.

9. If all of the information displayed on screen is correct, you should type Y and then press ↵. If any of it is wrong, type N and then press ↵. When you enter Y and press ↵, you will see the following string of messages

```
Adding login [dan] and making directory [/home/dan]

Adding the files from the /etc/skel directory:
./.kermrc -> /home/dan/./.kermrc
./.less -> /home/dan/./.less
./.lessrc -> /home/dan/./.lessrc
./.term -> /home/dan/./.term
./.term/termrc -> /home/dan/./.term/termrc
```

After these messages are displayed, you will again see the following shell prompt

```
#
```

You have just created your new account and it should be ready for you to use.

Logging In with Your New Account

Now that you've created a username and account for your own use, it's time to log in. If you are still logged into the system as root, type exit and then press ↵ to log off of the system. You should see the same login prompt that you saw at the beginning of this chapter.

```
darkstar login:
```

You are now ready to log into your system with your new username.

1. With the login prompt displayed on screen, type the username that you cre-ated for yourself in the last section and then press ↵. For example, I would type dan and then press ↵. As soon as you press ↵, you will see

   ```
   Password:
   ```

2. Now type in the password you assigned to your new account. Once you press ↵, you should see a few lines of text telling you the version of Linux that is running on the machine and the last time you logged into the system. After these two lines are displayed, you will see a command prompt.

As soon as you enter the password and press ↵, you should be logged into the sys-tem with your new username and will see the following shell prompt

```
darkstar:~$
```

telling you that Slackware Linux is ready for you to type in a command. To verify that you really did log in with your new username, you can type whoami and then press ↵. The whoami command displays the username that you are currently using. If you were to use the su command to become a superuser now, and then enter whoami and press ↵, the system would respond with

```
root
```

Since the su command turns you into the superuser, the whoami command will re-port that you are logged into the system as the root user.

You now have a user account, and should log in with this account whenever you use your Slackware Linux system. Whenever you need to access the privileges of the root user, use the su command.

Quitting Slackware Linux

As with most Unix machines, you should never just turn the power off or hit the reset button while Slackware Linux is running. Slackware Linux uses a number of common Unix tricks to speed up file I/O (input/ouput)—one is that it does not al-ways save changes to a file on disk immediately. Sometimes these changes are buff-ered in RAM until a better time. So, when you turn off the machine with the power switch or reset the machine with the reset button, not all of the files are written to disk.

The proper way to shut down your Slackware Linux machine is with the halt or shutdown command. You must be logged in as the superuser to use either of these commands. When you enter halt and then press ⏎, the system will stop as soon as possible. Once the system is halted, a message will be displayed on screen telling you so.

With the shutdown command, you can specify that the machine shut down after a certain period of time. For example, issuing the command shutdown 9:30 will cause the machine to shut down at 9:30AM. It is better to use the shutdown command when many people are using the machine at one time. If you are the only person using the machine, the halt command is the quickest and easiest way to quit Linux. (Hitting Ctrl-Alt-Del will do the same thing as executing the halt command. You can safely reset your machine at any time by pressing the Ctrl-Alt-Del key combination.)

WARNING You should never turn your machine off while Slackware Linux is running. Doing so may corrupt files needed for Linux to run. Always use either the halt or the shutdown command to quit.

What's Next?

You should now have Slackware Linux installed and running on your system, and a user account set up. This is the account you should use most of the time. You should only use the root account when you need to do system maintenance.

In the rest of Book I, I'll talk about two things you can do with your new system: run the X Window windowing system and the DOS Emulator. These are two features of Slackware Linux that are very popular. X Window is the standard windowing system used on Unix workstations, and its inclusion in Slackware Linux makes Slackware look like a real Unix operating system. The DOS Emulator allows you to run lots of DOS-based applications. Since application software is the one area where Slackware Linux—and Unix in general—is weakest, its presence makes using Slackware Linux as your primary operating system all the more possible.

As you continue to read Book I, you should refer frequently to Matt Welsh's book, *Linux Installation and Getting Started*, which is included as Book II in this kit. Appendix A in Book II includes a bibliography of useful books about Unix. Chapter 7 in Book I will point you to many sources of both on-line and printed information relative to Slackware Linux and Unix in general. You can also use most texts about Unix as a guide to using your Slackware Linux system. The one thing to remember is that Slackware Linux—and Unix in general—is a very powerful and complicated operating system. Many people have spent many years mastering how to use it. If you invest the time to learn how to use Slackware Linux, you will be rewarded by having a truly powerful and robust operating system at your disposal. And remember, everything you learn about Slackware Linux is directly applicable to other forms of Unix. I've known more than one Unix system administrator who got their start by learning how to maintain a Linux machine.

CHAPTER

FIVE

Configuring and Using the X Window System

5

- Installing the X Window System

- Configuring X Window

- Starting Up X Window

- A Quick Tour of X Window

- Exiting X Window

X Window is the standard windowing system on Unix workstations. The Slackware Linux CD-ROM that comes with this book includes XFree 86, a version of X Window Release 11 Version 6 customized for '386-based Unix and Unix-like operating systems like Linux. By installing the X Window system on your computer, you will have even easier access to the multitasking capabilities of Linux. With it you can run multiple applications, with each application displayed in its own window. You can also start using powerful graphics programs available for Linux (many of which are included on the CD-ROM that comes with this book). By using the X Window development tools also included on the CD-ROM, you can start developing your own windowing programs today.

A Note on the XFree86 Project

The X Window system was originally developed at the Massachusetts Institute of Technology, which has since made the source code for the X Window system freely available to the public, just like the source code to Linux. It is currently being refined and extended by the X Consortium, an organization of companies and groups with an interest in the future of the X Window system.

The XFree86 Project, a member of the X Consortium, is a non-profit organization whose aim is to develop and make freely available the X Window system for Intel-based computers. You can get more information about them via Internet e-mail by sending a message to Xfree86@Xfree86.org, or by accessing the World Wide Web document http://www.xfree86.org/. The XFree86 Project is supported by donations. They are always in need of both monetary and computer hardware donations.

Installing the X Window System

If you elected to install X Window while you were installing Slackware Linux on your system, you can skip installing it now. You should still take a look at "Hardware Requirements," below, to see if the X Window system will run on your computer.

Otherwise, you will now need to use the `setup` command to install the X Window system onto your computer.

Hardware Requirements

While Slackware Linux itself has rather modest hardware requirements, the X Window system requires a more substantial system. You should have at least 8 MB of RAM and a fast '386 or better CPU. You should also have at least 20 MB of disk space available to store the files for the X Window system.

The X Window system makes heavy use of your graphics card—it is the most important piece of hardware required by the system. The version that comes with this book should work with the following types of video cards:

Nonaccelerated Video Cards

- Tseng ET3000, ET4000AX, ET4000/W32
- Western Digital/Paradise PVGA1
- Western Digital WD90C00, WD90C10, WD90C11, WD90C24, WD90C30
- Genoa GVGA
- Trident TVGA8800CS, TVGA8900B, TVGA8900C, TVGA8900CL, TVGA9000, TVGA9000i, TVGA9100B, TVGA9200CX, TVGA9320, TVGA9400CX, TVGA9420
- ATI 28800-4, 28800-5, 28800-6, 28800-a
- NCR 77C22, 77C22E, 77C22E+
- Cirrus Logic CLGD6205, CLGD6215, CLGD6225, CLGD6235
- Compaq AVGA
- OAK OTI067, OTI077

Accelerated Video Cards

- Cirrus GLGD5420, CLGD5422, CLGD5424, CLGD5426, CLGD5428
- Western Digital WD90C31
- S3 86C911, 86C924, 86C801, 86C805, 86C928
- ATI mach8 supported by the XF86_Mach8 server
- ATI mach32
- IBM 8514/a and true clones

What to Install

You can use the setup program to install the X Window system on your computer. To run the setup program while logged into the system as the superuser, type /sbin/setup and then press ↵. We discussed using setup in Chapter 3. Here we will just cover how it relates to installing the X Window system.

NOTE To install the X Window system on your computer—or any additional Slackware Linux package—you will need to be logged in as the superuser. You should either log in as root or log in with your usual username and use the su command to become the superuser before proceeding.

Once you start up the setup program, you should select the Source option and then press ↵. Everything from this point on should look familiar to you. The procedure is almost identical to what you did in Chapter 3 to install Slackware Linux onto your computer. The only difference is that you should only select the X—and maybe the XAP—disk sets to install. The X disk set contains the X Window system. The XAP disk set contains applications that run under the X Window system.

When installing the X disk set, you will be given the choice of a number of different X Window servers. The following list will help you choose the server that works with the type of card you have.

Server	Designed to work with…
XF86_SVGA	most Super VGA cards
XF86_S3	cards built around the S3 chipset
XF86_Mach8	video cards build around ATI's Mach 8 chipset
XF86_Mach32	video cards built around ATI's Mach 32 chipset
XF86_8514	video cards built with IBM's 8514 chipset

The XAP disk set contains a number of the application programs for the X Window system. Installing the contents of this disk set will give you access to many graphical X Window applications, such as GNU Chess, a chess game; XPaint, a graphics program; and Seyon, a powerful telecommunications program.

Configuring X Window

Now that you have X Window installed on your computer, you are ready to configure it. You need to tell X Window what type of video adapter, monitor, and mouse you have installed in your system. Until recently, this has involved a long trial-and-error process of editing configuration files and then starting up X Window to see the results. But Slackware Linux now includes a program that will help you configure the X Window system. This program will ask you a series of questions and, based on your answers, set up the X Window system. By using this program, you do not have to edit any of the X Window configuration files yourself.

Using a Preconfigured Config File

Slackware Linux's X Window system comes with configuration files for a number of popular setups. If any of the following describes your configuration, you should use the instructions in this section to get Slackware Linux's X Window system up and running. If you do not see an entry that matches your computer, go ahead to the next section, where we'll cover using the `ConfigXF86` program to configure the X Window system on your computer.

To see a list of the preconfigured configurations that are available, follow these instructions:

1. Type `more /usr/X11/lib/X11/Xconfig/Xconfig.Index` and then press ↵. You will see a list of configurations displayed on screen. You can use the space bar to scroll down the list.

2. Determine which of the configurations listed most closely matches your computer, and remember the configuration number associated with it. If none of the configurations seem to match your computer, you will need to skip to the

next section, where I tell you how to use the `ConfigXF86` program to configure the X Window system.

3. Assuming that you found an entry in the index file that matches your computer, type `cp /usr/X11/lib/X11/Sample-Xconfig-files/Xconfig.n`
`/usr/X11/lib/X11/Xconfig` and then press ↵. Once this is done, the X Window system will use this sample for its configuration information.

That's all there is to it. You are now ready to start up the X Window system. Skip
ahead to the section, "Starting X Window." If X Window does not start as expected,
you can either replace X Window's configuration file with another of the sample
files and try again, or follow the directions in the next section for using the program
`ConfigXF86` to create a configuration file.

Creating a Config File

In this section I'll show you how to use the program `ConfigXF86` to create the configuration file for the X Window system by selecting options from menus. Just as
when you originally installed X Window on your computer, you will need to be
logged in to the system as the superuser in order to configure it. You should either
be logged in as `root` or use the `su` command to become the superuser before following these instructions.

1. From the Slackware Linux command line, type `ConfigXF86` and then press ↵.

2. Once `ConfigXF86` starts up, you will see a screen asking for information
about the mouse in your computer, along with a prompt at the bottom of the
screen, which looks like >. You should now enter the number that corresponds to the type of mouse that you have in your system. Use the table below to determine the number for your mouse.

Enter	If you have...
2	any type of bus mouse
3	a Logitech serial mouse
4	a Microsoft serial mouse
6	a Mouse Man serial mouse
7	a Mouse Systems serial mouse

TIP

Most serial mice are compatible with the Microsoft serial mouse. If you have a serial mouse that is not included on this list, you should pick Microsoft Serial mouse and continue.

3. If you selected a serial mouse in the above step, you will now be shown a screen in which you can specify to which serial port the mouse attaches. Type `/dev/tty0` if your mouse is attached to COM1 or `/dev/tty1` if your mouse is attached to COM2. If you properly answered the questions about your mouse when you first installed Slackware Linux, you can also enter `/dev/mouse` as the port to which your mouse is attached.

4. If you are using a serial mouse, you'll now have to enter the baud rate of the mouse. You can safely enter 1200 and then press ↵ regardless of the type of serial mouse attached to your computer. All serial mice should work at 1200 baud.

5. `ConfigXF86` now displays all the settings you have entered. If you see anything wrong with the information, type n and then press ↵. This will take you back to the start of the program and allow you to enter new information. If everything looks correct on screen, type y and then press ↵.

6. Next, you will be prompted to enter the font path. Press ↵ to accept the default font path and continue with the configuration process.

Next, `ConfigXF86` needs to configure the video adapter that the X Window system will use.

7. `ConfigXF86` will now display a screen full of information about setting up your video adapter. You should read this information and then press ↵ to continue to the next screen.

8. You will now be shown a list of video cards that are compatible with `ConfigXF86` and the X Window system. You should type in the number that appears to the left of the name of the video card that is in your computer. If you don't see your video card listed in the first screen, you can press ↵ without entering a number to display another screen of video cards.

WARNING   You may not be able to run the X Window system on your computer if you do not see your video card on this list. Picking the wrong video card from this list can do damage to your monitor. Be careful!

9. Once you have specified the video card that is in your computer, a list of monitors will appear. Specify the monitor that is attached to your computer by typing the number that appears to the right of its name, and then press ↵. You can press ↵ without entering a number to see more choices.

TIP   Choosing the wrong monitor from this list is less dangerous than choosing the wrong video card. If your exact monitor is not included on the list, pick one that closely matches your monitor.

Starting Up X Window

To start X Window, you should be logged into the system with your regular username—not as the superuser. If you are still logged in as root, use the exit command to log off and then log in again using the username that you created for your own use.

At the Slackware Linux prompt, type startx and then press ↵. You should see messages appear on your screen as X Window starts to run. Once the X Window system is running, it will put your computer into graphics mode and you will see a blank screen with your mouse pointer on it.

TIP

If X does not start after you type `startx`, there is most likely a problem with the X Window configuration files. Reread the sections earlier in this chapter about configuring X Window to see if you entered some incorrect information. You can also refer to Chapter 5 in Book II for an additional discussion about the X Window system.

A Quick Tour of X Window

5

In this section, you will learn how you can use the X Window system to do some basic computing tasks. A full discussion of the X Window system is beyond the scope of this book. See Chapter 5 in Book II for an X Window tutorial.

The X Window system has one major difference from other windowing systems such as Microsoft Windows and the Apple System. While other windowing systems include the user interface as part of the system, the X Window system runs a separate program to provide the user interface. This allows you to change the look and feel of your system by starting up a different window manager while still running X Window. This is not possible with, for example, Microsoft Windows—as long as you are using Microsoft Windows, you are using its user interface. The default window manager used when you install the X Window system with Slackware Linux is the Feeble Virtual Window Manager (aka `fvwm`).

TIP

If you install the XV disk set, the default window manager will be the Open Look window manager. Some people prefer Open Look to the Feeble Virtual Window Manager, though it makes greater demands on RAM.

`fvwm` assigns menus to each of the mouse buttons. For example, when you point at the desktop and click on the left mouse button, you will see a menu containing a list of X Window programs. Selecting xterm from the list and releasing the mouse button causes the xterm program to run. xterm is a very useful application that creates a terminal window, allowing you to type in commands. You can also quickly access other applications such as Seyon, an X Window-based communications program; GNU Plot, a graphics plotting package; and XPaint, a graphics program, via the left mouse button menu.

TIP Don't worry if you select one of these programs and it doesn't start up. You may be selecting a program from the XAP disk set that you have not installed. You can always go back and add more X Window applications by installing the XAP disk set with Slackare Linux's setup program.

Exiting X Window

Some people never want to exit X Window. They keep it running on their Slackware Linux computers all the time. But if you do want to exit it, follow these steps:

1. Point the mouse pointer at the desktop, away from any windows you have on screen.

2. Right click on the desktop. That is, point the mouse pointer at the desktop, and then click and hold down the left mouse button. A menu will appear.

3. While still holding down the left mouse button, drag the mouse around until the Exit menu is selected. A submenu should appear listing further options.

4. Now drag the mouse pointer until Yes, Really Exit is highlighted and then release the button.

The X Window system should now stop running. It will take it a few seconds to shut down, and then you will see the shell prompt on screen.

More About X Window

In this chapter we have just touched the surface in our description of the X Window system. X Window is one of the most powerful and versatile windowing systems available, and many Linux applications use it. Once you start using the X Window system regularly, you will find it an indispensable computing tool. For an X Window tutorial, see Chapter 5 in Book II.

5

CHAPTER

SIX

The DOS Emulator

6

- Creating a DOS Boot Disk

- Installing the DOS Emulator

- Configuring the Pseudo-Hard Drive

- Giving Other Users Access to the DOS Emulator

- Using the DOS Emulator

With Slackware Linux, you can run a whole host of programs that you could never use with DOS. While you can find software to address a wide range of scientific and technical problems, this new world of software is still lacking in one crucial area: applications. Fortunately, there is a way around this problem. The DOS Emulator is a program that allows you to "run" DOS just like any other Linux program on your Slackware Linux machine. With the DOS Emulator, you will be able to run a wide range of DOS-based software, including Quicken for DOS, Quattro Pro, and Microsoft Word for DOS.

NOTE   The DOS Emulator is not able to run with Microsoft Windows 3.1, nor any Windows 3.1 applications. But all hope is not lost, since there is a group of Linux programmers working on a project called WINE, which when finished, will allow you to run Microsoft Windows applications and X Window applications side by side on your screen. It is possible to run Microsoft Windows 3.0 under the DOS Emulator, but most current Windows applications will not work with Windows 3.0, so this feature is not very useful.

In this chapter, you will learn how to install and configure the DOS Emulator to work with Slackware Linux on your computer. Once the DOS Emulator is set up, you will be able to start some DOS-based applications right from Slackware Linux. Depending on the DOS software you usually use, you may find yourself never needing to boot up DOS again.

The DOS Emulator is not a part of the standard Slackware Linux distribution. It is, however, included on the CD-ROM that comes with this book.

In order to get the DOS Emulator running on your computer, you will have to do a number of things:

- Create a DOS boot disk containing the files needed to run DOS
- Install the DOS Emulator from the CD-ROM
- Install some DOS files that you already have
- Create a configuration file that will allow you to run the DOS Emulator while logged into the system as a normal user

Virtual Consoles

Slackware Linux includes a very useful feature called *virtual consoles*. virtual consoles are a simple and easy way to access the multiprocessing power of Linux; using virtual consoles, you'll be able to start up many programs all at the same time. When you first start up Slackware Linux, you are using virtual console 1. Each virtual console displays its output on its own screen. You can switch between the different virtual consoles by holding down the Alt key and pressing a function key. Each function key between F1 and F6 will switch you to a different virtual console. (It is possible to set the actual number of virtual consoles available by modifying some of Slackware Linux's configuration files.)

In addition to using virtual consoles to switch between Linux programs, you can also use them to switch between the DOS Emulator and other Linux programs. The only difference is that when you are switching to a virtual console from the DOS Emulator, you must hold down the Ctrl key, as well as the Alt key and function key. So, to switch to virtual console 2 when using the DOS Emulator, you would hold down Ctrl-Alt-F2. You can switch from a virtual console running another Linux program to one running the DOS Emulator just as if it were any Linux program—you just use Alt and the function key of the virtual console.

Creating a DOS Boot Disk

Since DOS is commercial software, it is not included with the DOS Emulator, so the first step in getting the DOS Emulator to work on your computer is to create a DOS boot disk. The DOS Emulator does not really "emulate" DOS, rather it allows a copy of it to run under Linux, just as if it were any other Linux program.

To create a DOS boot disk, you first need to have DOS booted up on your computer and a DOS prompt on screen. If you are currently running Slackware Linux, you should now boot DOS by removing any disk you may have in your A: drive and pressing the key combination Ctrl-Alt-Del. Linux should display a message telling you that the system is going down. Following this message, the machine will reset.

1. Once DOS is running and you have a DOS prompt, place a blank disk in your A: drive.

2. Type `format a:/s` and then press ↵. This will format the disk. Then, the three files needed to boot DOS, `msdos.sys`, `io.sys`, and `command.com` will be copied to the disk. You will see

```
Format complete
System transferred

Volume label (11 characters, ENTER for none)?
```

on screen. Go ahead and press ↵, since you do not need to assign a volume label to the disk.

3. When you see the DOS prompt again, you can start copying onto the disk the files needed to get the DOS Emulator running. Type `copy c:\dos\fdisk.exe a:` and then press ↵. The disk drive light should come on for a few seconds, and then a DOS prompt will appear on screen.

4. Now type `copy c:\dos\sys.com a:` and press ↵. Again, the drive light should go on for a few seconds, and then you will once again see a DOS prompt appear on screen. Both the `FDISK` and `SYS` programs are used later to make the DOS Emulator's pseudo-hard disk bootable.

The files that you need in order to run the DOS Emulator under Linux are now on the floppy disk, and you are ready to install the DOS Emulator.

Installing the DOS Emulator

Now that you have a disk from which you can boot up DOS, you are ready to install the DOS Emulator software. The following steps are done from Slackware Linux, so you should have Linux running now. If you still have DOS running, put the Slackware Linux boot disk that you created in Chapter 3 into your A: drive and press Ctrl-Alt-Del. Your machine should reboot. Once you get the Slackware Linux login prompt, log in with the username `root`. You must be logged in as the super-user in order to install the DOS Emulator.

You can always find the most up-to-date version of the DOS Emulator on the anonymous ftp site `tsx-11.mit.edu`, in the directory `/pub/linux/ALPHA/dosemu`. You will only find the *source code* for the emulator here. In order to compile it to use on your computer, you will need to install the Slackware Linux development system from the D disk set.

In the next section, you are going to install the files that make up the DOS Emulator. All of these files are combined into a single archive file on the CD-ROM. You will need to use the program `tar` to extract onto your Slackware Linux drive the files needed to run the DOS Emulator.

1. While logged in as `root`, type `cd /` and then press ↵. This will make the root directory the current directory.

2. Next type `mount -t iso9660 -O ro /dev/cdrom /mnt` to make the CD-ROM accessible from Slackware Linux.

3. Type `tar xf /mnt/dosemu-0.60.tar`, and then press ↵. This command installs the files you need to run the DOS Emulator on your computer.

You now have the DOS Emulator software installed on your computer, but you are not yet ready to start running DOS programs from within Linux. Remember the DOS boot disk we just made? Next we will use that boot disk to copy DOS to the DOS Emulator's pseudo-hard disk.

Configuring the Pseudo-Hard Drive

While you are using the DOS Emulator, you will have access to a special drive. Though it will appear as your C: drive while you are using the DOS Emulator, it is not at all the same as the C: drive you have when you are using regular DOS. The C: drive that you have access to in the DOS Emulator is a pseudo-hard drive—it's actually a disk file kept on your Slackware Linux drive. What you need to do now is place a copy of DOS onto this pseudo-hard disk so that you can quickly boot up DOS as a task under Slackware Linux.

1. Place the DOS boot disk you just created into the A: drive.

2. While still logged in as `root`, type `dos -A` and then press ↵. The `dos` command will start up the DOS Emulator, and the `-A` option will tell the DOS Emulator to boot DOS from your A: floppy drive.

As the DOS Emulator boots, you should see the following messages on screen

```
Linux DOS Emulator 0.53p128 $Date: 1994/10/14 17:58:38 $
Last configured at Oct 21 02:06:58 1994
on fuzzy, Linux 1.1.54 #1 Sun Oct 16 21:13:41 CDT 1994
Bugs, Patches & New Code to James MacLean, jmaclean@fox.nstn.ns.ca

Starting DOS...
```

3. This will be followed by a prompt to enter the current date. Your machine should already know the proper date, so just press ↵ to continue.

4. You are now asked for the current time. Again, your machine should already be set to the correct time, so just press ↵ again.

5. You will see the following typical DOS command prompt

   `A:\>`

   You are now ready to start copying the DOS system to the C: drive.

6. Type `fdisk /mbr` and then press ↵. This will write some special information that DOS needs to the C: drive.

7. Now type `sys c:`, and then press ↵. You should see some disk activity and then the message `System transferred` will be displayed on screen. That's all there is to it. You have just copied DOS to the C: drive that you use with Slackware Linux's DOS Emulator.

Since we have copied everything that we need to the new C: drive, we are now ready to exit the DOS Emulator and start it up, this time from the C: drive.

8. Type `c:\exitemu` and then press ↵. EXOTEMU is a special DOS program that you use to exit the DOS Emulator and return to Slackware Linux.

Now, you should once again be looking at a Slackware Linux prompt. If everything has gone well so far, you have started up the DOS Emulator using a copy of DOS on a floppy disk and copied the DOS files from that disk to the DOS Emulator's pseudo-hard disk. The DOS Emulator's pseudo-hard disk should now contain all the files needed to run DOS.

9. This time, start up the DOS Emulator by typing dos -C, and then press ↵. As before, the dos command will start up the DOS Emulator, but this time the -C option tells it to boot DOS from the C: drive. (Remember, you can boot from the C: drive now because we just copied the necessary DOS files to it.)

You should see a start-up banner for the DOS Emulator again.

```
Linux DOS Emulator 0.53p128 $Date: 1994/10/14 17:58:38 $
Last configured at Oct 21 02:06:58 1994
on fuzzy, Linux 1.1.54 #1 Sun Oct 16 21:13:41 CDT 1994
Bugs, Patches & New Code to James MacLean,
jmaclean@fox.nstn.ns.ca

Starting DOS...
```

10. When prompted to enter the date and time, just press ↵ as before. Your computer should already know the correct date and time. You should now see the following DOS prompt

   C:\>

11. Type c:\exitemu and then press ↵. You need to exit the DOS Emulator to continue configuring it to run properly.

The DOS Emulator is now set up to run on your computer. In the following sections, you will finish configuring it so it will be ready to run your DOS-based programs.

Giving Other Users Access to the DOS Emulator

So far, we have just been running the DOS Emulator while logged in as the super-user, root. Using root is fine when you are testing out the DOS Emulator, but as I have advised you before, it is better to use your normal login name whenever possible while using Slackware Linux. Immediately after installation, the DOS Emulator will only run when started by the superuser—no other users can start it. You will now create the configuration file that the DOS Emulator needs in order to know which users can use the program. You will only put your personal login name in this file. If you are sharing the machine with a number of different people, you might want to put their login names in the configuration file as well. It's up to you.

First, you must be logged in as the superuser. Either log in as root or use the su command to become root, if you are not already.

1. While logged in as the superuser, type cat > /etc/dosemu.users, and then press ↵. When you press ↵, the cursor will go to the next line. Linux is waiting for you to type in information that it will then place in the file dosemu.users.

2. Type your username and then press ↵. For example, I would type dan and then press ↵, since I use the username dan when I log in to my Slackware Linux machine.

3. Now hold down the Ctrl key and press D. Ctrl-D is a special character in Unix that means "end-of-file." You are telling Slackware Linux that you are finished entering this file. When you hit Ctrl-D, a Linux prompt should appear on the next line.

> **TIP** You can also use a text editor like vi to create this file. Refer to Chapter 3 in Book II for more information.

You are now done adding yourself as a user. To specify more than one user, repeat step 2. When you are done entering all of the usernames of the people who you want to be able to use the DOS Emulator, press Ctrl-D.

Using the DOS Emulator

Now that you have the DOS Emulator installed and running on your computer, it is time to start using it. The DOS Emulator comes with a number of special DOS programs that you can use while it is running. These programs control aspects of the DOS Emulator and give you access to some special features of Slackware Linux from within DOS.

1. Start up the DOS Emulator by typing dos -C at the Slackware Linux prompt, and then press ↵. The DOS Emulator banner should appear on screen, and, in a few seconds, you should see the DOS prompt.

2. Type dir, and then press ↵. You should see a listing of the files that are on the C: drive.

3. Now type d: and press ↵. The DOS Emulator's D: corresponds to the Slackware Linux file system. You can access all of the files on your Slackware Linux drive via the DOS Emulator's D: drive.

4. You can see the files available to you on the D: drive by typing dir and then pressing ↵. A list of files similar to that shown below will appear on screen.

```
Volume in drive C is DOSEMU49
Volume Serial Number is 374A-09CF
Directory of C:\

BOOTOFF  COM        12 05-04-94   7:36p
EXITEMU  COM        16 05-04-94   7:36p
CONFIG   SYS       183 07-21-93   2:57a
EMUFS    SYS       664 05-04-94   7:36p
AUTOEXEC BAT        44 05-04-94   8:52p
BOOTON   COM        12 05-04-94   7:36p
CONFIG   BAK        23 04-14-93   1:47a
AUTOEXEC BAK        34 04-14-93   1:48a
VGAON    COM        32 05-04-94   7:36p
```

(Continued)

```
    VGAOFF    COM          8 05-04-94    7:36p
    LREDIR    EXE      8,606 04-19-94    9:41p
    DOSDBG    EXE     13,580 04-19-94    9:41p
    PDIPX     COM     26,511 05-04-94    7:18p
    LANCHECK  EXE     49,890 04-19-94    9:41p
    EMS       SYS        416 05-04-94    7:36p
    COMMAND   COM     54,500 09-27-93    6:20a
            16 file(s)      154,531 bytes
                            864,256 bytes free
```

5. Notice that one of the files on the D: drive is called `dos`. This corresponds to the entire drive onto which you originally installed Slackware Linux. Type `cd \dos`, and then press ↵.

6. Now if you type `dir` and press ↵ again, you will see the contents of your entire "real" C: drive—not the pseudo-C: drive created by the DOS Emulator.

7. Type `cd dos` again to change into the DOS directory on your C: drive.

8. Now type `dir` and press ↵. You will see a listing of all the files that are usually in the DOS directory.

You now know how to access files on your normal DOS drive from within the DOS Emulator. Let's continue to set up the DOS Emulator by editing the `autoexec.bat` file.

1. With the `d:\dos\dos` directory still current, type `edit c:\autoexec.bat` and then press ↵. The DOS Edit window will appear, displaying the contents of the file `autoexec.bat`, as shown in Figure 6.1.

2. Use the ↓ key to move the cursor down to the bottom of the file.

3. Now type `path d:\dos\dos`, and then press ↵. You have just added your DOS directory to the search path. From now on, whenever you use the DOS Emulator, you can type in any DOS command and the DOS Emulator will find it in your DOS directory.

You can also add to the path a directory that holds any DOS-based programs that you usually use. So, if you use Quicken for DOS, which stores all of its files in the directory `quicken`, you would enter `path d:\dos\dos; d:\dos\quicken` to set the path to include both the DOS directory and Quicken's directory. You can add any number of directories in this manner.

FIGURE 6.1:

While running Slackware Linux's DOS Emulator, we have loaded the **autoexec.bat** file into the DOS Edit program.

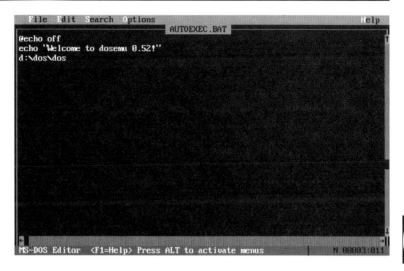

Once you have added the quicken directory to the path, you can start up Quicken for DOS by simply typing q and pressing ↵ at the DOS Emulator prompt. When you do this, Quicken will start up on your computer, as shown in Figure 6.2. This is the same procedure for starting up Quicken straight from DOS.

FIGURE 6.2:

The DOS Emulator allows you to run DOS-based application software such as Quicken.

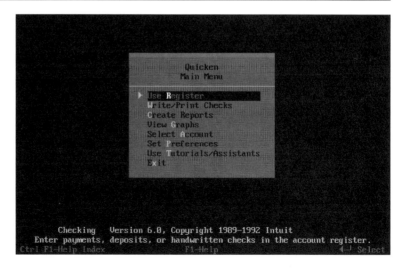

In Summary

The DOS Emulator enables you to run many thousands of DOS-based application programs from within Slackware Linux. By adding the DOS Emulator to your system, you have alleviated one of the major problems with all Unix distributions: the lack of application software.

CHAPTER

SEVEN

Linux Resources

- Electronic Sources of Information

- Printed Sources of Information

- User Groups

7

By now you have Slackware Linux installed and running on your computer and are ready to start learning more about it and Unix. While we have tried to give you the basic information needed to get Linux up and running, Linux is such a versatile and complicated operating system that I've been unable to cover even a fraction of the available features. It is because Linux is both such a popular and complicated operating system that you will find many sources of information about it. These days, you will find talk of Linux in many forums—both print and electronic. In this chapter, I'll give you some pointers on where to get more information. Some of it is specific to Linux and some of it is more general but still applicable to Linux.

Given the strong role that the Internet has played in the development of Linux, it's no surprise that much of the information available about Linux is located on the Internet. The Linux Usenet newsgroups are among the most popular newsgroups around. You can also receive information about Linux via e-mail, the World Wide Web, and from many other on-line sources.

While the number of books written specifically for Linux is still small, Linux is so close to Unix that the vast majority of Unix books contain useful information for Linux users.

Electronic Sources of Information

In this section, you will learn about some of the major sources of information about Linux available on the Internet.

> **TIP**
>
> We assume that you are familiar with the Internet and how to access Internet resources—particularly Usenet news, mailing lists, and the World Wide Web. *The Internet Road Map,* also published by Sybex, is a good general introduction to the Internet.

Usenet Newsgroups

Usenet is a worldwide electronic messaging system. With Usenet, you can exchange messages with other Linux users—and developers—from around the world. Even Linus Torvalds himself, the father of Linux, participates in some of the Linux newsgroups. If you have access to either the Internet or a commercial on-line service such as CompuServe or America Online, you probably have access to Usenet. Of the many thousands of *newsgroups*—discussion areas devoted to a single topic—that exist on Usenet, you will find many that contain information you can use to learn about Linux.

Methods for accessing Usenet news vary, depending on the Internet provider or on-line server you use. Many Unix machines directly connected to the Internet have the newsreader program `tin`. If you are unsure how to use Usenet with your service provider, contact your provider's technical support department.

As you start using Usenet to learn about Linux, you should keep a few basic rules in mind. Before you post a question to any newsgroup, you should spend some time looking for related articles that have already been posted. Often, when you have a common question, you will find that an answer has already been posted by someone else. You should also consult each newsgroup's FAQ (Frequently Asked Questions) document before posting a question. Most newsgroups have FAQs that contain the most common questions and answers from the newsgroup. Make sure that you only post a message to a newsgroup that is related to the topic of your message. Asking how to set up your e-mail system on the `comp.os.linux.development` newsgroup will not get you many answers.

A number of newsgroups are dedicated to talking about specific parts of Linux.

Newsgroup	Topic
comp.os.linux.admin	Linux system administration
comp.os.linux.advocacy	Arguments about the merits of Linux compared to other operating systems

Newsgroup	Topic
`comp.os.linux.announce`	Announcements of interest to the Linux community
`comp.os.linux.answers`	The latest HOWTO documents are regularly posted to this newsgroup
`comp.os.linux.development`	Linux kernel development
`comp.os.linux.development.apps`	Developing and porting applications to Linux
`comp.os.linux.development.system`	Tools to help in developing and porting applications to Linux
`comp.os.linux.hardware`	Linux-compatible hardware
`comp.os.linux.help`	General questions and answers about running Linux
`comp.os.linux.misc`	A catch-all newsgroup for discussions about Linux that do not fit into any other newsgroup
`comp.os.linux.networking`	Networking with Linux
`comp.os.linux.setup`	Problems setting up Linux
`comp.os.linux.x`	Running the X Window system and its applications under Linux

In addition to newsgroups dedicated to the discussion of Linux, you can find useful information in many of the thousands of general newsgroups carried by Usenet. Some of the more useful groups include:

Newsgroup	Topic
comp.os.unix	General discussions about the Unix operating system
comp.windows.x.announce	Announcements about the X Window system
comp.mail.sendmail	The sendmail program. This is the program that comes with Slackware Linux and handles sending and receiving e-mail from the Internet.
gnu.announce	Announcements about the Free Software Foundation's GNU project. Much of the software that makes up Slackware originated from the Free Software Foundation.
gnu.emacs	The emacs text editor. (emacs is available for Slackware Linux on the E disk set.)
alt.dcom.slip-emulators	Software that allows you to emulate a SLIP connection with a regular shell Unix account. Many Linux users use this type of software to attach their Linux machines to the Internet.
comp.security.unix	Unix security issues

7

Newsgroup	Topic
comp.unix.admin	Administering a Unix system
comp.unix.shell	Different Unix shells—like bash—and shell programming
comp.protocols.tcp-ip	TCP/IP networking
comp.windows.x	The X Window system
comp.windows.x.i386	Running the X Window system on Intel 386-based operating systems

All of the newsgroups listed above are available worldwide. In addition to these newsgroups, some local and regional newsgroups also address issues related to Linux. Local newsgroups are usually restricted to people in a certain organization, such as a university. Regional newsgroups are usually restricted to a certain part of the United States, like California, or a foreign country. By reading one of these newsgroups, you'll find other Linux users in your area.

Linux Mailing Lists

Another very popular way to distribute information about Linux is through *mailing lists.* A mailing list is similar to a Usenet newsgroup, but the messages are sent via electronic mail. Mailing lists dedicated to Linux are run from two different mailing list server sites on the Internet. The original location of the Linux mailing lists is niksula.hut.fi in Finland. E-mail traveling between this site and the United States tends to be rather slow, so a second site, vger.rutgers.edu, was set up. Both of these sites maintain a similar set of mailing lists, although they are different. Messages posted to a mailing list that is run from one of these servers will not automatically appear on the corresponding mailing list run on the other machine.

The following table lists all of the mailing lists currently maintained at vger.rutgers.edu. See below for information on how to subscribe.

TIP

You can retrieve the most up-to-date version of this list by sending e-mail to majordomo@vger.rutgers.edu, that contains only the text lists in the body of the message. You will receive a copy of the list by e-mail within minutes of sending your message.

List Name	Topic
linux-680x0	Porting Linux to the 68000 processor
linux-admin	Administrating a Linux machine
linux-all	General discussions about Linux
linux-alpha	Porting Linux to the Alpha processor
linux-announce	Announcements of interest to all Linux users. These are the same announcements that are posted to Usenet's comp.os.linux.announce newsgroup.
linux-apps	Applications running under Linux
linux-bbs	Running a bulletin board system under Linux
linux-c-programming	Writing programs for Linux in the C computer language
linux-config	Configuring a Linux system

7

List Name	Topic
`linux-diald`	The program `diald`, which is used to create a dial-up connection to the Internet
`linux-doc`	The Linux Documentation Project
`linux-fido`	Transferring e-mail between a Linux machine and the FIDO network of BBSs
`linux-fsf`	The Free Software Foundation
`linux-gcc`	The GNU C compiler (`gcc` is the C compiler that comes with Slackware Linux)
`linux-gcc-digest`	A digested form of the `linux-gcc` mailing list
`linux-hams`	Using Linux with a ham radio
`linux-interviews`	The Interviews windowing system that can run with Linux
`linux-ipx`	Integrating Novell's IPX protocol with Linux
`linux-japanese`	Japanese language extensions to Linux
`linux-kernel`	The Linux kernel and kernel development
`linux-kernel-digest`	A digested version of the `linux-kernel` mailing list

List Name	Topic
linux-kernel-patch	A forum for information about patches to the Linux kernel
linux-laptop	Running Linux on laptop computers
linux-linuxbsd	Running a BBS under Linux
linux-localbus	Using Linux on a local bus-based machine
linux-mca	Using Linux on an MCA-based machine
linux-mgr	Using the mgr package under Linux
linux-mips	Porting Linux to the MIPS processor
linux-msdos	Running DOS-based programs under Linux
linux-msdos-digest	A digested version of the linux-msdos mailing list
linux-net	Networking issues related to Linux
linux-newbie	A mailing list dedicated to new Linux users
linux-oi	Using the Object Interface tool kit
linux-pkg	Making package installation easier
linux-ppc	The Power-PC port of Linux

7

List Name	Topic
linux-ppp	Using PPP networking under Linux
linux-pro	The Linux PRO distribution
linux-qag	Linux Quality Assurance Group
linux-scsi	SCSI drive development and usage
linux-serial	Using serial devices under Linux
linux-seyon	Seyon, an X Window terminal program
linux-sound	Using sound cards and utilities under Linux
linux-standards	Standardizing various aspects of Linux
linux-svgalib	The SVGA graphics library
linux-tape	Using tape storage devices under Linux
linux-term	Using the term suite of programs
linux-uucp	Using UUCP under Linux
linux-wabi	The Windows Binary Application Interface (WABI) project, a project to allow Linux and other Unix-like operating systems to run Microsoft Windows applications

List Name	Topic
`linux-word`	Creating a word processing program for Linux
`linux-x11`	Using the X Window system under Linux

For complete instructions on using any of these mailing lists, send an e-mail message to `majodomo@vger.rutgers.edu`, putting only the word `help` in the body of the message. To join any of the above mailing lists, send an e-mail message to `majodomo@vger.rutgers.edu`, with only the text `subscribe` *list-name* in the body of the message, where *list-name* is the mailing list you've chosen from above.

The other large set of mailing lists for Linux is maintained on the European machine `niksula.hut.fi`. You can obtain a list of the mailing lists available on `niksula.hut.fi` by sending a message containing only the word `help` to `linux-activists@niksula.hut.fi`. You should receive a list of mailing lists by return e-mail. Note that this system is in Finland and the turn-around time for messages sent from the United States can be rather long. We do not cover this mail server in detail because the list server based in the United States provides better service in America.

TIP
If you do not currently have access to the Internet or e-mail, you should take a look at Appendix D in Book II. It contains a list of BBSs that offer files and other information about Linux. Some of these BBSs also give you access to Usenet newsgroups and Internet e-mail.

Linux on the World Wide Web

The latest way to distribute information on the Internet is through the World Wide Web. All types of information are starting to appear on the Web, including lots of information about Linux. In order to view the Web, you will need both an Internet connection and a Web browser. Once you have an Internet connection set up, you can use a Web browser like NCSA Mosaic or Netscape. Both NCSA Mosaic and Netscape for Linux require that you have both the X Window system and an Internet connection. NCSA Mosaic is available for anonymous ftp from `sunsite.unc.edu` in the /pub/Linux/system/Network/info-systems/Mosaic directory. You retrieve Netscape via anonymous ftp from ftp.netscape.com in the /netscape/unix directory. The best jumping off point for information about Linux is Matt Welsh's Linux Documentation Project home page. You can access this page via the *URL* http://sunsite.unc.edu/mdw (a URL is how you specify a document on the World Wide Web). The Linux Documentation Project's home page includes links to many other Linux resources available on the Web. The following are some of the pages about Linux available on the Web.

http://www.xfree86.org contains the XFree86 Project Web server. These are the people who make the version of X Window that comes with Slackware Linux.

http://www.leo.org/archiv/linux/archiv/ann_index.html is a searchable database of announcements that have been posted to the comp.os.linux.announce Usenet newsgroup.

http://liber.stanford.edu/linuxppc/linux-ppc-FAQ.html contains information about creating a version of Linux for Power PC-based computers.

http://whirligig.ecs.soton.ac.uk/~rmk92/armlinux.html contains information about creating a version of Linux for computers based on the ARM processor.

These are just a few of the many pages about Linux accessible from the World Wide Web. You will find links to many other Linux resources on the Internet located on all of the above pages.

On-Line Documentation

The two most popular on-line documentation projects for Linux are included on the CD-ROM that comes with this book. These are the Linux Documentation Project's manuals, which include *The Kernel Hacker's Guide* and *The Network Administrator's Guide,* and the Linux HOWTO documents.

The HOWTO documents are stored on the CD in the /HOWTO directory. They are all stored as ASCII text files, so you should be able to access them from either DOS or Linux. To access them from Linux, do the following:

1. Type mount -t iso9660 -o ro /dev/ cdrom /mnt while logged in as the superuser, and then press ↵. This will mount your CD-ROM drive so it is accessible from the directory /mnt.

2. Now type cd /mnt/HOWTO and then press ↵. This will make the directory that contains the HOWTO documents on the CD-ROM your current directory.

3. You can now see a list of all the HOWTO documents by typing ls and then pressing ↵.

4. To display the contents of any of these HOWTO documents on screen, use the more command. For example, to display the contents of the CD-ROM HOWTO, type more CDROM-HOWTO and then press ↵.

NOTE Since all of the HOWTO files are in ASCII text format, you can also access them from DOS. You can open them in any text editor, such as DOS Edit or Windows' Notepad, or a word processing program.

In addition to having a complete set of Linux HOWTO documents, the CD-ROM also contains manuals produced by the Linux Documentation Project. You can find these documents in the CD-ROM's /linux-doc-project directory. After mounting the CD-ROM as described above, this directory will be called /mnt/linux-doc-project. The manuals are stored on the CD-ROM in a number of formats—the most usable are in ASCII text and Postscript. You can display The ASCII text files on screen, either from Linux or from DOS. The Postscript files are ready to be sent to a Postscript-compatible printer for printing.

NOTE The Linux Documentation Project's *Linux Installation and Getting Started* manual is included as Book II of this package.

Printed Sources of Information

Not only is Linux well represented in electronic documents, but there are also quite a few printed documents that can help you make the most of your system.

Unix Books

The first thing you should read after getting Slackware Linux installed and running on your computer is Matt Welsh's *Linux Installation and Getting Started*, which is included as Book II in this package. It will give you a good overview of using Linux and how it relates to other forms of Unix. Once you have read *Linux Installation and Getting Started*, you will be in a much better position to start reading other Unix titles. There are many thousands of books about the Unix operating system that contain information useful for learning about Linux. See Appendix A of Book II for a list of books about Linux and Unix.

Magazines

Many computer magazines now include articles about Linux from time to time. *Dr. Dobb's Journal* recently printed an interview with Linus Torvalds, Linux's creator, and named him Programmer of the Year. Articles about Linux also appear in Unix and X Window magazines as well. In addition to articles specifically about Linux, you will find articles about software that runs under Linux, such as `emacs` or Mosaic, in many other magazines, such as *Unix Review*.

There is one magazine that is dedicated to talking just about Linux—the *Linux Journal*. Each month, the *Linux Journal* features articles about how to use your system to do new things, such as access the Internet or use it with a ham radio, and how other people are using Linux. You can contact them via e-mail at `subs@ssc.com`, or write them at:

Linux Journal
P.O. Box 85867
Seattle, WA 98145-1867
FAX: (206) 526-0803

User Groups

Another growing source of information about Linux is local user groups. More and more user groups dedicated to either Unix or Linux are appearing, and many Unix user groups now have Linux special interests groups, called SIGs. You can find a listing of user groups in your area in a local computer newspaper like *MicroTimes* or *Computer Currents*.

In Summary

As you can see from this chapter, learning about Slackware Linux—and Unix in general—is a continuous process. Slackware Linux is such a large and complex operating system that there will always be some new area for you to study. You will find that as you continue to use Slackware Linux, and take advantage of the resources discussed in this chapter, you will learn more about the system. As soon as you understand one feature, you will find another feature to study.

7

CHAPTER

EIGHT

Using Internet Tools to Retrieve Linux Material

8

- Connecting to the Internet

- Viewing Linux Documents on the World Wide Web

- Using `ftp` to Retrieve Software

In this chapter, you'll learn how to use some common tools, such as `ftp`, Netscape and Mosaic to retrieve information about Linux from the Internet. First, you will learn about your options for connecting your computer to the Internet. Then, you'll find out how to access a selection of the Linux resources on the Internet that were covered in the last chapter. Finally, you'll see how you can use `ftp`—a method for copying files between machines on the Internet—to download new software to your computer, including both software that runs under Slackware Linux, and entire new releases of Slackware Linux.

> **TIP**
>
> While Slackware Linux is available free from the Internet, its size makes it impractical to completely download to your computer. Slackware Linux itself is about 90 MB in size, so it takes a prohibitively long time to transfer from the Internet to your machine via modem. Also, once you get the entire Slackware Linux archive downloaded to your machine, you'll need to store all those files. These are the two reasons why it is worthwhile to get Slackware Linux on a CD-ROM, such as the one provided with this book.

Connecting to the Internet

This year, the Internet is one of the biggest news stories around. It is hard to read a magazine, glance at a newspaper, or watch television without hearing some reference to the Internet. The Internet is used by the people developing Linux to share ideas and transfer source code between them. Linux is, by its very existence, a testament to what can be accomplished with the Internet. When you take a look at the Internet, you'll find that it is mostly made up of Unix-based workstations. Since it was built with Unix machines, your Slackware Linux machine fits on the Internet much better than machines running different operating systems. So by running Slackware Linux on your computer, you are in a far better position to take advantage of the Internet than most other people. With Slackware Linux running, you will be able to run the same e-mail, news, `ftp`, and other applications on your computer that are commonplace throughout the Internet.

Slackware Linux not only provides you with many different options for accessing the Internet, but also makes a great platform on which to run Internet server software, such as a World Wide Web server or an ftp server. All the software needed to do this either comes with Slackware Linux or is easily accessible from the Internet.

While it is possible to run Internet servers on your machine using SLIP or PPP to connect to the Internet (see "Using a SLIP/PPP Connection," below), it is not practical for a real Internet site. When you use SLIP or PPP to connect via a modem, the transfer rate between your computer and the Internet is very slow compared to a dedicated link. Also, you probably won't keep your Internet connection going 24 hours a day, so other people on the Internet will not be able to reliably access the information that you make available. In other words, SLIP/PPP just doesn't cut it when it comes to running an Internet server.

NOTE Although a SLIP or PPP connection is not suitable for running a server offering public information on the Internet, it's fine for your own educational purposes. Running a World Wide Web server on your Slackware Linux machine, regardless of your connection to the Internet, is an excellent way to learn how to maintain and operate a Web server.

8

Using a SLIP/PPP Connection

SLIP (Serial Line Internet Protocol) and PPP (Point-to-Point Protocol) are methods for sending TCP/IP packets—the pieces of data that make up the Internet—over a serial link like that created over phone lines between two modems. When you use SLIP or PPP to connect to the Internet, your computer becomes one more node on the Internet—just like any other Internet-connected computer.

The program you use on your Slackware Linux machine to start up a SLIP or PPP session is called `dip`. `dip` reads a *script* file that tells it how to call up your Internet service provider and log into your SLIP or PPP account. It then executes those instructions, and once connected and logged in, starts to route Internet packets between your local computer and the Internet. You can learn more about configuring `dip` in the Linux Documentation Project's *Networking Administrators Guide*, which is included on the CD-ROM in the `/linux-doc-project` directory.

Using an Ethernet Connection

If your Linux machine sits on a local area network (LAN) that is attached to the Internet, you may be able to configure your Linux machine to use the Internet without the need for SLIP or PPP. Slackware Linux comes with drivers for many popular Ethernet cards, including:

- 3Com 3c501, 3c503, and 3c509/3c570
- Novell NE1000 and NE2000 and compatibles
- Western Digital WD80x3

If you have one of these cards in your computer, you should be able to access Internet resources right over your LAN. To start networking on your Slackware Linux machine, use the Slackware Linux setup program to install the networking packages from the N disk set. The N disk set contains all the networking programs you'll need to gain access to the Internet.

> **TIP** Chapter 5 in Book II provides more details about using Linux on a network. You should also see the Linux Documentation Project's *Linux Networking Administrator's Guide*, which is available in the /linux-doc-project directory on the CD-ROM, and the Net-2 HOWTO document, located in the HOWTO directory. Both of these include information about connecting to the Internet via your local area network.

Viewing Linux Documents on the World Wide Web

In the last chapter, I discussed some of the Linux resources available on the World Wide Web. Here, I'll go into more detail about how you can use two popular Internet tools: Netscape, an X Window-based Web browser; and lynx, a text-based browser, to access the Web.

NOTE

In order to access either the World Wide Web or `ftp`, you must be using a computer that is attached to the Internet. This connection can be via any of the ways discussed earlier in this chapter. Once you are connected to the Internet, you can run software like Netscape Navigator and `lynx` right on your own computer. If you have an account on another Unix machine that is connected to the Internet, you can run text-based Web browsing software like `lynx`.

Using Netscape to Connect to Sunsite's Linux Documentation Project Home Page

One of the most popular Web browsers these days is Netscape Navigator. While Netscape is copyrighted software (and as such, could not be included on the CD-ROM that comes with this book), you can download it from Netscape's own ftp server at `ftp.netscape.com`.

TIP

Another popular World Wide Web browser for X Window is NCSA Mosaic. It is available via anonymous `ftp` from `ftp.ncsa.uiuc.edu`.

To use Netscape:

1. You must be using a machine that is running the X Window system, is connected to the Internet, and has the Linux version of Netscape installed. Type `netscape` at the Slackware Linux shell prompt and then press ↵. Netscape will load and then display a window.

2. You can now view information on the World Wide Web by selecting File ➤ Open Location. In the dialog box that appears, enter a URL of a World Wide Web resource, like the ones listed in the last chapter. For example, to view the Linux Documentation Project's home page, type `http://sun-site.unc.edu/mdw` and then press ↵. The Linux Documenatation Project home page will load and be displayed on screen, as shown in Figure 8.1.

FIGURE 8.1:

Netscape is a popular World Wide Web browser for X Window. With Netscape you can access information from Web servers located all over the world. Displayed here is the Linux Documentation Project's home page, which is a very good launching point for finding Linux information on the Web.

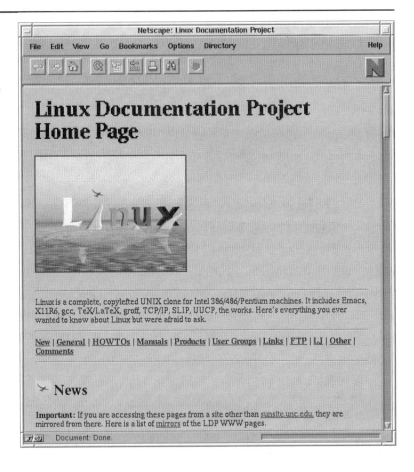

As you view documents in Netscape, links to other documents appear in blue. You can display these other documents by clicking on the links. By following the links that appear in the Linux Documentation home page, you will find lots of other documents that pertain to Linux. See the list of home pages listed in Chapter 7— these should provide a good starting point for your Web travels.

Using lynx: A Text-Based Web Browser

If you don't have access to a graphical Web browser like Netscape, or prefer a faster, text-based Web browser, you can use lynx.

lynx supports all the same hypertext features as its graphical relatives. The only drawback is that it does not support graphics or other forms of multimedia. lynx is, however, perfectly suited to searching and reading all of the text-based information about Linux on the Web.

TIP   lynx is just one of many text-based World Wide Web browsers. If the Unix machine you are using to access the Internet does not have lynx installed, you should trying using the browser www, which is another text-based World Wide Web browser.

To use lynx:

1. On a Unix machine that is connected to the Internet and has lynx installed, type lynx and then press ↵. A page of information, including *links*—or words which you can select to load other pages—will appear.

2. When lynx loads, the first link on the page is highlighted. Pressing ↵ will load the page that link points to. You can use the Ctrl-N and Ctrl-P keys to move the highlight to other links on the page. Every time you press Ctrl-N, the following link becomes highlighted. Pressing Ctrl-P causes the previous link to become highlighted.

3. Once a link is selected, press ↵ to load the page. (Figure 8.2 shows the Linux Documentation home page.)

Using ftp to Retrieve Linux Software

ftp, which stands for file transfer protocol, is a program that copies files between different computers on the Internet. Anonymous ftp is a way in which people can make files available to anyone on the Internet.

When you start up ftp, you give it the name of an ftp site on the Internet. It then contacts an ftp server program on the other computer, and the two start communicating. Once this connection is made, the first thing you need to do is identify yourself to the ftp server program. You do this by entering a username and a password. The username can be on the remote machine—just as your Slackware Linux

FIGURE 8.2:

lynx gives you access to all the features of the Web except graphics. Here you see the same Web page as shown in the previous figure, only this time it does not include any graphic elements, such as a logo or different fonts.

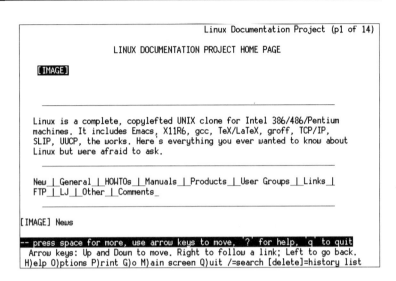

```
                                              Linux Documentation Project (p1 of 14)

                          LINUX DOCUMENTATION PROJECT HOME PAGE

      [IMAGE]


      _____

      Linux is a complete, copylefted UNIX clone for Intel 386/486/Pentium
      machines. It includes Emacs, X11R6, gcc, TeX/LaTeX, groff, TCP/IP,
      SLIP, UUCP, the works. Here's everything you ever wanted to know about
      Linux but were afraid to ask.


      _____

      New | General | HOWTOs | Manuals | Products | User Groups | Links |
      FTP | LJ | Other | Comments_


     _____

  [IMAGE] News

-- press space for more, use arrow keys to move, '?' for help, 'q' to quit
   Arrow keys: Up and Down to move. Right to follow a link; Left to go back.
   H)elp O)ptions P)rint G)o M)ain screen Q)uit /=search [delete]=history list
```

machine keeps a list of usernames and passwords, so do remote machines. An alternative to having a username and password on the remote machine is to use anonymous ftp. Anyone can log into an anonymous ftp server from a remote machine and retrieve files without using a username or password.

ftp is one of the Internet tools that made the development of Linux possible. Without ftp and a few central ftp sites, the many hundreds of Linux developers would not have been able to share source code between them. Since ftp is such an important tool in the development of Linux, it's not suprising that many files of interest to the Slackware Linux user are available via anonymous ftp. In the next section, we'll cover how to access and download files from two important Linux ftp sites: ftp.cdrom.com and tsx-11.mit.edu. Both of these sites contain many thousands of files that relate to Linux and Slackware Linux.

Connecting to ftp.cdrom.com to Download Slackware Linux

This session assumes that you are using a Unix machine that is connected to the Internet. It can either be your Slackware Linux machine, connected either by ethernet, SLIP or PPP, or it can be a machine that belongs to an Internet service provider or university.

ncftp: A Better ftp than ftp

ftp is one of the oldest methods for distributing information on the Internet, and over the years, many improvements have been made to it. Slackware Linux comes with an improved version called ncftp, which automates the process of logging into the anonymous account on remote machines. You don't need to type in the anonymous username and your e-mail address as a password—ncftp takes care of that for you by automatically logging you into the remote machine with the username anonymous, and sending your e-mail address as the password. ncftp also remembers the ftp sites you frequent and can use shortened names for each of them. To access an ftp site you use frequently, all you need to do is enter the first part of its name when you start up ncftp. With ncftp, you view remote text files on screen by using the page command. All you need to do is type page followed by the name of the text file you wish to view, and the contents of the file will appear on screen. This saves you from having to download the file to your computer, exit the ftp program, and then view the file. These features of ncftp make it a real time saver. You should use ncftp if it is available on the machine from which you access the Internet.

8

1. At the shell prompt, enter ftp ftp.cdrom.com and then press ↵ to start up the ftp program and connect to the machine ftp.cdrom.com. This machine is the official repository for Slackware Linux. Here you will always find the most up-to-date version of Slackware Linux.

2. Once the ftp program connects to the remote machine, you will be asked to provide a password with the line

```
Connected to wcarchive.cdrom.com.
220 wcarchive.cdrom.com FTP server (Version wu-2.4(1) Mon Aug 15
13:35:59 PDT 1994) ready.
Name (ftp.cdrom.com:dat):
```

3. Since you only need to access the anonymous areas of this machine, type anonymous and then press ↲. You will see

```
331 Guest login ok, send your complete e-mail address as password.
Password:
```

4. Now enter your e-mail address as a password and press ↲. When you use anonymous ftp to access ftp servers, it is customary to provide your e-mail address as your password. ftp site administrators use this information to track who is using their ftp site. A welcome message will appear on screen, and then you will see the following ftp prompt.

```
ftp>
```

This means that the ftp program is waiting for you to enter a command. Try the ls command first. The ls command works with ftp just as it does when you enter it at the Slackware Linux shell prompt. The only difference is that now you are listing the contents of a directory that is located on a remote machine, not your local machine.

5. Type ls and then press ↲. You should see

```
200 PORT command successful.
150 Opening ASCII mode data connection for file list.
.1
.2
.3
.4
.5
.6
.7
.8
pub
bin
etc
catalog
incoming
.10
README
```

(Continued)

```
.cache
cache+
ls-1R
.9
.14
.15
ls-1R.Z
.forward
.16
.17
jobs
catalog.fre
.rhosts
.11
.12
.13
config
catalog.ita
226 Transfer complete.
210 bytes received in 0.12 seconds (1.7 Kbytes/s)
```

8

NOTE   **The list of files that you see may be different than what is shown here. This list is current as of the writing of this book.**

6. Most anonymous ftp sites keep their publicly accessible software in a public directory called /pub. The actual location of Slackware Linux on this machine is /pub/linux/slackware. To change into this directory, type cd /pub/linux/slackware and then press ↵.

7. Now that we have changed into the directory that contains Slackware Linux, we can display the contents of the directory with the ls command. This time, use the command ls -C. This will display the files in a column format.

```
.BOOTING            README.INS            link2cd/
COPYING             SLAKWARE.FAQ          non-commercial-use/
ChangeLog           UPGRADE.TXT           rootdsks.12/
Copyright           bootdsks.12/          rootdsks.144/
INSTALL.TXT         bootdsks.144/         slaktest/
INS_1_2.MEG         contents/             slakware/
LOWMEM.TXT          contrib/              source/
MIRRORS.TXT         install/
README.220          kernels/
```

You should recognize some of the directory names here—this is the same version of Slackware Linux that comes on the CD-ROM with this book. As new versions of Slackware Linux are created, they will appear in this directory.

8. Type bin and then press ⏎. You should always use the bin command before transferring binary files with ftp. If you do not use the bin command, the files are just transferred as text files and the result will not be usable.

9. You can now use ftp's get command to transfer files from the ftp server to your local machine. Typing get README.220 will cause the file README.220 to be copied from the ftp.cdrom.com machine to the machine on which you are running ftp. The ftp server that runs on ftp.cdrom.com includes a special feature to make transferring entire directories simpler. You can add the extension .tar to any directory and use that with the get command. This will convert the directory and its contents into a tar archive file and save this file to the machine on which you are running ftp. tar, which comes with Slackware Linux, is a standard Unix program for creating file archives.

TIP

If your Internet connection is via a modem, watch out for large files while you are using ftp. Large files take lots of time to transfer over a modem. Since Slackware Linux is so large, you may end up transferring many 100s of megabytes. When this book was written, Slackware's slakware directory contained over 90 MB of data.

10. You can use the cd command to change into any other directory on ftp.cdrom.com, and the get command to copy additional files to the computer on which you are running ftp.

11. Once you are done using ftp, you should type quit and then press ↵. This will exit you from the ftp program and return you to the shell prompt.

Connecting to tsx-11.mit.edu to Retrieve Linux Software

In this section, you'll learn how to use ftp to connect to another large Linux archive site—tsx-11.mit.edu. This site, located at MIT, contains software for Linux, such as games, graphic programs, and much more, all of which work with Slackware Linux. Since I just gave you rather detailed, step-by-step instructions for using ftp to access an ftp site, we won't go into as much detail here.

1. Start up the ftp program by entering ftp tsx-11.mit.edu and then pressing ↵. You will see the following on screen

```
220 tsx-11 FTP server (Version wu-2.4(2) Thu Jul 21 21:54:33 EDT 1994)
ready.
Name (tsx-11.mit.edu:dan):
```

2. Type anonymous and then press ↵. The ftp server should respond with the following message

```
331 Guest login ok, send your complete e-mail address as password.
Password:
```

3. You should now type in your e-mail address and press ↵. Whenever you are using anonymous ftp, you should enter your e-mail address as your password. This allows the ftp site administrators to keep track of who is using their site.

105

4. A welcome message will now be displayed on screen, followed by the `ftp` prompt

   `ftp>`

   We are now logged into the `tsx-11.mit.edu` ftp server and are ready to re-trieve files. As I said earlier, some of the more valuable resources available on this ftp site are the Linux Documentation Project manuals and HOWTO documents. You can always find updated copies of these documents on this machine.

5. The Linux Documentation Project documents are kept in the directory `/pub/linux/docs/linux-doc-project`. Type `cd /pub/Linux/docs/linux-doc-project` and then press ↵ to make this the current directory.

6. You can now type `ls` and then press ↵ to see a list of the files in the directory. When I did it, I saw a list of filenames that included `nag-1.0.as-cii.tar.gz`, which is version 1.0 of the Linux Documentation Project's *Network Administrator's Guide*.

7. You can use the `get` command to retrieve one of the files you see listed. Type `get nag-1.0.ascii.tar.gz` and then press ↵ to retrieve the file. When the file is finished copying to your local machine, you will see a message telling you how big the file is. At this point, the `ftp` prompt will reappear on screen. To retrieve multiple files from this directory, repeat this command.

8. Now let's take a look at the HOWTO documents kept in the directory `/pub/linux/docs/HOWTO`. Type `cd /pub/linux/docs/HOWTO` and then press ↵. When you press ↵, a message will appear saying that the command was successfully completed. The `ftp` prompt will then reappear.

9. Now type `ls` and then press ↵ to see a list of files in the directory. When I did this, I saw the file `SCSI-HOWTO` listed.

10. You can now use the `get` command to retrieve any of the files. For example, to retrieve the file `SCSI-HOWTO`, type `get SCSI-HOWTO` and then press ↵.

11. Once you are done using `ftp`, type `quit` and then press ↵. You will be re-turned to the shell prompt.

You should now be comfortable accessing information about Linux from the Internet. With tools such as Netscape, lynx, and ftp you have access to many thou-sands of files. All you need to retrieve this information is access to the Internet.

In Summary

Throughout this book I have concentrated on the basics of getting Slackware Linux up and running. You should now be in a good position to continue to use Linux, as well as increase your knowledge of Unix. The *Linux Installation and Getting Started* manual, which is included as Book II, is a good next step for learning about Linux.

8

BOOK II

Linux Installation and Getting Started

Matt Welsh

The Linux Documentation Project

PREFACE

"You are in a maze of twisty little passages, all alike."

Before you looms one of the most complex and utterly intimidating systems ever written: Linux, the free operating system for the 80386 and 80486. Linux, the great accomplishment of the free software world. Linux—the name is enough to strike terror into the hearts of men and women. Not only is it difficult to pronounce, it's almost impossible to comprehend.

Linux was produced by a mishmash team of Unix gurus, hackers, and the occasional loon. The system itself reflects this complex heritage. The jungle is deep and dangerous. You are entering the realm of black magic and deep wizardry, of voodoo programming and subtle obfuscation. Monsters lurk behind every tree, ready to pounce. Making your way though it alone—well, you can forget about that.

You hold in your very hands the map and guidebook to the many-faceted world of Linux. Armed with this guide, neither the novice nor the guru need fear this system ever again. In fact, setting up your own Linux system can be a great deal of fun. Sit back. Relax. Read on.

This is the second edition of this book. The first edition was specific to the then-popular SLS distribution of Linux. Since that time, Linux has diversified in many ways, and many separate distributions are becoming available. This version is a complete installation and new-user guide, intended to be general for any distribution. The first three chapters have been bagged, and replaced with two new chapters that are much more comprehensive than the original. The appendices have been revised, and various sections have been tweaked to remain up-to-date with the many changes taking place within the Linux community.

Audience

This book is for any personal computer user who wants to install and use Linux on their system. We assume that you have basic knowledge about personal computers and operating systems such as MS-DOS. No previous knowledge about Linux or Unix is assumed.

Despite this, we strongly suggest that Unix novices invest in one of the many good Unix books out there. (Several of them are listed in Appendix A.) This book contains information useful to new Linux users, but for more advanced information, you'll have to look elsewhere!

Organization

This book contains the following chapters:

Chapter 1, *Introduction to Linux*, gives a general introduction to what Linux is, what it can do for you, and what is required to run it on your system. It also provides helpful hints for getting help and reducing overall stress.

Chapter 2, *Obtaining and Installing Linux*, explains how to obtain the Linux software, as well as how to install it—from repartitioning your drive to creating filesystems and loading the software on the system. It contains instructions meant to be general for any distribution of Linux, and relies on the documentation provided for your particular release to fill in any gaps.

Chapter 3, *Linux Tutorial*, is a complete introduction to using the Linux system for Unix novices. If you have previous Unix experience, most of this material should be familiar.

Chapter 4, *System Administration*, introduces many of the important concepts of system administration under Linux. This will also be of interest to Unix system administrators who want to know about the Linux-specific issues of running a system.

Chapter 5, *Advanced Features*, introduces the reader to a number of advanced features supported by Linux, such as the X Window System and TCP/IP networking.

Appendix A, *Sources of Linux Information*, is a listing of other sources of information about Linux, including newsgroups, mailing lists, on-line documents, and books.

Appendix B, *Linux Distribution and Mail Order List*, provides a short list of available Linux distributions and where to get them.

Appendix C, *ftp Tutorial and Site List*, is a tutorial for downloading files from the Internet with `ftp`. This appendix also includes a listing of ftp archive sites that carry Linux software.

Appendix D, *Linux BBS List*, is a listing of bulletin board systems worldwide that carry Linux software. Because most Linux users do not have access to the Internet, it is important that information on BBS systems becomes available.

Appendix E, *The GNU General Public License*, contains a copy of the GNU GPL, the license agreement under which Linux is distributed. It is very important that Linux users understand the GPL; many disagreements over the terms of the GPL have been raised in recent months.

Acknowledgments

This book has been long in the making, and many people are responsible for the outcome. In particular, I would like to thank Larry Greenfield and Karl Fogel for their work on the first version of Chapter 3, and Lars Wirzenius for his work on Chapter 4. Thanks to Michael K. Johnson for his assistance with the LDP and the LaTeX conventions used in this manual, and to Ed Chi, who sent me a printed copy of the book for edition.

Special thanks to Melinda A. McBride at SSC, Inc., who did an excellent job completing the index for Chapters 3, 4, and 5. I would also like to thank Andy Oram, Lar Kaufman, and Bill Hahn at O'Reilly and Associates for their assistance and interest in the Linux Documentation Project.

And, of course, much thanks to the many activists, from Linus Torvalds to Peter MacDonald, for devoting so much time and energy to this project, and without whom none of this would be possible.

Last but not least, thanks to the myriad of readers who have sent their helpful comments and corrections. Who needs a spell checker when you have an audience?

Matt Welsh
January 13, 1994

Credits and Legalese

The Linux Documentation Project is a loose team of writers, proofreaders, and editors who are working on a set of definitive Linux manuals. The overall coordinator of the project is Matt Welsh, aided by Lars Wirzenius and Michael K. Johnson.

This manual is but one in a set of several being distributed by the Linux Documentation Project, including a *Linux User's Guide*, *System Administrator's Guide*, and *Kernel Hacker's Guide*. These manuals are all available in LaTeX source format and PostScript output for anonymous ftp from `sunsite.unc.edu`, in the directory `/pub/Linux/docs/LDP`.

We encourage anyone with a penchant for writing or editing to join us in improving Linux documentation. If you have Internet e-mail access, you can join the DOC channel of the `Linux-Activists` mailing list by sending mail to:

`linux-activists-request@niksula.hut.fi`

with the line

`X-Mn-Admin: join DOC`

as the first line of the message body.

Feel free to get in touch with the author and coordinator of this manual if you have questions, postcards, money, or ideas. Matt Welsh can be reached via Internet e-mail at `mdw@sunsite.unc.edu`, and in real life at

205 Gray Street
Wilson, N.C. 27893
U.S.A.

UNIX is a trademark of X/Open.

Linux is not a trademark, and has no connection to UNIX™ or X/Open.

The X Window System is a trademark of the Massachusetts Institute of Technology.

MS-DOS and Microsoft Windows are trademarks of Microsoft, Corp.

this book either free of charge or for profit. If doing so, you may wish to include a short "installation supplement" for your release.

The author would like to know of any plans to publish and distribute this book commercially. In this way, we can ensure that you are kept up-to-date with new revisions. And, should a new version be right around the corner, you might wish to delay your publication of the book until it is available.

If you are distributing this book commercially, donations, royalties, and/or printed copies are greatly appreciated by the author. Contributing in this way shows your support for free software and the Linux Documentation Project.

All source code in *Linux Installation and Getting Started* is placed under the GNU General Public License. See Appendix E for a copy of the GNU "GPL."

Documentation Conventions

These conventions should be obvious, but we'll include them here for the pedantic.

Italic	Used to mark new concepts and keywords, emphasis in text, and occasionally quotes or introductions at the beginning of a section. Also used to indicate commands for the user to type when showing screen interaction (see below).
<Italics>	Used to mark meta-variables in the text, especially in representations of the command line. For example,

ls -l *<foo>*

where *<foo>* would "stand for" a filename, such as /bin/cp.

Mono-spaced	Used to represent screen interaction, as in

$ ls -l /bin/cp

-rwxr-xr-x 1 root wheel 12104 Sep 25 15:53 /bin/cp

⏎, ↓, ↑, ←, →   Represent a key to press. You will often see one of these in this form:

Press ⏎ to continue.

NOTE   This is a note that supplements the text or that refers you to another section for more information.

WARNING   This is a warning that alerts you to problems you may encounter in carrying out a function discussed in the text.

CHAPTER

ONE

Introduction to Linux

Linux is quite possibly the most important achievement of free software since the original *Space War*, or, more recently, emacs. This book will be your guide to its shifting and many-faceted world. Linux has developed into the operating system for businesses, education, and personal productivity. It is no longer just for Unix wizards who sit for hours in front of the glowing console (although we assure you that quite a number of users still fall into this category). This book will help you get the most out of it.

Linux (pronounced with a short *i*, as in *LIH-nucks*) is a clone of the Unix operating system that runs on Intel 80386 and 80486 computers. It supports a wide range of software, from TEX to X Window to the GNU C/C++ compiler to TCP/IP. It's a versatile, bona fide implementation of Unix, freely distributed by the terms of the GNU General Public License (see Appendix E).

Linux can turn any 386 or 486 PC into a workstation. It will give you the full power of Unix at your fingertips. Businesses are installing Linux on entire networks of machines, using the operating system to manage financial and hospital records, a distributed user computing environment, telecommunications, and more. Universities worldwide are using Linux for teaching courses on operating systems programming and design. And, of course, computing enthusiasts everywhere are using Linux at home for programming, productivity, and all-around hacking.

What makes Linux so different is that it is a *free* implementation of Unix. It was and still is developed by a group of volunteers, primarily on the Internet, exchanging code, reporting bugs, and fixing problems in an open-ended environment. Anyone is welcome to join in the Linux development effort: all it takes is an interest in hacking a free Unix clone and some kind of programming know-how. The book that you hold in your hands is your tour guide.

About This Book

This book is an installation and entry-level guide to the Linux system. The purpose is to get new users up and running with the system by consolidating as much important material as possible into one book. Instead of covering many of the volatile technical details, those things which tend to change with rapid development, we give you enough background to find out more on your own.

Linux is not difficult to install and use. However, as with any implementation of Unix, there is often some black magic involved to get everything working correctly. We hope that this book will get you on the Linux tourbus and show you how groovy this operating system can be.

In this book, we cover the following topics:

- What is Linux? The design and philosophy of this unique operating system, and what it can do for you.

- All of the details of what is needed to run Linux, including suggestions on what kind of hardware configuration is recommended for a complete system.

- How to obtain and install Linux. There are many distributions of Linux software. We present a general discussion of Linux software distributions, how to obtain them, and generic instructions for installing the software (which should be applicable to any distribution).

- A brief introductory Unix tutorial, for those users who have never had experience with Unix before. This tutorial should, hopefully, provide enough material for complete novices to have enough basic know-how to find their way around the system.

- An introduction to systems administration with Linux. This covers the most important tasks that new Linux administrators will need to be familiar with, such as creating users, managing filesystems, and so forth.

- A cursory overview of advanced features of Linux, such as the X Window System, networking with TCP/IP and SLIP, and the setup of electronic mail and news systems.

This book is for the personal computer user wishing to get started with Linux. We don't assume previous Unix experience, but do expect novices to refer to other materials along the way. For those unfamiliar with Unix, a list of useful sources of information is given in Appendix A. In general, this book is meant to be read along with another book on basic Unix concepts.

A Brief History of Linux

Unix is one of the most popular operating systems worldwide because of its large support base and distribution. It was originally developed as a multitasking system for minicomputers and mainframes in the mid-1970s, but has since grown to become one of the most widely used operating systems anywhere, despite its sometimes confusing interface and lack of central standardization.

The real reason for Unix's popularity? Many hackers feel that Unix is the Right Thing—the One True Operating System. Hence the development of Linux by an expanding group of Unix hackers who want to get their hands dirty with their own system.

Versions of Unix exist for many systems—ranging from personal computers to supercomputers such as the Cray Y-MP. Most versions of Unix for personal computers are quite expensive and cumbersome. At the time of this writing, a one-machine version of AT&T's System V for the 386 runs at about U.S. $1500.

Linux is a freely distributable version of Unix developed primarily by Linus Torvalds (`torvalds@kruuna.helsinki.fi`) at the University of Helsinki in Finland. Linux was developed with the help of many Unix programmers and wizards across the Internet, allowing anyone with enough know-how and gumption the ability to develop and change the system. The Linux kernel uses no code from AT&T or any other proprietary source, and much of the software available for Linux is developed by the GNU project at the Free Software Foundation in Cambridge, Massachusetts. However, programmers all over the world have contributed to the growing pool of Linux software.

Linux was originally developed as a hobby project by Linus Torvalds. It was inspired by Minix, a small Unix system developed by Andy Tanenbaum, and the first discussions about Linux were on the Usenet newsgroup `comp.os.minix`. These discussions were concerned mostly with the development of a small, academic Unix system for Minix users who wanted more.

The very early development of Linux was mostly dealing with the task-switching features of the 80386 protected-mode interface, all written in assembly code. Linus writes,

> "After that it was plain sailing: hairy coding still, but I had some devices, and debugging was easier. I started using C at this stage, and it certainly speeds

up development. This is also when I start to get serious about my megaloma-
niac ideas to make 'a better Minix than Minix'. I was hoping I'd be able to recompile gcc under Linux some day....

"Two months for basic setup, but then only slightly longer until I had a disk-
driver (seriously buggy, but it happened to work on my machine) and a small
filesystem. That was about when I made 0.01 available (around late August of
1991): it wasn't pretty, it had no floppy driver, and it couldn't do much of anything. I don't think anybody ever compiled that version. But by then I was
hooked, and didn't want to stop until I could chuck out Minix."

No announcement was ever made for Linux version 0.01. The 0.01 sources weren't
even executable: they contained only the bare rudiments of the kernel source, and
assumed that you had access to a Minix machine to compile and play with them.

On October 5, 1991, Linus announced the first *official* version of Linux: version 0.02.
At this point, Linus was able to run bash (the GNU Bourne Again Shell) and gcc
(the GNU C compiler), but not very much else was working. Again, this was intended as a hacker's system. The primary focus was kernel development—none of
the issues of user support, documentation, distribution, and so on had even been
addressed. Today, the Linux community still seems to treat these ergonomic issues
as secondary to the *real programming*—kernel development.

Linus wrote in comp.os.minix,

"Do you pine for the nice days of Minix-1.1, when men were men and wrote
their own device drivers? Are you without a nice project and just dying to cut
your teeth on an OS you can try to modify for your needs? Are you finding it
frustrating when everything works on Minix? No more all-nighters to get a
nifty program working? Then this post might be just for you.

"As I mentioned a month ago, I'm working on a free version of a Minix-look-
alike for AT-386 computers. It has finally reached the stage where it's even usable (though [it] may not be depending on what you want), and I am willing
to put out the sources for wider distribution. It is just version 0.02...but I've
successfully run bash, gcc, gnu-make, gnu-sed, compress, etc. under it."

After version 0.03, Linus bumped the version number up to 0.10, as more people
started to work on the system. After several further revisions, Linus increased the version number to 0.95, to reflect his expectation that the system was ready for an *official*
release very soon. (Generally, software is not assigned the version number 1.0 until
it is theoretically complete or bug-free.) This was in March of 1992. Almost a year and
a half later, in late December of 1993, the Linux kernel was still at version 0.99.pl14—
asymptotically approaching 1.0. Some felt that version 1.0 would never make it.

Today, Linux is a complete Unix, capable of running X Window, TCP/IP, `emacs`, UUCP, mail, and news software...you name it. Almost all of the major free software packages have been ported to Linux, and commercial software is becoming available. Much more hardware is supported than in original versions of the kernel. Many people have executed benchmarks on 80486 Linux systems and found them comparable with midrange workstations from Sun Microsystems and Digital Equipment Corporation. Who would have ever guessed that this *little* Unix clone would have grown up to take on the entire world of personal computing?

System Features

Linux supports most of the features found in other implementations of Unix, plus quite a few that aren't found elsewhere. This section is a nickel tour of the Linux kernel features.

Linux is a complete multitasking, multiuser operating system (just like all other versions of Unix). This means that many users can be logged into the same machine at once, running multiple programs simultaneously.

The Linux system is mostly compatible with a number of Unix standards (inasmuch as Unix has standards) on the source level, including IEEE POSIX.1, System V, and BSD features. It was developed with source portability in mind: therefore, you are most likely to find commonly-used features in the Linux system which are shared across multiple implementations. A great deal of free Unix software available on the Internet and elsewhere compiles on Linux out of the box. In addition, all source code for the Linux system, including the kernel, device drivers, libraries, user programs, and development tools, is freely distributable.

Other specific internal features of Linux include POSIX job control (used by shells such as `csh` and `bash`), pseudoterminals (`pty` devices), and support for national or customized keyboards using dynamically-loadable keyboard drivers. Linux also supports *virtual consoles*, which allow you to switch between multiple login sessions from the system console in text mode. Users of the `screen` program will find the Linux virtual console implementation familiar.

The kernel is able to emulate 387-FPU instructions itself, so that systems without a math coprocessor can run programs that require floating-point math instructions.

Linux supports various file system types for storing data. Various file systems, such as the *ext2fs* file system, have been developed specifically for Linux. Other file system types, such as the Minix-1 and Xenix file systems, are also supported. The MS-DOS file system has been implemented as well, allowing you to access MS-DOS files directly by mounting an MS-DOS partition or floppy. The ISO 9660 CD-ROM file system type, which reads all standard formats of CD-ROMs, is also supported. We'll talk more about file systems in Chapters 2 and 4.

Linux provides a complete implementation of TCP/IP networking. This includes device drivers for many popular Ethernet cards, SLIP (Serial Line Internet Protocol, allowing you to access a TCP/IP network via a serial connection), PLIP (Parallel Line Internet Protocol), PPP (Point-to-Point Protocol), NFS, and so on. The complete range of TCP/IP clients and services is supported, such as ftp, `telnet`, NNTP, and SMTP. We'll talk more about networking in Chapter 5.

The Linux kernel is developed to use the special protected-mode features of the Intel 80386 and 80486 processors. In particular, Linux makes use of the protected-mode descriptor-based memory management paradigm and many of the other advanced features of these processors. Anyone familiar with 80386 protected-mode programming knows that this chip was designed for a multitasking system such as Unix (or, actually, Multics). Linux exploits this functionality.

The Linux kernel supports demand-paged loaded executables. That is, only those segments of a program which are actually used are read into memory from disk. Also, copy-on-write pages are shared among executables, meaning that if several instances of a program are running at once, they will share pages in physical memory, reducing overall memory usage.

In order to increase the amount of available memory, Linux also implements disk paging: that is, up to 256 MB of *swap space* can be allocated on disk. When the system requires more physical memory, it will swap out inactive pages to disk, thus allowing you to run larger applications and support more users at once. However, swap is no substitute for physical RAM—it is much slower due to drive access latency times.

> **NOTE**
> Swap space is inappropriately named: entire processes are not swapped, but rather individual pages. Of course, in many cases, entire processes will be swapped out, but this is not always the case.

The kernel also implements a unified memory pool for user programs and disk cache. In this way, all free memory is used for caching, and the cache is reduced when running large programs.

Executables use dynamically linked shared libraries, meaning that executables share common library code in a single library file found on disk, not unlike the SunOS shared library mechanism. This allows executable files to occupy much less space on disk, especially those that use many library functions. There are also statically-linked libraries for those who wish to use object debugging or maintain "complete" executables without the need for shared libraries to be in place. Linux shared libraries are dynamically linked at run-time, allowing the programmer to replace modules of the libraries with their own routines.

To facilitate debugging, the Linux kernel does core dumps for post-mortem analysis. Using a core dump and an executable linked with debugging support, it is possible to determine what caused a program to crash.

Software Features

In this section, we'll introduce you to many of the software applications available for Linux, and talk about a number of common computing tasks. After all, the most important part of the system is the wide range of software available for it. The fact that most of this software is freely distributable is even more impressive.

Basic Commands and Utilities

Virtually every utility that you would expect to find on standard implementations of Unix has been ported to Linux. This includes basic commands such as `ls`, `awk`, `tr`, `sed`, `bc`, `more`, and so on. You name it...Linux has it. Therefore, you can expect your familiar working environment on other Unix systems to be duplicated on

Linux. All of the standard commands and utilities are there. (Novice Linux users should see Chapter 3 for an introduction to these basic Unix commands.)

Many text editors are available, including vi, ex, pico, and jove, as well as GNU emacs and variants such as Lucid emacs (which incorporates extensions for use under X Window) and joe. Whatever text editor you're accustomed to using has more than likely been ported to Linux.

The choice of a text editor is an interesting one. Many Unix users still use "simple" editors such as vi (in fact, the author wrote this book using vi under Linux). However, vi has many limitations, due to its age, and more modern (and complex) editors such as emacs are gaining popularity. emacs supports a complete LISP-based macro language and interpreter, a powerful command syntax, and other fun-filled extensions. emacs macro packages exist to allow you to read electronic mail and news, edit the contents of directories, and even engage in an artificially intelligent psychotherapy session (indispensable for stressed-out Linux hackers).

One interesting note is that most of the basic Linux utilities are GNU software. These GNU utilities support advanced features not found in the standard versions from BSD or AT&T. For example, GNU's version of the vi editor, elvis, includes a structured macro language which differs from the original AT&T implementation. However, the GNU utilities strive to remain compatible with their BSD and System V counterparts. Many people consider the GNU versions of these programs superior to the originals.

The most important utility to many users is the *shell*. The shell is a program which reads and executes commands from the user. In addition, many shells provide features such as *job control* (allowing the user to manage several running processes at once—not as Orwellian as it sounds), input and output redirection, and a command language for writing *shell scripts*. A shell script is a file containing a program in the shell command language, analogous to a *batch file* under MS-DOS.

There are many types of shells available for Linux. The most important difference between shells is the command language. For example, the *C Shell* (csh) uses a command language somewhat like the C programming language. The classic *Bourne Shell* uses a different command language. One's choice of a shell is often based on the command language that it provides. The shell that you use defines, to some extent, your working environment under Linux.

No matter what shell you're accustomed to, some version of it has probably been ported to Linux. The most popular shell is the *GNU Bourne Again Shell* (bash), a

Bourne shell variant which includes many advanced features such as job control, command history, command and filename completion, an emacs-like interface for editing the command line, and powerful extensions to the standard Bourne shell language. Another popular shell is tcsh, a version of the C Shell with advanced functionality similar to that found in bash. Other shells include zsh, a small Bourne-like shell; the Korn shell (ksh); BSD's ash; and rc, the Plan 9 shell.

What's so important about these basic utilities? Linux gives you the unique opportunity to tailor a custom system to your needs. For example, if you're the only person who uses your system, and you prefer to exclusively use the vi editor, and bash as your shell, there's no reason to install other editors or shells. The "do it yourself" attitude is prevalent among Linux hackers and users.

Text Processing and Word Processing

Almost every computer user has a need for some kind of document preparation system. (How many computer enthusiasts do you know who still use pen and paper? Not many, we'll wager.) In the PC world, *word processing* is the norm: it involves editing and manipulating text (often in a "What-You-See-Is-What-You-Get" environment) and producing printed copies of the text, complete with figures, tables, and other garnishes.

In the Unix world, *text processing* is much more common, which is quite different than the classical concept of word processing. With a text processing system, text is entered by the author using a "typesetting language", which describes how the text should be formatted. Instead of entering the text within a special word processing environment, the source may be modified with any text editor such as vi or emacs. Once the source text (in the typesetting language) is complete, the user formats the text with a separate program, which converts the source to a format suitable for printing. This is somewhat analogous to programming in a language such as C, and "compiling" the document into a printable form.

There are many text processing systems available for Linux. One is groff, the GNU version of the classic nroff text formatter originally developed by Bell Labs and still used on many Unix systems worldwide. Another modern text processing system is TEX, developed by Donald Knuth of computer science fame. Dialects of TEX, such as LaTEX, are also available.

Text processors such as TeX and `groff` differ mostly in the syntax of their formatting languages. The choice of one formatting system over another is also based upon what utilities are available to satisfy your needs, as well as personal taste.

For example, some people consider the `groff` formatting language to be a bit obscure, so they use TeX, which is more readable by humans. However, `groff` is capable of producing plain ASCII output, viewable on a terminal, while TeX is intended primarily for output to a printing device. However, various programs exist to produce plain ASCII from TeX-formatted documents, or to convert TeX to `groff`, for example.

Another text processing system is `texinfo`, an extension to TeX used for software documentation by the Free Software Foundation. `texinfo` is capable of producing a printed document, or an online-browsable hyper text *Info* document from a single source file. Info files are the main format of documentation used by GNU software such as `emacs`.

Text processors are used widely in the computing community for producing papers, theses, magazine articles, and books (in fact, this book was produced using LaTeX). The ability to process the source language as a plain text file opens the door to many extensions to the text processor itself. Because source documents are not stored in an obscure format, readable only by a particular word processor, programmers are able to write parsers and translators for the formatting language, extending the system.

What does such a formatting language look like? In general, the formatting language source consists mostly of the text itself, along with *control codes* to produce a particular effect, such as changing fonts, setting margins, creating lists, and so on.

As an example, take the following text:

Mr. Torvalds:

We are very upset with your current plans to implement *post-hypnotic suggestion* in the **Linux** terminal driver code. We feel this way for three reasons:

1. Planting subliminal messages in the terminal driver is not only immoral, it is a waste of time;
2. It has been proven that "post-hypnotic suggestions" are ineffective when used upon unsuspecting Unix hackers;
3. We have already implemented high-voltage electric shocks, as a security measure, in the code for `login`.

We hope you will reconsider.

This text would appear in the LaTeX formatting language as the following:

```
\begin{quote}
Mr. Torvalds:

We are very upset with your current plans to implement {\em post-hypnotic
suggestion\/} in the {\bf Linux} terminal driver code. We feel this
way for three reasons:
\begin{enumerate}
\item Planting subliminal messages in the kernel driver is not only
      immoral, it is a waste of time;
\item It has been proven that "post-hypnotic suggestions" are ineffective
      when used upon unsuspecting Unix hackers;
\item We have already implemented high-voltage electric shocks, as a
      security measure, in the code for {\tt login}.
\end{enumerate}
We hope you will reconsider.
\end{quote}
```

The author enters the above "source" text using any text editor, and generates the formatted output by processing the source with LATEX. At first glance, the typesetting language may appear to be obscure, but it's actually quite easy to learn. Using a text processing system enforces typographical standards when writing. For example, all enumerated lists within a document will look the same, unless the author modifies the definition of the enumerated list "environment". The primary goal is to allow the author to concentrate on writing the actual text, instead of worrying about typesetting conventions.

WYSIWYG word processors are attractive for many reasons; they provide a powerful (and sometimes complex) visual interface for editing the document. However, this interface is inherently limited to those aspects of text layout which are accessible to the user. For example, many word processors provide a special *format language* for producing complicated expressions such as mathematical formulae. This is identical to text processing, albeit on a much smaller scale.

The subtle benefit of text processing is that the system allows you to specify exactly what you mean. Also, text processing systems allow you to edit the source text with any text editor, and the source is easily converted to other formats. The tradeoff for this flexibility and power is the lack of a WYSIWYG interface.

Many users of word processors are used to seeing the formatted text as they edit it. On the other hand, when writing with a text processor, one generally does not worry about how the text will appear when formatted. The writer learns to expect how the text should look from the formatting commands used in the source.

There are programs which allow you to view the formatted document on a graphics display before printing. For example, the xdvi program displays a "device independent" file generated by the TEX system under the X Window environment. Other software applications, such as xfig, provide a WYSIWYG graphics interface for drawing figures and diagrams, which are subsequently converted to the text processing language for inclusion in your document.

Admittedly, text processors such as nroff were around long before word processing was available. However, many people still prefer to use text processing, because it is more versatile and independent of a graphics environment. In either case, the idoc word processor is also available for Linux, and before long we expect to see commercial word processors becoming available as well. If you absolutely don't want to give up word processing for text processing, you can always run MS-DOS, or some other operating system, in addition to Linux.

There are many other text-processing-related utilities available. The powerful METAFONT system, used for designing fonts for TEX, is included with the Linux port of TEX. Other programs include ispell, an interactive spell checker and corrector, makeindex, used for generating indicies in LATEX documents; as well as many groff and TEX-based macro packages for formatting many types of documents and mathematical texts. Conversion programs to translate between TEX or groff source to a myriad of other formats are available.

Programming Languages and Utilities

Linux provides a complete Unix programming environment, including all of the standard libraries, programming tools, compilers, and debuggers that you would expect to find on other Unix systems. Within the Unix software development world, applications and systems programming is usually done in C or C++. The standard C and C++ compiler for Linux is GNU's gcc, which is an advanced, modern compiler supporting many options. It is also capable of compiling C++ (including AT&T 3.0 features) as well as Objective-C, another object-oriented dialect of C.

Besides C and C++, many other compiled and interpreted programming languages have been ported to Linux, such as Smalltalk, FORTRAN, Pascal, LISP, Scheme, and Ada (if you're masochistic enough to program in Ada...we're not going to stop you). In addition, various assemblers for writing protected-mode 80386 code are available, as are Unix hacking favorites such as Perl (the script language to end all script languages) and Tcl/Tk (a shell-like command processing system including support for developing simple X Window applications).

The advanced `gdb` debugger has been ported, which allows you to step through a program to find bugs, or examine the cause for a crash using a core dump. `gprof`, a profiling utility, will give you performance statistics for your program, letting you know where your program is spending most of its time executing. The `emacs` text editor provides an interactive editing and compilation environment for various programming languages. Other tools include GNU `make` and `imake`, used to manage compilation of large applications; and RCS, a system for source locking and revision control.

Linux implements dynamically-linked shared libraries, which allow binaries to be much smaller as the subroutine code is linked at run-time. These DLL libraries also allow the applications programmer to override function definitions with their own code. For example, if a programmer wished to write her own version of the `malloc()` library routine, the linker would use the programmer's new routine instead of the one found in the libraries.

Linux is ideal for developing Unix applications. It provides a modern programming environment with all of the bells and whistles. Various standards such as POSIX.1 are supported, allowing software written for Linux to be easily ported to other systems. Professional Unix programmers and system administrators can use Linux to develop software at home, and then transfer the software to Unix systems at work. This can not only save a great deal of time and money, but will also let you work in the comfort of your own home, on a single-user system. Computer Science students can use Linux to learn Unix programming and to explore other aspects of the system, such as kernel architecture.

The author uses his Linux system to develop and test X Window applications at home, which can be directly compiled on workstations elsewhere.

With Linux, not only do you have access to the complete set of libraries and programming utilities, but you also have the complete kernel and library source code at your fingertips. (Just imagine the endless mischief arising there!)

The X Window System

The X Window System is the standard graphics interface for Unix machines. It is a powerful environment supporting many applications. Using X Window, the user can have multiple terminal windows on the screen at once, each one containing a different login session. A pointing device such as a mouse is often used with the X interface, although it isn't required.

Many X-specific applications have been written, such as games, graphics utilities, programming and documentation tools, and so on. With Linux and X, your system is a bona fide workstation. Coupled with TCP/IP networking, you can even display X applications running on other machines on your Linux display, as is possible with other systems running X.

The X Window System was originally developed at MIT, and is freely distributable. However, many commercial vendors have distributed proprietary enhancements to the original X Window software. The version of X Window available for Linux is known as XFree86, a port of X11R5 made freely distributable for 80386-based Unix systems such as Linux. XFree86 supports a wide range of video hardware, including VGA, Super VGA, and a number of accelerated video adaptors. This is a complete distribution of the X Window software, containing the X server itself, many applications and utilities, programming libraries, and documentation.

Standard X applications include `xterm` (a terminal emulator used for most text-based applications within an X window); `xdm` (the X Session Manager, which handles logins); `xclock` (a simple clock display); `xman` (an X-based man page reader), and more. The many X applications available for Linux are too numerous to mention here, but the base XFree86 distribution includes the "standard" applications found in the original MIT release. Many others are available separately, and theoretically any application written for X Window should compile cleanly under Linux.

The look and feel of the X Window interface is controlled to a large extent by the *window manager*. This friendly program is in charge of the placement of windows, the user interface for resizing, iconifying, and moving windows, the appearance of window frames, and so on. The standard XFree86 distribution includes twm, the classic MIT window manager, although more advanced window managers such as the Open Look Virtual Window Manager (olvwm) are available as well. One window manager that is popular among Linux users is fvwm. This is a small window manager, requiring less than half of the memory used by twm. It provides a 3-D appearance for windows, as well as a virtual desktop—if the user moves the mouse to the edge of the screen, the entire desktop is shifted as if the display were much larger than it actually is. fvwm is greatly customizable, and allows all functions to be accessed from the keyboard as well as the mouse. Many Linux distributions use fvwm as the standard window manager.

The XFree86 distribution contains programming libraries and includes files for those wily programmers who wish to develop X applications. Various widget sets, such as Athena, Open Look, and Xaw3D are supported. All of the standard fonts, bitmaps, man pages, and documentation are included. PEX (a programming interface for 3-D graphics) is also supported.

Many X applications programmers use the proprietary Motif widget set for development. Several vendors sell single and multiple-user licenses for a binary version of Motif for Linux. Because Motif itself is relatively expensive, not many Linux users own it. However, binaries statically linked with Motif routines may be freely distributed. Therefore, if you write a program using Motif and wish to distribute it freely, you may provide a binary so that users without Motif can use the program.

The only major caveats with X Window are the hardware and memory requirements. A 386 with 4 MB of RAM is capable of running X, but 8 MB or more of physical RAM are needed to use it comfortably. A faster processor is nice to have as well, but having enough physical RAM is much more important. In addition, to achieve really slick video performance, an accelerated video card (such as a local bus S3-chipset card) is strongly recommended. Performance ratings in excess of 140,000 xstones have been acheived with Linux and XFree86. With sufficient hardware, you'll find that running X and Linux is as fast, or faster, than running X on other Unix workstations.

In Chapter 5 we'll discuss how to install and use X on your system.

Networking

Interested in communicating with the world? Yes? No? Maybe? Linux supports the two primary networking protocols for Unix systems: *TCP/IP* and *UUCP*. TCP/IP (Transmission Control Protocol/Internet Protocol, for acronym afficionados) is the set of networking paradigms that allow systems all over the world to communicate on a single network known as the Internet. With Linux, TCP/IP, and a connection to the network, you can communicate with users and machines across the Internet via electronic mail, Usenet news, file transfers with `ftp`, and more. There are many Linux systems currently on the Internet.

Most TCP/IP networks use Ethernet as the physical network transport. Linux supports many popular Ethernet cards and interfaces for personal computers, including the D-Link pocket Ethernet adaptor for laptops.

However, because not everyone has an Ethernet drop at home, Linux also supports *SLIP* (Serial Line Internet Protocol), which allows you to connect to the Internet via modem. In order to use SLIP, you'll need to have access to a SLIP server, a machine connected to the network which allows dial-in access. Many businesses and universities provide such SLIP servers. In fact, if your Linux system has an Ethernet connection as well as a modem, you can configure it as a SLIP server for other hosts.

`nfs` (Network File System) allows your system to seamlessly share files with other machines on the network. `ftp` (file transfer protocol) allows you to transfer files between other machines. Other applications include `sendmail`, a system for sending and receiving electronic mail using the SMTP protocol; NNTP-based electronic news systems such as C-News and INN; `telnet`, `rlogin`, and `rsh`, which allow you to login and execute commands on other machines on the network; and `finger`, which allows you to get information on other Internet users. There are literally tons of TCP/IP-based applications and protocols out there.

The full range of mail and news readers are available for Linux, such as `elm`, `pine`, `rn`, `nn`, and `tin`. Whatever your preference, you can configure your Linux system to send and receive electronic mail and news from all over the world.

If you have experience with TCP/IP applications on other Unix systems, Linux will be very familiar to you. The system provides a standard socket programming interface, so virtually any program which uses TCP/IP can be ported to Linux. The

Linux X server also supports TCP/IP, allowing you to display applications running on other systems on your Linux display.

In Chapter 5 we'll discuss configuration and setup of TCP/IP, including SLIP, for Linux.

UUCP (Unix-to-Unix Copy) is an older mechanism used to transfer files with UUCP machines connected to each other over the phone lines via modem, but UUCP is able to transport over a TCP/IP network as well. If you do not have access to a TCP/IP network or a SLIP server, you can configure your system to send and receive files and electronic mail using UUCP. See Chapter 5 for more information.

Telecommunications and BBS Software

If you have a modem, you will be able to communicate with other machines using one of the telecommunications packages available for Linux. Many people use telecommunications software to access bulletin board systems (BBSs), as well as commercial on-line services such as Prodigy, CompuServe, and America Online. Other people use their modems to connect to a Unix system at work or school. You can even use your modem and Linux system to send and receive facsimiles. Telecommunications software under Linux is very similar to that found under MS-DOS or other operating systems. Anyone who has ever used a telecommunications package will find the Linux equivalent familiar.

One of the most popular communications packages for Linux is Seyon, an X application providing a customizable, ergonomic interface, with built-in support for various file transfer protocols such as Kermit, ZModem, and so on. Other telecommunications programs include C-Kermit, pcomm, and minicom. These are similar to communications programs found on other operating systems, and are quite easy to use.

If you do not have access to a SLIP server (see the previous section), you can use term to multiplex your serial line. term will allow you to open multiple login sessions over the modem connection to a remote machine. term will also allow you to redirect X client connections to your local X server, through the serial line, allowing you to display remote X applications on your Linux system. Another software package, KA9Q, implements a similar SLIP-like interface.

Running a bulletin board system (BBS) is a favorite hobby (and means of income) for many people. Linux supports a wide range of BBS software, most of which is more powerful than what is available for other operating systems. With a phone line, a modem, and Linux, you can turn your system into a BBS, providing dial-in access to your system to users worldwide. BBS software for Linux includes XBBS and the UniBoard BBS packages.

Most BBS software locks the user into a menu-based system where only certain functions and applications are available. An alternative to BBS access is full Unix access, which would allow users to dial into your system and login as a regular user. While this would require a fair amount of maintenance on the part of the system administrator, it can be done, and providing public Unix access from your Linux system is not difficult to do. Along with a TCP/IP network, you can provide electronic mail and news access to users on your system.

If you do not have access to a TCP/IP network or UUCP feed, Linux will also allow you to communicate with a number of BBS networks, such as FidoNet, with which you can exchange electronic news and mail via the phone line. More information on telecommunications and BBS software under Linux can be found in Chapter 5.

Interfacing with MS-DOS

Various utilities exist to interface with the (somewhat perverse, we admit) world of MS-DOS. The most well-known application is the Linux MS-DOS Emulator, which allows you to run many MS-DOS applications directly from Linux. Although Linux and MS-DOS are completely different operating systems, the 80386 protected-mode environment allows certain tasks to behave as if they were running in 8086-emulation mode, as MS-DOS applications do.

The MS-DOS Emulator is still under development, yet many popular applications run under it. Understandably, however, MS-DOS applications which use bizarre or esoteric features of the system may never be supported, because it is only an emulator. For example, you wouldn't expect to be able to run any programs which use 80386 protected-mode features, such as Microsoft Windows (in 386 enhanced mode, that is).

Applications which run successfully under the Linux MS-DOS Emulator include 4DOS (a command interpreter), Foxpro 2.0, Harvard Graphics, MathCad, Stacker 3.1, Turbo Assembler, Turbo C/C++, Turbo Pascal, Microsoft Windows 3.0 (in real mode), and WordPerfect 5.1. Standard MS-DOS commands and utilities (such as PKZIP, and so on) work with the emulator as well.

The MS-DOS Emulator is meant mostly as an ad hoc solution for those people who need MS-DOS only for a few applications, but use Linux for everything else. It's not meant to be a complete implementation of MS-DOS. Of course, if the Emulator doesn't satisfy your needs, you can always run MS-DOS as well as Linux on the same system. Using the LILO boot loader, you can specify at boot time which operating system to start. Linux can coexist with other operating systems, such as OS/2, as well.

Linux provides a seamless interface for transferring files between Linux and MS-DOS. You can mount an MS-DOS partition or floppy under Linux, and directly access MS-DOS files as you would any other.

Currently under development is a project known as *WINE*—a Microsoft Windows emulator for the X Window System under Linux. Once WINE is complete, users will be able to run MS-Windows applications directly from Linux. This is similar to the proprietary WABI Windows emulator from Sun Microsystems. At the time of this writing, WINE is still in the early stages of development, but the outlook is good.

In Chapter 5, we'll talk about the MS-DOS tools available for Linux.

Other Applications

A host of miscellany is available for Linux, as one would expect from such a hodge-podge operating system. Linux's primary focus is currently for personal Unix computing, but this is rapidly changing. Business and scientific software is expanding, and commercial software vendors are beginning to contribute to the growing pool of applications.

Several relational databases are available for Linux, including Postgres, Ingres, and Mbase. These are full-featured, professional client/server database applications similar to those found on other Unix platforms. /rdb, a commercial database system, is available as well.

Scientific computing applications include FELT (a finite element analysis tool); gnuplot (a plotting and data analysis application); Octave (a symbolic mathematics package similar to MATLAB); xspread (a spreadsheet calculator); xfractint, an X-based port of the popular Fractint fractal generator; xlispstat (a statistics package), and more. Other applications include Spice (a circuit design and analysis tool) and Khoros (an image/digital signal processing and visualization system).

Of course, there are many more such applications which have been, and can be, ported to run on Linux. Whatever your field, porting Unix-based applications to

Linux should be quite straightforward. Linux provides a complete Unix programming interface, sufficient to serve as the base for any scientific application.

As with any operating system, Linux has its share of games. Classic text-based dungeon games such as Nethack and Moria; MUDs (multi user dungeons, which allow many users to interact in a text-based adventure) such as DikuMUD and TinyMUD; as well as a slew of X games such as `xtetris`, `netrek`, and `gnuchess`. True, Unix never has lent itself to the modern trend of dazzling shoot-em-up arcade games, but you know what they say: "All work and no play makes Linux a dull toy."

For audiophiles, Linux has support for various sound cards and related software, such as CDplayer (a program which can control a CD-ROM drive as a conventional CD player, surprisingly enough), MIDI sequencers and editors (allowing you to compose music for playback through a synthesizer or other MIDI-controlled instrument), and sound editors for digitized sounds.

Can't find the application you're looking for? The Linux Software Map (see Appendix A) contains a list of many software packages which have been written and ported to Linux. While this list is far from complete, it contains a great deal of software. Another way to find Linux applications is to look at the `INDEX` files found on Linux ftp sites, if you have Internet access. Just by poking around you'll find a great deal of software just waiting to be played with.

If you absolutely can't find what you need, you can always attempt to port the application from another platform to Linux. Most freely distributable Unix-based software will compile on Linux with few problems. Or, if all else fails, you can write the application yourself. If it's a commercial application you're looking for, there may be a free *clone* available. Or, you can encourage the software company to consider releasing a Linux binary version. Several individuals have contacted software companies, asking them to port their applications to Linux, and have met with varying degrees of success.

About Linux's Copyright

Linux is covered by what is known as the GNU *General Public License*, or *GPL*. The GPL was developed for the GNU project by the Free Software Foundation. It makes a number of provisions for the distribution and modification of *free software*. *Free* in this sense refers to freedom, not just cost. The GPL has always been subject to misinterpretation, and we hope that this summary will help you to understand the extent and goals of the GPL and its effect on Linux. A complete copy of the GPL is included in Appendix E.

Originally, Linus Torvalds released Linux under a license more restrictive than the GPL, which allowed the software to be freely distributed and modified, but prevented any money changing hands for its distribution and use. On the other hand, the GPL allows people to sell and make profit from free software, but does not allow them to restrict the right for others to distribute the software in any way.

First, it should be explained that free software covered by the GPL is *not* in the public domain. Public domain software is software that is not copyrighted, and is literally owned by the public. Software covered by the GPL, on the other hand, is copyrighted to the author or authors. This means that the software is protected by standard international copyright laws, and that the author of the software is legally defined. Just because the software may be freely distributed does not mean that it is in the public domain.

GPL-licensed software is also not *shareware*. Generally, shareware software is owned and copyrighted by the author, but the author requires users to send in money for its use after distribution. On the other hand, software covered by the GPL may be distributed and used free of charge.

The GPL also allows people to take and modify free software, and distribute their own versions of the software. However, any derived works from GPL software must also be covered by the GPL. In other words, a company could not take Linux, modify it, and sell it under a restrictive license. If any software is derived from Linux, that software must be covered by the GPL as well.

The GPL allows free software to be distributed and used free of charge. However, it also allows a person or organization to distribute GPL software for a fee, and even to make a profit from its sale and distribution. However, in selling GPL software, the distributor cannot take those rights away from the purchaser; that is, if you purchase GPL software from some source, you may distribute the software for free, or sell it yourself as well.

This might sound like a contradiction at first. Why sell software for profit when the GPL allows anyone to obtain it for free? As an example, let's say that some company decided to bundle a large amount of free software on a CD-ROM and distribute it. That company would need to charge for the overhead of producing and distributing the CD-ROM, and the company may even decide to make a profit from the sale of the software. This is allowed by the GPL.

Organizations that sell free software must follow certain restrictions set forth in the GPL. First, they cannot restrict the rights of users who purchase the software. This means that if you buy a CD-ROM of GPL software, you can copy and distribute that CD-ROM free of charge, or resell it yourself. Secondly, distributors must make it obvious to users that the software is indeed covered by the GPL. Thirdly, distributors must provide, free of charge, the complete source code for the software being distributed. This will allow anyone who purchases GPL software to make modifications to that software.

Allowing a company to distribute and sell free software is a very good thing. Not everyone has access to the Internet to download software, such as Linux, for free. The GPL allows companies to sell and distribute software to those people who do not have free (cost-wise) access to the software. For example, many organizations sell Linux on diskette, tape, or CD-ROM via mail order, and make a profit from these sales. The developers of Linux may never see any of this profit; that is the understanding that is reached between the developer and the distributor when software is licensed by the GPL. In other words, Linus knew that companies may wish to sell Linux, and that he may not see a penny of the profits from those sales.

In the free software world, the important issue is not money. The goal of free software is always to develop and distribute fantastic software and to allow anyone to obtain and use it. In the next section, we'll discuss how this applies to the development of Linux.

The Design and Philosophy of Linux

When new users encounter Linux, they often have a few misconceptions and false expectations of the system. Linux is a unique operating system, and it is important to understand its philosophy and design in order to use it effectively. Time enough for a soapbox. Even if you are a seasoned Unix guru, what follows is probably of interest to you.

In commercial Unix development houses, the entire system is developed with a rigorous policy of quality assurance, source and revision control systems, documentation, and bug reporting and resolution. Developers are not allowed to add features or to change key sections of code on a whim: they must validate the change as a response to a bug report and consequently "check in" all changes to the source control system, so that the changes can be backed out of if necessary. Each developer is assigned one or more parts of the system code, and only that developer may alter those sections of the code while it is "checked out".

Internally, the quality assurance department runs rigorous regression test suites on each new pass of the operating system, and reports any bugs. It is the responsibility of the developers to fix these bugs as reported. A complicated system of statistical analysis is employed to ensure that a certain percentage of bugs are fixed before the next release, and that the operating system as a whole passes certain release criteria.

In all, the process used by commercial Unix developers to maintain and support their code is very complicated, and quite reasonably so. The company must have quantitative proof that the next revision of the operating system is ready to be shipped; hence, the gathering and analysis of statistics about the operating system's performance. It is a big job to develop a commercial Unix system, often large enough to employ hundreds (if not thousands) of programmers, testers, documentors, and administrative personnel. Of course, no two commercial Unix vendors are alike, but you get the general picture.

With Linux, you can throw out the entire concept of organized development, source control systems, structured bug reporting, or statistical analysis. Linux is, and more than likely always will be, a hacker's operating system.

NOTE   What I mean by *hacker* is a feverishly dedicated programmer; a person who enjoys exploiting computers and generally doing interesting things with them. This is in contrast to the common denotation of a hacker as a computer wrongdoer or outlaw.

Linux is primarily developed as a group effort by volunteers on the Internet from all over the world. Across the Internet and beyond, anyone with enough know-how has the opportunity to aid in developing and debugging the kernel, porting new software, writing documentation, or helping new users. There is no single organization responsible for developing the system. For the most part, the Linux community communicates via various mailing lists and Usenet newsgroups. A number of conventions have sprung up around the development effort: for example, anyone wishing to have their code included in the "official" kernel should mail it to Linus Torvalds. He will test it and more than likely include it in the kernel, as long as it doesn't break things or go against the overall design of the system.

The system itself is designed with a very open-ended, feature-minded approach. While recently the number of new features and critical changes to the system have diminished, the general rule is that a new version of the kernel will be released about every few months (sometimes even more frequently than this). Of course, this is a very rough figure: it depends on several factors, including the number of bugs to be fixed, the amount of feedback from users testing pre-release versions of the code, and the amount of sleep that Linus has had this week.

Let it suffice to say that not every single bug has been fixed, and not every problem ironed out between releases. As long as the system appears to be free of critical or oft-manifesting bugs, it is considered "stable" and new revisions will be released. The thrust behind Linux development is not an effort to release perfect, bug-free code: it is to develop a free implementation of Unix. Linux is for the developers, more than anyone else.

Anyone who has a new feature or software application to add to the system generally makes it available in an *alpha* stage—that is, a stage for testing by those brave or unwary users who want to bash out problems with the initial code. Because the Linux community is largely based on the Internet, alpha software is usually uploaded to one or more of the various Linux ftp sites (see Appendix C) and a message posted to one of the Linux Usenet newsgroups about how to get and test the code. Users who download and test alpha software can then mail results, bug fixes, or questions to the author.

After the initial problems in the alpha code have been fixed, the code enters a *beta* stage, in which it is usually considered stable but not complete (that is, it works, but not all of the features may be present). Otherwise, it may go directly to a *final* stage in which the software is considered complete and usable. For kernel code, once it is complete the developer may ask Linus to include it in the standard kernel, or as an optional add-on feature to the kernel.

Keep in mind that these are only conventions—not rules. Some people feel so confident with their software that they don't need to release an alpha or test version. It is always up to the developer to make these decisions.

You might be amazed that such a nonstructured system of volunteers, programming and debugging a complete Unix system, could get anything done at all. As it turns out, it is one of the most efficient and motivated development efforts ever employed. The entire Linux kernel was written "from scratch", without employing any code from proprietary sources. A great deal of work was put forth by volunteers to port all of the free software under the sun to the Linux system. Libraries were written and ported, file systems developed, and hardware drivers written for many popular devices.

The Linux software is generally released as a *distribution*, which is a set of prepackaged software making up an entire system. It would be quite difficult for most users to build a complete system from the ground up, starting with the kernel, adding utilities, and installing all of the necessary software by hand. Instead, there are a number of software distributions including everything that you need to install and run a complete system. Again, there is no standard distribution—there are many, each with their own advantages and disadvantages. We'll talk more about the various available Linux distributions in "Distribution of Linux" in Chapter 2.

Despite the completeness of the Linux software, you will still need a bit of Unix know-how to install and run a complete system. No distribution of Linux is completely bug-free, so you may be required to fix small problems by hand after installation. Running a Unix system is not an easy task, not even for commercial versions of Unix. If you're serious about Linux, bear in mind that it will take a considerable amount of effort and attention on your part to keep the system running and to take care of things: this is true of *any* Unix system, and Linux is no exception. Because of the diversity of the Linux community and the many needs the software is attempting to meet, not everything can be taken care of for you all of the time.

Hints for Unix Novices

One of the greatest mistakes often made by new Unix users is attempting to install and run a complete Linux system without much background Unix knowledge. To put it simply, without previous Unix experience, installing and running Linux is going to prove difficult at best. This is the case with all implementations of Unix. Nobody can expect to go from being a Unix novice to a Unix system administrator overnight. Too much of the time, MS-DOS users are tempted to dive into the Linux world, expecting that it will be easy to pick up "as you go along" without any external help. As the expression goes, "This isn't Kansas any more." Unix is not like MS-DOS or Microsoft Windows. No implementation of Unix is expected to run trouble- and maintenance-free. Every Unix system needs a system administrator, and if you are the system administrator for your soon-to-be-Linux system, you need to learn quite a few things about using and running Unix before you begin.

This may sound like a tall order, but it really isn't so bad. There are many good introductory Unix books on the market: See Appendix A for a list. Many new Unix users expect to install Linux in order to *learn* Unix, but we're afraid that it's supposed to work the other way around. Installing and setting up a Unix system of your own is a challenging task even for very experienced system administrators. This is not to say that it is difficult, but only that you will benefit greatly from Unix experience and an understanding of the process. Should you have trouble installing the system, you will know how to investigate and fix the problem yourself without having to find outside help. You must be aptly prepared for the journey that lies ahead. Otherwise, if you're new to Unix, you may very well become overly frustrated with the system. It is very important to do some reading and experimentation with Unix systems before attempting to run your own Linux system.

Hints for Unix Gurus

Even those people with years of Unix programming and systems administration experience may need assistance before they are able to pick up and install Linux. There are still aspects of the system that Unix wizards will need to be familiar with before diving in. For one thing, Linux is not a commercial Unix system. It does not attempt to uphold the same standards as other Unix systems you may have come across. To be more specific, while stability is an important factor in the development of Linux, it is not the *only* factor.

More important, perhaps, is functionality. In many cases, new code will make it into the standard kernel even though it is still buggy and not functionally complete. The assumption is that it is more important to release code that users can test and use than to delay a release until it is "complete." As an example, WINE (the Microsoft Windows Emulator for Linux) had an "official" alpha release before it was completely tested. In this way, the Linux community at large had a chance to work with the code, test it, and help develop it, while those who found the alpha code good enough for their needs could use it. Commercial Unix vendors rarely, if ever, release software in this manner.

If you have been a Unix systems administrator for more than a decade, and have used every commercial Unix system under the Sun (no pun intended), Linux may take some getting used to. The system is very modern and dynamic. A new kernel release is made approximately every few months. New software is constantly being released. One day your system may be completely up-to-date with the current trend, and the next day the same system is considered to be in the Stone Age.

With all of this dynamic activity, how can you be expected to keep up with the ever-changing Linux world? For the most part, it is best to upgrade incrementally; that is, upgrade only those parts of the system that *need* upgrading, and then only when you think an upgrade is necessary. For example, if you never use emacs, there is little reason to continuously install every new release of emacs on your system. Furthermore, even if you are an avid emacs user, there is usually no reason to upgrade it unless you find that some feature is missing that is in the next release. There is little or no reason to always be on top of the newest version of software.

We hope that Linux will meet or exceed your expectations of a home brew Unix system. At the very core of Linux is the spirit of free software, of constant development and growth. The Linux community favors expansion over stability, and that is a difficult concept to swallow for many people, especially those so steeped in the world of commercial Unix. You cannot expect Linux to be perfect; nothing ever is in the free software world. However, we believe that Linux really is as complete and useful as any other implementation of Unix.

Differences Between Linux and Other Operating Systems

It is important to understand the differences between Linux and other operating systems, such as MS-DOS, OS/2, and other implementations of Unix for the personal computer. First of all, it should be made clear that Linux will coexist happily with other operating systems on the same machine: that is, you can run MS-DOS and OS/2 along with Linux on the same system without problems. There are even ways to interact between the various operating systems, as we'll see.

Why Use Linux?

Why use Linux instead of a well-known, well-tested, and well-documented commercial operating system? We could give you a thousand reasons. One of the most important, however, is that Linux is an excellent choice for personal Unix computing. If you're a Unix software developer, why use MS-DOS at home? Linux will allow you to develop and test Unix software on your PC, including database and X Window applications. If you're a student, chances are that your university computing systems run Unix. With Linux, you can run your own Unix system and tailor it to your own needs. Installing and running Linux is also an excellent way to learn Unix if you don't have access to other Unix machines.

But let's not lose sight. Linux isn't just for personal Unix users. It is robust and complete enough to handle large tasks, as well as distributed computing needs. Many businesses—especially small ones—are moving to Linux in lieu of other Unix-based workstation environments. Universities are finding Linux to be perfect for teaching courses in operating systems design. Larger commercial software vendors are starting to realize the opportunities that a free operating system can provide.

The following sections should point out the most important differences between Linux and other operating systems. We hope that you'll find that Linux can meet your computing needs, or (at least) enhance your current computing environment. Keep in mind that the best way to get a taste for Linux is just to try it out—you needn't even install a complete system to get a feel for it. In Chapter 2, we'll show you how.

Linux vs. MS-DOS

It's not uncommon to run both Linux and MS-DOS on the same system. Many Linux users rely on MS-DOS for applications such as word processing. While Linux provides its own analogs for these applications (for example, TEX), there are various reasons why a particular user would want to run MS-DOS as well as Linux. If your entire dissertation is written using WordPerfect for MS-DOS, you may not be able to easily convert it to TEX or some other format. There are many commercial applications for MS-DOS which aren't available for Linux, and there's no reason why you can't use both.

As you might know, MS-DOS does not fully utilize the functionality of the 80386 and 80486 processors. On the other hand, Linux runs completely in the processor's protected mode, and exploits all of the features of the processor. You can directly access all of your available memory (and beyond, using virtual RAM). Linux provides a complete Unix interface not available under MS-DOS—developing and porting Unix applications under Linux is easily done, while under MS-DOS you are limited to a small subset of the Unix programming functionality. Because Linux is a true Unix system, you do not have these limitations.

We could debate the pros and cons of MS-DOS and Linux for pages on end. However, let it suffice to say that Linux and MS-DOS are completely different entities. MS-DOS is inexpensive (compared to other commercial operating systems), and has a strong foothold in the PC computing world. No other operating system for the PC has reached the level of popularity of MS-DOS—largely because the cost of these other operating systems is unapproachable to most personal computer users. Very few PC users can imagine spending $1000 or more on the operating system alone. Linux, however, is free, and you finally have the chance to decide.

We will allow you to make your own judgments of Linux and MS-DOS based on your expectations and needs. Linux is not for everybody. If you have always wanted to run a complete Unix system at home, without the high cost of other Unix implementations for the PC, Linux may be what you're looking for.

There are tools available to allow you to interact between Linux and MS-DOS. For example, it is easy to access MS-DOS files from Linux. There is also an MS-DOS emulator available, which allows you to run many popular MS-DOS applications. A Microsoft Windows emulator is currently under development.

Linux vs. The Other Guys

A number of other advanced operating systems are on the rise in the PC world. Specifically, IBM's OS/2 and Microsoft's Windows NT are becoming very popular as more users move away from MS-DOS.

Both OS/2 and Windows NT are full multitasking operating systems, much like Linux. Technically, OS/2, Windows NT, and Linux are quite similar: they support roughly the same features in terms of user interface, networking, security, and so forth. However, the real difference between Linux and The Other Guys is the fact that Linux is a version of Unix, and hence benefits from the contributions of the Unix community at large.

What makes Unix so important? Not only is it the most popular operating system for multiuser machines, it is also the foundation for the majority of the free software world. If you have access to the Internet, nearly all of the free software available there is written specifically for Unix systems. (The Internet itself is largely Unix-based.)

There are many implementations of Unix from many vendors, and no single organization is responsible for distribution. There is a large push in the Unix community for standardization in the form of open systems, but no single corporation controls this design. Hence, any vendor (or, as it turns out, any hacker) may implement these standards in an implementation of Unix.

OS/2 and Windows NT, on the other hand, are proprietary systems. The interface and design are controlled by a single corporation, and only that corporation may implement that design. (Don't expect to see a free version of OS/2 anytime in the near future.) In one sense, this kind of organization is beneficial: it sets a strict standard for the programming and user interface unlike that found even in the open systems community. OS/2 is OS/2 wherever you go—the same holds for Windows NT.

However, the Unix interface is constantly developing and changing. Several organizations are attempting to standardize the programming model, but the task is very difficult. Linux, in particular, is mostly compliant with the POSIX.1 standard for the Unix programming interface. As time goes on, it is expected that the system will adhere to other such standards, but standardization is not the primary issue in the Linux development community.

Other Implementations of Unix

There are several other implementations of Unix for the 80386 and 80486. The 80386 architecture lends itself to the Unix design, and a number of vendors have taken advantage of this.

Feature-wise, other implementations of Unix for the PC are quite similar to Linux. You will see that almost all commercial versions of Unix support roughly the same software, programming environment, and networking features. However, there are some strong differences between Linux and commercial versions of Unix.

First of all, Linux supports a different range of hardware from commercial implementations. In general, Linux supports the most well-known hardware devices, but support is still limited to that hardware which developers actually have access to.

However, commercial Unix vendors generally have a wider support base, and tend to support more hardware, although Linux is not far behind. We'll cover the hardware requirements for Linux in "Hardware Requirements" later in this chapter.

Secondly, commercial implementations of Unix usually come bundled with a complete set of documentation as well as user support from the vendor. In contrast, most of the documentation for Linux is limited to documents available on the Internet—and books such as this one (See "Sources of Linux Documentation" later in this chapter.

As far as stability and robustness are concerned, many users have reported that Linux is at least as stable as commercial Unix systems. Linux is still under development, and certain features (such as TCP/IP networking) are less stable but improve as time goes by.

The most important factor to consider for many users is price. The Linux software is free, if you have access to the Internet (or another computer network) and can download it. If you do not have access to such a network, you may need to purchase it via mail order on diskette, tape, or CD-ROM (see Appendix B). Of course, you may copy Linux from a friend who may already have the software, or share the cost of purchasing it with someone else. If you are planning to install Linux on a large number of machines, you need only purchase a single copy of the software—Linux is not distributed on a "single machine" license.

The value of commercial Unix implementations should not be demeaned: along with the price of the software itself, one usually pays for documentation, support, and assurance of quality. These are very important factors for large institutions, but personal computer users may not require these benefits. In any case, many businesses and universities are finding that running Linux on a lab of inexpensive personal computers is preferable to running a commercial version of Unix in a lab of workstations. Linux can provide the functionality of a workstation on PC hardware at a fraction of the cost.

As a real-world example of Linux's use within the computing community, Linux systems have traveled the high seas of the North Pacific, managing telecommunications and data analysis for an oceanographic research vessel. Linux systems are being used at research stations in Antarctica. As a more mundane example, perhaps, several hospitals are using Linux to maintain patient records. It is proving to be as reliable and useful as other implementations of Unix.

There are other free or inexpensive implementations of Unix for the 386 and 486. One of the most well-known is 386BSD, an implementation and port of BSD Unix for the 386. 386BSD is comparable to Linux in many ways, but which one is better depends on your own personal needs and expectations. The only strong distinction that we can make is that Linux is developed openly (where any volunteer can aid in the development process), while 386BSD is developed within a closed team of programmers who maintain the system. Because of this, serious philosophical and design differences exist between the two projects. The goals of the two projects are entirely different: the goal of Linux is to develop a complete Unix system from scratch (and have a lot of fun in the process), and the goal of 386BSD is in part to modify the existing BSD code for use on the 386.

NetBSD is another port of the BSD NET/2 distribution to a number of machines, including the 386. NetBSD has a slightly more open development structure, and is comparable to 386BSD in many respects.

Another project of note is HURD, an effort by the Free Software Foundation to develop and distribute a free version of Unix for many platforms. Contact the Free Software Foundation (see Appendix E) for more information about this project. At the time of this writing, HURD is still in the early stages of development.

Other inexpensive versions of Unix exist as well, such as Coherent (available for about $99) and Minix (an academic but useful Unix clone upon which early development of Linux was based). Some of these implementations are of mostly academic interest, while others are full-fledged systems for real productivity. Needless to say, however, many personal Unix users are moving to Linux.

Hardware Requirements

Now you must be convinced of how wonderful Linux is, and all of the great things that it can do for you. However, before you rush out and install the software, you need to be aware of the hardware requirements and limitations that Linux has.

Keep in mind that Linux was developed by its users. This means, for the most part, that the hardware which is supported by Linux is only the hardware the users and developers actually have access to. As it turns out, most of the popular hardware and peripherals for 80386/80486 systems are supported (in fact, Linux supports more hardware than some commercial implementations of Unix). However, some of the more obscure and esoteric devices aren't supported yet. As time goes on, a wider range of hardware is supported, so if your favorite devices aren't listed here, chances are that support for them is forthcoming.

Another drawback for hardware support under Linux is that many companies have decided to keep the hardware interface proprietary. The upshot of this is that volunteer Linux developers simply can't write drivers for those devices (if they could, those drivers would be owned by the company that owned the interface, which would violate the GPL). The companies that maintain proprietary interfaces write their own drivers for operating systems such as MS-DOS and Microsoft Windows; the end user (that's you) never needs to know about the interface. Unfortunately, this does not allow Linux developers to write drivers for those devices.

There is very little that can be done about the situation. In some cases, programmers have attempted to write hackish drivers based on assumptions about the interface. In other cases, developers will work with the company in question and attempt to obtain information about the device interface, with varying degrees of success.

In the following sections, we'll attempt to summarize the hardware requirements for Linux. The Linux Hardware HOWTO, discussed in "On-line Documents" in Appendix A, contains a more complete listing of hardware supported by Linux.

Disclaimer: a good deal of hardware support for Linux is currently in the development stage. Some distributions may or may not support these experimental features. This section primarily lists hardware which has been supported for some time and is known to be stable. When in doubt, consult the documentation for the distribution of Linux you are using (see "Distributions of Linux" in Chapter 2).

Motherboard and CPU Requirements

Linux currently supports systems with an Intel 80386 or 80486 CPU. This includes all variations on this CPU type, such as the 386SX, 486SX, 486DX, and 486DX2. Linux should also work on Intel's Pentium processor with minor changes. Non-Intel "clones", such as AMD and Cyrix processors, work with Linux as well.

If you have an 80386 or 80486SX, you may also wish to use a math coprocessor, although one isn't required (the Linux kernel can do FPU emulation if you do not have a math coprocessor). All standard FPU couplings are supported, such as IIT,

Cyrix FasMath, and Intel coprocessors.

The system motherboard must use ISA or EISA bus architecture. Their terms define how the system interfaces with peripherals and other components on the main bus. Most systems sold today are either ISA or EISA bus. IBM's MicroChannel (MCA) bus, found on machines such as the IBM PS/2, is not currently supported.

Systems that use a local bus architecture (for faster video and disk access) are supported as well. It is suggested that you have a standard local bus architecture such as the VESA Local Bus (VLB).

Memory Requirements

Linux requires very little memory to run compared to other advanced operating systems. You should have at the very least 2 MB of RAM; however, it is strongly suggested that you have 4 MB. The more memory you have, the faster the system will run.

Linux can support the full 32-bit address range of the 386/486; in other words, it will utilize all of your RAM automatically.

Linux will run happily with only 4 MB of RAM, including all of the bells and whistles such as X Window, emacs, and so on. However, having more memory is almost as important as having a faster processor. 8 MB is more than enough for personal use; 16 MB or more may be needed if you are expecting a heavy user load on the system.

Most Linux users allocate a portion of their hard drive as swap space, which is used as virtual RAM. Even if you have a great deal of physical RAM in your machine, you may wish to use swap space. While swap space is no replacement for actual physical RAM, it can allow your system to run larger applications by swapping out inactive portions of code to disk. The amount of swap space that you should allocate depends on several factors; we'll come back to this question in "Linux Partition Requirements" in Chapter 2.

Hard Drive Controller Requirements

You do not need to have a hard drive to run Linux; you can run a minimal system completely from floppy. However, this is slow and very limited, and many users have access to hard drive storage anyway. You must have an AT-standard (16-bit) controller. There is support in the kernel for XT-standard (8 bit) controllers; however, most controllers used today are AT-standard. Linux should support all MFM, RLL, ESDI, and IDE controllers.

The general rule for non-SCSI hard drive and floppy controllers is that if you can access the drive from MS-DOS or another operating system, you should be able to access it from Linux.

Linux also supports a number of popular SCSI drive controllers, although support for SCSI is more limited because of the wide range of controller interface standards. Supported SCSI controllers include the Adaptec AHA1542B, AHA1742A (BIOS version 1.34), AHA1522, AHA1740, AHA1740 (SCSI-2 controller, BIOS 1.34 in Enhanced mode); Future Domain 1680, TMC-850, TMC-950; Seagate ST-02; UltraStor SCSI; Western Digital WD7000FASST. Clones that are based on these cards should work as well.

Hard Drive Space Requirements

Of course, to install Linux, you'll need to have some amount of free space on your hard drive. Linux will support multiple hard drives in the same machine; you can allocate space for Linux across multiple drives if necessary.

The amount of hard drive space that you will require depends greatly on your needs and the amount of software that you're installing. Linux is relatively small as Unix implementations go; you could run a complete system in 10 to 20 MB of space on your drive. However, if you want to have room for expansion, and for larger packages such as X Window, you will need more space. If you plan to allow multiple users to use the machine, you will need to allocate storage for their files.

Also, unless you have a large amount of physical RAM (16 MB or more), you will more than likely want to allocate swap space, to be used as virtual RAM. We will discuss all of the details of installing and using swap space in "Linux Partition Requirements" in Chapter 2.

Each distribution of Linux usually comes with some literature that should help you to gauge the precise amount of required storage depending on the amount of software you plan to install. You can run a minimal system with less than 20 MB; a complete system with all of the bells and whistles in 80 MB or less; and a very large system with room for many users and space for future expansion in the range of

100-150 MB. Again, these figures are meant only as a ballpark approximation; you will have to look at your own needs and goals in order to determine your specific storage requirements.

Monitor and Video Adaptor Requirements

Linux supports all standard Hercules, CGA, EGA, VGA, and Super VGA video cards and monitors for the default text-based interface. In general, if the video card and monitor coupling works under another operating system such as MS-DOS, it should work fine with Linux.

Graphical environments such as the X Window System have video hardware requirements of their own. Instead of listing these requirements here, we relegate the discussion to "Hardware Requirements" in Chapter 5.

Miscellaneous Hardware

The above sections described the hardware which is required to run a Linux system. However, most users have a number of optional devices such as tape and CD-ROM storage, sound boards, and so on, and are interested in whether or not this hardware is supported by Linux. Read on.

Mice and Other Pointing Devices

For the most part, you will only be using a mouse under a graphical environment such as the X Window System. However, several Linux applications not associated with a graphics environment do make use of the mouse.

Linux supports all standard serial mice, including Logitech, MM series, Mouseman, Microsoft (2-button) and Mouse Systems (3-button). Linux also supports Microsoft, Logitech, and ATIXL busmice. The PS/2 mouse interface is supported as well.

All other pointing devices, such as trackballs, which emulate the above mice, should work as well.

CD-ROM Storage

Almost all CD-ROM drives use the SCSI interface. As long as you have a SCSI adaptor supported by Linux, then your CD-ROM drive should work. A number of CD-ROM drives have been verified to work under Linux, including the NEC CDR-74, Sony CDU-541, and Texel DM-3024. The Sony internal CDU-31a and the Mistsumi CD-ROM drives are supported by Linux as well.

Linux supports the standard ISO-9660 file system for CD-ROMs.

Tape Drives

There are several types of tape drives available on the market. Most of them use the SCSI interface, all of which should be supported by Linux. Among the verified SCSI tape drives are the Sankyo CP150SE; Tandberg 3600; Wangtek 5525ES, 5150ES, and 5099EN with the PC36 adaptor. Other QIC-02 drives should be supported as well.

Drivers are currently under development for various other tape devices, such as Colorado drives, which hang off of the floppy controller.

Printers

Linux supports the complete range of parallel printers. If you are able to access your printer via the parallel port from MS-DOS or another operating system, you should be able to access it from Linux as well. The Linux printing software consists of the Unix standard lp and lpr software. This software also allows you to print remotely via the network, if you have one available.

Modems

As with printer support, Linux supports the full range of serial modems, both internal and external. There is a great deal of telecommunications software available for Linux, including Kermit, pcomm, minicom, and Seyon. If your modem is accessible from another operating system on the same machine, you should be able to access it from Linux with no difficulty.

Ethernet Cards

Many popular Ethernet cards and LAN adaptors are supported by Linux. These include:

- 3com 3c503, 3c503/16
- Novell NE1000, NE2000

- Western Digital WD8003, WD8013

- Hewlett Packard HP27245, HP27247, HP27250

The following clones are reported to work:

- LANNET LEC-45

- Alta Combo

- Artisoft LANtastic AE-2

- Asante Etherpak 2001/2003

- D-Link Ethernet II

- LTC E-NET/16 P/N 8300-200-002

- Network Solutions HE-203

- SVEC 4 Dimension Ethernet

- 4-Dimension FD0490 EtherBoard 16

- D-Link DE-600

Clones which are compatible with any of the above cards should work as well.

Sources of Linux Information

As you have probably guessed, there are many sources of information about Linux available apart from this book. In particular, there are a number of books, not specific to Linux but rather about Unix in general, that will be of importance, especially to those readers without previous Unix experience. If you are new to the Unix world, we seriously suggest that you take the time to peruse one of these books before you attempt to brave the jungles of Linux. Specifically, the book *Learning the Unix Operating System,* by Grace Todino and John Strang, is a good place to start.

Many of the following sources of information are available online in some electronic form. That is, you must have access to an online network, such as the Internet, Usenet, or Fidonet, in order to access the information contained therein. If you do not have online access to any of this material, you might be able to find someone kind enough to give you hardcopies of the documents in question. Read on.

On-Line Documents

If you have access to the Internet, there are many Linux documents available via anonymous ftp from archive sites all over the world. If you do not have direct Internet access, these documents may still be available to you: they are distributed on many other networks as well, such as Fidonet and CompuServe. If you are able to send mail to Internet sites, you may be able to retrieve these files using one of the `ftpmail` servers which will electronically mail you the documents or files from ftp archive sites. See "Using ftpmail" in Appendix C for more information on using `ftpmail`.

There are a great number of ftp archive sites that carry Linux software and related documents. A list of well-known Linux archive sites is given in Appendix C. In order to reduce network traffic, you should always use the ftp site which is geographically (network-wise) closest to you.

Appendix A contains a listing of some of the Linux documents which are available via anonymous ftp. The filenames will differ depending on the archive site in question; most sites keep Linux-related documents in the `docs` subdirectory of their Linux archive space. For example, on the ftp site `sunsite.unc.edu`, Linux files are stored in the directory `/pub/Linux`, with Linux-related documentation being found in `/pub/Linux/docs`.

Examples of available on-line documents are the *Linux FAQ*, a collection of frequently asked questions about Linux; the *Linux HOWTO* documents, each describing a specific aspect of the system—including the *Installation HOWTO*, the *Printing HOWTO*, and the *Ethernet HOWTO*; and, the Linux META-FAQ, a list of other sources of Linux information on the Internet.

Most of these documents are also regularly posted to one or more Linux-related Usenet newsgroups; see "Usenet Newsgroups" below.

Books and Other
Published Works

At this time, there are few published works specifically about Linux. Most noteworthy are the books from the Linux Documentation Project, a project carried out over the Internet to write and distribute a bona fide set of "manuals" for Linux. These manuals are analogues to the documentation sets available with commercial versions of Unix: they cover everything from installing Linux, to using and running the system, programming, networking, kernel development, and more.

The Linux Documentation Project manuals are available via anonymous ftp from the Internet, as well as via mail order from several sources. Appendix A lists the manuals that are available and covers means of obtaining them in detail.

There are not many books specifically about Linux currently available. Several books have been published in Germany and Japan, including a translation of the Linux Documentation Project book *Linux Installation and Getting Started*. However, there are a large number of books about Unix in general which are certainly applicable to Linux—as far as using and programming the system is concerned, Linux does not differ greatly from other implementations of Unix. In short, almost everything you want to know about using and programming Linux can be found in sources meant for a general Unix audience. In fact, this book is meant to be complemented by the large library of Unix books currently available; here, we present the most important Linux-specific details and hope that you will look to other sources for more in-depth information.

Armed with a number of good books about using Unix, as well as the book you hold in your hands, you should be able to tackle just about anything. Appendix A includes a list of highly-recommended Unix books, both for Unix newcomers and Unix wizards alike.

There is also a monthly magazine about Linux, called the *Linux Journal*. It is distributed worldwide, and is an excellent way to keep in touch with the many goings-on in the Linux community—especially if you do not have access to Usenet news (see below). See Appendix B for information on subscribing to the *Linux Journal*.

Usenet Newsgroups

Usenet is a worldwide electronic news and discussion forum with a heavy contingent of so-called *newsgroups*—discussion areas devoted to a particular topic. Much of the development of Linux has been done over the waves of the Internet and Usenet, and not surprisingly there are a number of Usenet newsgroups available for discussions about Linux.

The original Linux newsgroup was `alt.os.linux`, and was created to move some of the discussions about Linux out of `comp.os.minix` and the various mailing lists. Soon, the traffic on `alt.os.linux` grew to be large enough that a newsgroup in the `comp` hierarchy was warranted; a vote was taken in February of 1992, and `comp.os.linux` was created.

comp.os.linux quickly became one of the most popular (and loudest) Usenet groups; more popular than any other `comp.os` group. In December of 1992, a vote was taken to split the newsgroup in order to reduce traffic; only `comp.os.linux.announce` passed this vote. In July of 1993, the group was finally split into the new hierarchy. Almost 2000 people voted in the `comp.os.linux` reorganization, making it one of the largest Usenet CFV's ever.

If you do not have direct Usenet access, but are able to send and receive electronic mail from the Internet, there are mail-to-news gateways available for each of the newsgroups below.

`comp.os.linux.announce` is a moderated newsgroup for announcements and important postings about the Linux system (such as bug reports, important patches to software, and so on). If you read any Linux newsgroups at all, read this one. Often, the important postings in this group are not crossposted to other groups. This group also contains many periodic postings about Linux, including many of the on-line documents described in the last section and listed in Appendix A.

Postings to this newsgroup must be approved by the moderators, Matt Welsh and Lars Wirzenius. If you wish to submit an article to this group, in most cases you can simply post the article as you normally would (using pnews or whatever posting software that you have available); the news software will automatically forward the article to the moderators for approval. However, if your news system is not set up correctly, you may need to mail the article directly; the submission address is linux-announce@tc.cornell.edu.

The rest of the Linux newsgroups listed below are unmoderated.

`comp.os.linux.help` This is the most popular Linux newsgroup. It is for questions and answers about using, setting up, or otherwise running a Linux system. If you are having problems with Linux, you may post to this newsgroup, and hopefully receive a reply from someone who might be able to help. However, it is strongly suggested that you read all of the available Linux documentation before posting questions to this newsgroup.

`comp.os.linux.admin` This newsgroup is for questions and discussion about running a Linux system, most commonly in an active, multi-user environment. Any discussion about administrative issues of Linux (such as packaging software, making backups, handling users, and so on) is welcome here.

`comp.os.linux.development` This is a newsgroup for discussions about development of the Linux system. All issues related to kernel and system software development should be discussed here. For example, if you are writing a kernel driver and need help with certain aspects of the programming, this would be the place to ask. This newsgroup is also for discussions about the direction and goals behind the Linux development effort, as described (somewhat) in "The Design and Philosophy of Linux" earlier in this chapter.

It should be noted that `comp.os.linux.development` is not (technically) for discussions about development of software *for* Linux, but rather for discussions of development *of* Linux. That is, issues dealing with applications programming under Linux should be discussed in another Linux newsgroup; `comp.os.linux.development` is about developing the Linux system itself, including the kernel, system libraries, and so on.

`comp.os.linux.misc` This newsgroup is for all discussion that doesn't quite fit into the other available Linux groups. In particular, advocacy wars (the incessant "Linux versus Windows NT" thread, for example), should be waged here, as opposed to in the technical Linux groups. Any nontechnical or metadiscourse about the Linux system should remain in this newsgroup.

It should be noted that the newsgroup `comp.os.linux`, which was originally the only Linux group, has been superseded by the new hierarchy of groups. If you have access to `comp.os.linux`, but not to the newer Linux groups listed above, encourage your news administrator to create the new groups on your system.

Internet Mailing Lists

If you have access to Internet electronic mail, you can participate in a number of mailing lists even if you do not have Usenet access. Note that if you are not directly on the Internet, you can join one of these mailing lists as long as you are able to exchange electronic mail with the Internet (for example, UUCP, FidoNET, CompuServe, and other networks all have access to Internet mail).

The "Linux Activists" mailing list is primarily for Linux developers and people interested in aiding the development process. This is a "multi-channel" mailing list, in which you join one or more "channels" based on your particular interests. Some of the available channels include: NORMAL, for general Linux-related issues; KERNEL, for kernel development; GCC, for discussions relating to the gcc compiler and library development; NET, for discussions about the TCP/IP networking code; DOC, for issues relating to writing and distributing Linux documentation; and more.

For more information about the Linux Activists mailing list, send mail to

```
linux-activists@niksula.hut.fi
```

You will receive a list of currently available channels, including information on how to subscribe and unsubscribe to particular channels on the list.

Quite a few special-purpose mailing lists about and for Linux exist as well. The best way to find out about these is to watch the Linux Usenet newsgroups for announcements, as well as to read the list of publicly-available mailing lists, periodically posted to the Usenet group `news.answers`.

Getting Help

You will undoubtedly require some degree of assistance during your adventures in the Linux world. Even the most wizardly of Unix wizards occasionally is stumped by some quirk or feature of Linux, and it's important to know how and where to find help when you need it.

The primary means of getting help in the Linux world are via Internet mailing lists and Usenet newsgroups, as discussed in "Sources of Linux Information" earlier in this chapter. If you don't have on-line access to these sources, you might be able to find comparable Linux discussion forums on other on-line services, such as on local BBS's, CompuServe, and so on.

A number of businesses are providing commercial support for Linux. This will allow you to pay a *subscription fee*, which will allow you to call the constants for help with your Linux problems. Appendix B contains a list of commercial sources for Linux support. However, if you have access to Usenet and Internet mail, you may find the free support found there to be just as useful.

Keeping the following suggestions in mind will greatly improve your experiences with Linux and will guarantee you more success in finding help to your problems.

Consult all available documentation…first! The first thing you should do when encountering a problem is consult the various sources of information listed in "Sources of Linux Information" in Chapter 1 and Appendix A. These documents were laboriously written for people like you—people who need help with the

Linux system. Even books written for Unix in general are applicable to Linux, and you should take advantage of them. More than likely, you will find the answer to your problems somewhere in this documentation, as impossible as it may seem.

If you have access to Usenet news or any of the Linux-related mailing lists, be sure to actually *read* the information there before posting for help with your problem. Many times, solutions to common problems are not easy to find in documentation, and instead are well-covered in the newsgroups and mailing lists devoted to Linux. If you only post to these groups, and don't actually read them, you are asking for trouble.

Learn to appreciate self-maintenance. In most cases, it is preferable to do as much independent research and investigation into the problem as possible before seeking outside help. After all, you asked for it by running Linux in the first place! Remember that Linux is all about hacking and fixing problems yourself. It is not a commercial operating system, nor does it try to look like one. Hacking won't kill you. In fact, it will teach you a great deal about the system to investigate and solve problems yourself—maybe even enough to one day call yourself a Linux guru. Learn to appreciate the value of hacking the system, and how to fix problems yourself. You can't expect to run a complete, home brew Linux system without some degree of handiwork.

Remain calm. It is vital to refrain from getting frustrated with the system, at all costs. Nothing is earned by taking an axe—or worse, a powerful electromagnet—to your Linux system in a fit of anger. The authors have found that a large punching bag or similar inanimate object is a wonderful way to relieve the occasional stress attack. As Linux matures and distributions become more reliable, we hope that this problem will go away. However, even commercial Unix implementations can be tricky at times. When all else fails, sit back, take a few deep breaths, and go after the problem again when you feel relaxed. Your mind and conscience will be clearer.

Refrain from posting spuriously. Many people make the mistake of posting or mailing messages pleading for help prematurely. When encountering a problem, do not— we repeat, do *not*—rush immediately to your nearest terminal and post a message to one of the Linux Usenet newsgroups. Often, you will catch your own mistake five minutes later and find yourself in the curious situation of defending your own sanity in a public forum. Before posting anything on any of the Linux mailing lists or newsgroups, first attempt to resolve the problem yourself and be absolutely certain what the problem is. Does your system not respond when switched on? Perhaps the machine is unplugged.

If you do post for help, make it worthwhile. If all else fails, you may wish to post a message for help in any of the number of electronic forums dedicated to Linux, such as Usenet newsgroups and mailing lists. When posting, remember that the people reading your post are not there to help you. The network is not your personal consulting service. Therefore, it is important to remain as polite, terse, and informative as possible.

How can one accomplish this? First, you should include as much (relevant) information about your system and your problem as possible. Posting the simple request, "I cannot seem to get e-mail to work" will probably get you nowhere unless you include information on your system, what software you are using, what you have attempted to do so far and what the results were. When including technical information, it is usually a good idea to include general information on the version(s) of your software (Linux kernel version, for example), as well as a brief summary of your hardware configuration. However, don't overdo it—including information on the brand and type of monitor that you have probably is irrelevant if you're trying to configure networking software.

Secondly, remember that you need to make some attempt—however feeble—at solving your problem before you go to the Net. If you have never attempted to set up electronic mail, for instance, and first decide to ask folks on the Net how to go about doing it, you are making a big mistake. There are a number of documents available (see "Sources of Linux Information" earlier in this chapter) on how to get started with many common tasks under Linux. The idea is to get as far along as possible on your own and *then* ask for help if and when you get stuck.

Also remember that the people reading your message, however helpful, may occasionally get frustrated by seeing the same problem over and over again. Be sure to actually read the Linux newsgroups and mailing lists before posting your problems. Many times, the solution to your problem has been discussed repeatedly, and all that's required to find it is to browse the current messages.

Lastly, when posting to electronic newsgroups and mailing lists, try to be as polite as possible. It is much more effective and worthwhile to be polite, direct, and informative—more people will be willing to help you if you master a humble tone. To be sure, the flame war is an art form across many forms of electronic communication, but don't allow that to preoccupy your and other people's time. Save the network undue wear and tear by keeping bandwidth as low as possible, and by paying as much attention to other sources of information which are available to you. The network is an excellent way to get help with your Linux problems—but it is important to know how to use the network *effectively*.

CHAPTER

TWO

2

Obtaining and Installing Linux

In this chapter, we'll describe how to obtain the Linux software, in the form of one of the various pre-packaged distributions, and how to install the distribution that you choose.

As we have mentioned, there is no single *official* distribution of the Linux software; there are, in fact, many distributions, each of which serves a particular purpose and set of goals. These distributions are available via anonymous ftp from the Internet, on BBS systems worldwide, and via mail on diskette, tape, and CD-ROM.

Here, we present only a general overview of the installation process. Each distribution has its own specific installation instructions, but armed with the concepts presented here you should be able to feel your way through any installation. Appendix A lists sources of information for installation instructions and other help if you're at a total loss.

Distributions of Linux

Because Linux is free software, no single organization or entity is responsible for releasing and distributing the software. Therefore, almost anyone is free to put together and distribute the Linux software, as long as the restrictions in the GPL are observed. The upshot of this is that there are many distributions of Linux, available via anonymous ftp or via mail order.

You are now faced with the task of deciding upon a particular distribution of Linux that will suit your needs. Not all distributions are alike. Many of them come with just about all of the software you need to run a complete system—and then some. Other Linux distributions are "small" distributions intended for users without copious amounts of diskspace. Many distributions contain only the core Linux software, and you are expected to install larger software packages, such as the X Window System, yourself. (In Chapter 5, we'll show you how.)

In Appendix B, a brief list of Linux distributions is given. You should be able to contact the maintainers of each distribution for more information, should you need it.

This is only a cursory list of Linux releases; for a more complete list, including information on other services, see "The Linux Distribution HOWTO" in Appendix A.

How can you decide among all of these distributions? If you have access to Usenet news, or another computer conferencing system, you might want to ask there for personal opinions from people who have installed Linux. Even better, if you know someone who has installed Linux, ask them for help and advice. There are many factors to consider when choosing a distribution; however, everyone's needs and opinions are different. In actuality, most of the popular Linux distributions contain roughly the same set of software, so the distribution that you select is more or less arbitrary.

Getting Linux from the Internet

If you have access to the Internet, the easiest way to obtain Linux may be via anonymous ftp. Appendix C lists a number of ftp archive sites that carry Linux software. One of these is `sunsite.unc.edu`, where you'll find the various Linux distributions can be found in the directory

`/pub/Linux/distributions`

NOTE   If you do not have direct Internet access, you can obtain Linux via the ftpmail service, provided that you have the ability to exchange e-mail with the Internet. See Appendix C for details.

Many distributions are released via anonymous ftp as a set of disk images. That is, the distribution consists of a set of files, and each file contains the binary image of a floppy. In order to copy the contents of the image file onto the floppy, you can use the `RAWRITE.EXE` program under MS-DOS. This program copies, block-for-block, the contents of a file to a floppy, without regard for disk format.

NOTE

If you have access to a Unix workstation with a floppy drive, you can use the `dd` command to copy the file image directly to the floppy. A command such as `dd of=/dev/rfd0 if=foo bs=16k` will *raw write* the contents of the file `foo` to the floppy device on a Sun workstation. Consult your local Unix gurus for more information on your system's floppy devices and the use of `dd`.

RAWRITE.EXE is available on the various Linux ftp sites, including `sunsite.unc.edu` in the directory

```
/pub/Linux/system/Install/rawwrite
```

Therefore, in many cases, you simply download the set of diskette images, and use `RAWRITE.EXE` with each image in turn to create a set of diskettes. You boot from the so-called *boot diskette* and you're ready to roll. The software is usually installed directly from the floppies, although some distributions allow you to install from an MS-DOS partition on your hard drive. Some distributions allow you to install over a TCP/IP network. The documentation for each distribution should describe these installation methods if they are available.

Other Linux distributions are installed from a set of MS-DOS format floppies. For example, the SLS distribution of Linux requires only one of the image—the *a1* diskette—to be written to diskette using `RAWRITE.EXE`. The rest of the files are copied to MS-DOS format diskettes labeled a2, a3, and so forth, using the MS-DOS `COPY` command. The system installs the software directly from the MS-DOS floppies. This saves you the trouble of having to use `RAWRITE.EXE` for many image files, although it requires you to have access to an MS-DOS system to create the diskettes.

Each distribution of Linux available via anonymous ftp should include a `README` file describing how to download and prepare the diskettes for installation. Be sure to read all of the available documentation for the release that you are using—this book is only meant to give you the general idea.

When downloading the Linux software, be sure to use binary mode for all file transfers (with most ftp clients, the command `binary` enables this mode).

Getting Linux from Other
On-Line Sources

If you have access to another computer network such as CompuServe or Prodigy, there may be a means to download the Linux software from these sources. In addition, many bulletin board (BBS) systems carry Linux software. A list of Linux BBS sites is given in Appendix D. Not all Linux distributions are available from these computer networks, however—many of them, especially the various CD-ROM distributions, are only available via mail order.

Getting Linux via Mail Order

If you don't have Internet or BBS access, many Linux distributions are available via mail order on diskette, tape, or CD-ROM. Appendix B lists a number of these distributors. Many of them accept credit cards as well as international orders, so if you're not in the United States or Canada you still should be able to obtain Linux in this way.

Linux is free software, although distributors are allowed by the GPL to charge a fee for it. Therefore, ordering Linux via mail order might cost you between U.S. $30 and U.S. $150, depending on the distribution. However, if you know someone who has already purchased or downloaded a release of Linux, you are free to borrow or copy their software for your own use. Linux distributors are not allowed to restrict the license or redistribution of the software in any way. If you are thinking about installing an entire lab of machines with Linux, for example, you only need to purchase a single copy of one of the distributions, which can be used to install all of the machines.

Preparing to Install Linux

After you have obtained a distribution of Linux, you're ready to prepare your system for installation. This takes a certain degree of planning, especially if you're already running other operating systems. In the following sections, we'll describe how to plan for the Linux installation.

Installation Overview

While each release of Linux is different, in general the method used to install the software is as follows:

1. **Repartition your hard drive(s)**. If you have other operating systems already installed, you will need to *repartition* the drives in order to allocate space for Linux. This is discussed in "Repartitioning Your Drives," below.

2. **Boot the Linux installation media**. Each distribution of Linux has some kind of installation media—usually a *boot floppy*—which is used to install the software. Booting this media will either present you with some kind of installation program, which will step you through the Linux installation, or allow you to install the software by hand.

3. **Create Linux partitions**. After repartitioning to allocate space for Linux, you create Linux partitions on that empty space. This is accomplished with the Linux fdisk program, covered in "Creating Linux Partitions," below.

4. **Create file systems and swap space**. At this point, you will create one or more *file systems*, used to store files, on the newly created partitions. In addition, if you plan to use swap space, you will create the swap space on one of your Linux partitions. This is covered in "Creating the Swap Space" and "Creating the file systems," below.

5. **Install the software on the new file systems**. Finally, you will install the Linux software on your newly created file systems. After this, it's smooth sailing—if all goes well. This is covered in "Installing the Software." Later, in "Running into Trouble," we describe what to do if anything goes wrong.

Many distributions of Linux provide an installation program which will step you through the installation process and automate one or more of the above steps for you. Keep in mind throughout this chapter that any number of the above steps may be automated for you, depending on the distribution.

Important hint: While preparing to install Linux, the best advice that we can give is to *take notes* during the entire procedure. Write down everything that you do, everything that you type, and everything that you see that might be out of the ordinary. The idea here is simple: if (or when!) you run into trouble, you want to be able to retrace your steps and find out what went wrong. Installing Linux isn't difficult, but there are many details to remember. You want to have a record of all of these details so that you can experiment with other methods if something goes wrong. Also, keeping a notebook of your Linux installation experience is useful when you want to ask other people for help, for example, when posting a message to one of the Linux-related Usenet groups. Your notebook is also something that you'll want to show to your grandchildren someday.

NOTE The author shamefully admits that he kept a notebook of all his tribulations with Linux for the first few months of working with the system. It is now gathering dust on his bookshelf.

Repartitioning Concepts

In general, hard drives are divided into *partitions*, where a single partition is devoted to a single operating system. For example, on one hard drive, you may have several separate partitions—one devoted to, say, MS-DOS, another to OS/2, and another to Linux.

If you already have other software installed on your system, you may need to resize those partitions in order to free up space for Linux. You will then create one or more Linux partitions on the resulting free space for storing the Linux software and swap space. We call this process *repartitioning*.

Many MS-DOS systems utilize a single partition inhabiting the entire drive. To MS-DOS, this partition is known as C:. If you have more than one partition, MS-DOS names them D:, E:, and so on. In a way, each partition acts like a separate hard drive.

On the first sector of the disk is a *master boot record* along with a *partition table*. The boot record (as the name implies) is used to boot the system. The partition table contains information about the locations and sizes of your partitions.

There are three kinds of partitions: *primary, extended,* and *logical*. Of these, primary partitions are used most often. However, because of a limit in the size of the partition table, you can only have four primary partitions on any given drive.

The way around this four-partition limit is to use an extended partition. An extended partition doesn't hold any data by itself; instead, it acts as a *container* for logical partitions. Therefore, you could create one extended partition, covering the entire drive, and within it create many logical partitions. However, you may have only one extended partition per drive.

Linux Partition Requirements

Before we explain how to repartition your drives, you need to have an idea of how much space you will be allocating for Linux. We will be discussing how to create these partitions later, in "Creating Linux Partitions."

On Unix systems, files are stored on a *file system*, which is essentially a section of the hard drive (or other medium, such as CD-ROM or diskette) formatted to hold files. Each file system is associated with a specific part of the directory tree; for example, on many systems, there is a file system for all of the files in the directory /usr, another for /tmp, and so on. The *root file system* is the primary file system, which corresponds to the topmost directory, /.

Under Linux, each file system lives on a separate partition on the hard drive. For instance, if you have a file system for / and another for /usr, you will need two partitions to hold the two file systems.

Before you install Linux, you will need to prepare file systems for storing the Linux software. You must have at least one file system (the root file system), and therefore one partition, allocated to Linux. Many Linux users opt to store all of their files on the root file system, which is in most cases easier to manage than several file systems and partitions.

However, you may create multiple file systems for Linux if you wish—for example, you may want to use separate file systems for /usr and /home. Those readers with Unix system administration experience will know how to use multiple file systems creatively. In Chapter 4, we discuss the use of multiple partitions and file systems.

Why use more than one file system? The most commonly stated reason is safety: if, for some reason, one of your file systems is damaged, the others will (usually) be unharmed. On the other hand, if you store all of your files on the root file system, and for some reason the file system is damaged, then you may lose all of your files in one fell swoop. This is, however, rather uncommon; if you backup the system regularly you should be quite safe.

Another reason to use multiple file systems is to divvy up storage between multiple hard drives. If you have, say, 40 MB free on one hard drive, and 50 MB free on another, you might want to create a 40-MB root file system on the first drive and a 50-MB /usr file system on the other. Currently it is not possible for a single file system to span multiple drives; if your free hard drive storage is fragmented between drives, you will need to use multiple file systems to utilize it all.

In summary, Linux requires at least one partition for the root file system. If you wish to create multiple file systems, you will need a separate partition for each additional file system. Some distributions of Linux automatically create partitions and file systems for you, so you may not need to worry about these issues at all.

Another issue to consider when planning your partitions is swap space. If you wish to use swap space with Linux, you have two options. The first is to use a *swap file* which exists on one of your Linux file systems. You will create the swap file for use as virtual RAM after you install the software. The second option is to create a *swap partition*, an individual partition to be used only as swap space. Most people use a swap partition instead of a swap file.

A single swap file or partition may be up to 16 MB in size. If you wish to use more than 16 MB of swap, you can create multiple swap partitions or files—up to eight in all. For example, if you need 32 MB of swap, you can create two 16-MB swap partitions.

Setting up a swap partition is covered in "Creating the Swap Space," below, and setting up a swap file in Chapter 4.

Therefore, in general, you will create at least two partitions for Linux: one for use as the root file system and the other for use as swap space. There are, of course, many variations on the above, but this is the minimal setup. You are not required to use swap space with Linux, but if you have less than 16 MB of physical RAM, it is strongly suggested that you do.

Of course, you need to be aware of how much *space* these partitions will require. The size of your Linux file systems (containing the software itself) depends greatly on how much software you're installing and what distribution of Linux you are using. Hopefully, the documentation that came with your distribution will give you an approximation of the space requirements. A small Linux system can use 20 MB or less; a larger system anywhere from 80 to 100 MB, or more. Keep in mind that in addition to the space required by the software itself, you need to allocate extra space for user directories, room for future expansion, and so forth.

The size of your swap partition (should you elect to use one) depends on how much virtual RAM you require. A rule of thumb is to use a swap partition that is twice the space of your physical RAM; for example, if you have 4 MB of physical RAM, an 8-MB swap partition should suffice. Of course, this is mere speculation—the actual amount of swap space that you require depends on the software which you will be running. If you have a great deal of physical RAM (say, 16 MB or more), you may not wish to use swap space at all.

WARNING Many SCSI adaptors are incapable of booting software from partitions using cylinders numbered over 1024. Therefore, when setting aside space for Linux, keep in mind that you may not want to use a partition in the >1024-cylinder range for your Linux root file system. Linux can still *use* partitions with cylinders numbered over 1024, however, you may not be able to *boot* Linux from such a partition. This advice may seem premature, but it is important to know while planning your drive layout.

If you absolutely must use a partition with cylinders numbered over 1024 for your Linux root file system, you can always boot Linux from floppy. This is not so bad, actually—it only takes a few seconds longer to boot than from the hard drive. At any rate, it's always an option.

Repartitioning Your Drives

In this section, we'll describe how to resize your current partitions (if any) to make space for Linux. If you are installing Linux on a "clean" hard drive, you can skip this section and proceed to "Installing the Linux Software," below.

The usual way to resize an existing partition is to delete it (thus destroying all of the data on that partition) and recreate it. Before repartitioning your drives, backup your system. After resizing the partitions, you can reinstall your original software from the backup. However, there are several programs available for MS-DOS which are able to resize partitions nondestructively. One of these is known as FIPS, and can be found on many Linux ftp sites.

Also, keep in mind that because you'll be shrinking your original partitions, you may not have space to reinstall everything. In this case, you need to delete enough unwanted software to allow the rest to fit on the smaller partitions.

The program used to repartition is known as fdisk. Each operating system has its own analogue of this program; for example, under MS-DOS, it is invoked with the FDISK command. You should consult your documentation for whatever operating systems you are currently running for information on repartitioning. Here, we'll discuss how to resize partitions for MS-DOS using FDISK, but this information should be easily extrapolated to other operating systems.

Please consult the documentation for your current operating systems before repartitioning your drive. This section is meant to be a general overview of the process; there are many subtleties that we do not cover here. You can lose all of the software on your system if you do not repartition the drive correctly.

WARNING Do not modify or create partitions for any other operating systems (including Linux) using FDISK under MS-DOS. You should only modify partitions for a particular operating system with the version of fdisk included with that operating system; for example, you will create Linux partitions using a version of fdisk for Linux. Later, in "Creating Linux Partitions," we describe how to create Linux partitions, but for now we are concerned with resizing your current ones.

Let's say that you have a single hard drive on your system, currently devoted entirely to MS-DOS. Hence, your drive consists of a single MS-DOS partition, commonly known as "C:". Because this repartitioning method will destroy the data on that partition, you need to create a bootable MS-DOS *system disk* which contains everything necessary to run FDISK and restore the software from backup after the repartitioning is complete.

In many cases, you can use the MS-DOS installation disks for this purpose. However, if you need to create your own system disk, format a floppy with the command

```
FORMAT /s A:
```

Copy onto this floppy all of the necessary MS-DOS utilities (usually most of the software in the directory \DOS on your drive), as well as the programs FORMAT.COM and FDISK.EXE. You should now be able to boot this floppy, and run the command

```
FDISK C:
```

to start up FDISK.

Use of FDISK should be self-explanatory, but consult the MS-DOS documentation for details. When you start FDISK, use the menu option to display the partition table, and *write down* the information displayed there. It is important to keep a record of your original setup in case you want to back out of the Linux installation.

To delete an existing partition, choose the FDISK menu option Delete An MS-DOS Partition Or Logical DOS Drive. Specify the type of partition that you wish to delete (primary, extended, or logical) and the number of the partition. Verify all of the warnings. Poof!

To create a new (smaller) partition for MS-DOS, just choose the FDISK option Create An MS-DOS Partition Or Logical DOS Drive. Specify the type of partition (primary, extended, or logical), and the size of the partition to create (specified in megabytes). FDISK should create the partition and you're ready to roll.

After you're done using FDISK, you should exit the program and reformat any new partitions. For example, if you resized the first DOS partition on your drive (C:), you should run the command

```
FORMAT /s C:
```

You may now reinstall your original software from backup.

Installing the Linux Software

After you have resized your existing partitions to make space for Linux, you are ready to install the software. Here is a brief overview of the procedure:

- Boot the Linux installation media;

- Run `fdisk` under Linux to create Linux partitions;

- Run `mke2fs` and `mkswap` to create Linux file systems and swap space;

- Install the Linux software;

- Finally, either install the `LILO` boot loader on your hard drive or create a boot floppy in order to boot your new Linux system.

As we have said, one (or more) of these steps may be automated for you by the installation procedure, depending on the distribution of Linux which you are using. Please consult the documentation for your distribution for specific instructions.

Booting Linux

The first step is to boot the Linux installation media. This may be a floppy, tape, or CD-ROM, depending on the distribution.

In most cases, the installation media is a *boot floppy* which contains a small Linux system. Upon booting the floppy, you will be presented with an installation menu of some kind which will lead you through the steps of installing the software. On other distributions, you will be presented with a login prompt when booting this floppy. Here, you usually login as `root` or `install` to begin the installation process.

The documentation that came with your particular distribution will explain what is necessary to boot Linux from the installation media.

Drives and Partitions under Linux

Many distributions require you to create Linux partitions by hand using the `fdisk` program. Others may automatically create partitions for you. Either way, you should know the following information about Linux partitions and device names.

Drives and partitions under Linux are given different names than their counterparts under other operating systems. Under MS-DOS, floppy drives are referred to as A: and B:, while hard drive partitions are named C:, D:, and so on. Under Linux, the naming convention is quite different.

Device drivers, found in the directory /dev, are used to communicate with devices on your system (such as hard drives, mice, and so on). For example, if you have a mouse on your system, you access it through the driver /dev/mouse. Floppy drives, hard drives, and individual partitions are all given individual device drivers of their own. Don't worry about the device driver interface for now; it is important only to understand how the various devices are named in order to use them. Table 2.1 lists the names of these various device drivers.

A few notes about this table. Note that /dev/fd0 corresponds to the first floppy drive (A: under MS-DOS) and /dev/fd1 corresponds to the second floppy (B:).

Also, SCSI hard drives are named differently than other drives. IDE, MFM, and RLL drives are accessed through the devices /dev/hda, /dev/hdb, and so on. The individual partitions on the drive /dev/hda are /dev/hda1, /dev/hda2, and so on. However, SCSI drives are named /dev/sda, /dev/sdb, etc., with partition names such as /dev/sda1 and /dev/sda2.

Here's an example. Let's say that you have a single IDE hard drive with 3 primary partitions. The first two are set aside for MS-DOS, and the third is an extended partition which contains two logical partitions, both for use by Linux. The devices referring to these partitions are shown in Table 2.1.

Note that /dev/hda4 is skipped; it corresponds to the fourth primary partition, which we don't have in this example. Logical partitions are named consecutively starting with /dev/hda5.

Creating Linux Partitions

Now you are ready to create Linux partitions with the fdisk command. As described in "Linux Partition Requirements," in general you will need to create at least one partition for the Linux software itself and another partition for swap space.

TABLE 2.1: Linux Partition Names

Device	Name
First floppy (A:)	/dev/fd0
Second floppy (B:)	/dev/fd1
First hard drive (entire drive)	/dev/hda
First hard drive, primary partition 1	/dev/hda1
First hard drive, primary partition 2	/dev/hda2
First hard drive, primary partition 3	/dev/hda3
First hard drive, primary partition 4	/dev/hda4
First hard drive, logical partition 1	/dev/hda5
First hard drive, logical partition 2	/dev/hda6
…	
Second hard drive (entire drive)	/dev/hdb
Second hard drive, primary partition 1	/dev/hdb1
…	
First SCSI hard drive (entire drive)	/dev/sda
First SCSI hard drive, primary partition 1	/dev/sda1
…	
Second SCSI hard drive (entire drive)	/dev/sdb
Second SCSI hard drive, primary partition 1	/dev/sdb1
…	
First MS-DOS partition (C:)	/dev/hda1
Second MS-DOS partition (D:)	/dev/hda2
Extended partition	/dev/hda3
First Linux logical partition	/dev/hda5
Second Linux logical partition	/dev/hda6

After booting the installation media, run fdisk by typing

```
fdisk <drive>
```

where *drive* is the Linux device name of the drive you plan to add partitions to (see Table 2.1). For instance, if you want to run fdisk on the first SCSI disk in your system, use the command fdisk /dev/sda. /dev/hda (the first IDE drive) is the default if you don't specify one.

If you are creating Linux partitions on more than one drive, run fdisk once for each drive.

```
# fdisk /dev/hda
Command (m for help):
```

Here fdisk is waiting for a command; you can type m to get a list of options.

```
Command (m for help): m
Command action
a toggle a bootable flag
d delete a partition
l list known partition types
m print this menu
n add a new partition
p print the partition table
q quit without saving changes
t change a partition's system id
u change display/entry units
v verify the partition table
w write table to disk and exit
x extra functionality (experts only)

Command (m for help):
```

The n command is used to create a new partition. Most of the other options you won't need to worry about. To quit fdisk without saving any changes, use the q command. To quit fdisk and write the changes to the partition table to disk, use the w command.

The first thing you should do is display your current partition table and write the information down, for later reference. Use the p command.

```
Command (m for help): p
Disk /dev/hda:  16 heads, 38 sectors, 683 cylinders
Units = cylinders of 608 * 512 bytes
```

```
    Device Boot  Begin   Start    End   Blocks   Id   System
/dev/hda1     *      1       1    203    61693    6   DOS 16-bit >=32M
```

```
Command (m for help):
```

In this example, we have a single MS-DOS partition on /dev/hda1, which is 61693 blocks (about 60 MB). This partition starts at cylinder number 1 and ends on cylinder 203. We have a total of 683 cylinders in this disk, so there are 480 cylinders left to create Linux partitions on.

To create a new partition, use the n command. In this example, we'll create two primary partitions (/dev/hda2 and /dev/hda3) for Linux.

```
Command (m for help): n
Command action
e extended
p primary partition (1-4)
p
```

Here, fdisk is asking for the type of the partition to create: extended or primary. In our example, we're creating only primary partitions, so we choose p.

```
Partition number (1-4):
```

fdisk will then ask for the number of the partition to create; since partition 1 is already used, our first Linux partition will be number 2.

```
Partition number (1-4): 2
First cylinder (204-683):
```

Now enter the starting cylinder number of the partition. Since cylinders 204 through 683 are unused, we'll use the first available one (numbered 204). There's no reason to leave empty space between partitions.

```
First cylinder (204-683): 204
Last cylinder or +size or +sizeM or +sizeK (204-683):
```

fdisk is asking for the size of the partition to create. We can either specify an ending cylinder number, or a size in bytes, kilobytes, or MB. Since we want our partition to be 80 MB in size, we specify +80M. When specifying a partition size in this way, fdisk will round the actual partition size to the nearest number of cylinders.

```
Last cylinder or +size or +sizeM or +sizeK (204-683): +80M
```

```
Warning: Linux cannot currently use 33090 sectors of this partition
```

If you see a warning message such as this, it can be ignored. `fdisk` prints the warning because it's an older program and dates before the time that Linux partitions were allowed to be larger than 64 MB.

Now we're ready to create our second Linux partition. For sake of demonstration, we'll create it with a size of 10 MB.

```
Command (m for help): n
Command action
e extended
p primary partition (1-4)
p
Partition number (1-4): 3
First cylinder (474-683): 474
Last cylinder or +size or +sizeM or +sizeK (474-683): +10M
```

At last, we'll display the partition table. Again, write down all of this information—especially the block sizes of your new partitions. You'll need to know the sizes of the partitions when creating file systems later. Also, verify that none of your partitions overlap.

```
Command (m for help): p
Disk /dev/hda:  16 heads, 38 sectors, 683 cylinders
Units = cylinders of 608 * 512 bytes

Device     Boot   Begin   Start    End   Blocks   Id   System
/dev/hda1    *       1       1     203    61693    6   DOS 16-bit >=32M
/dev/hda2          204     204     473    82080   81   Linux/MINIX
/dev/hda3          474     474     507    10336   81   Linux/MINIX
```

As you can see, `/dev/hda2` is now a partition of size 82080 blocks (which corresponds to about 80 MB), and `/dev/hda3` is 10336 blocks (about 10 MB).

Note that many distributions (such as Slackware) require you to use the t command in `fdisk` to change the type of the swap partition to *Linux swap*, which is usually numbered 82. You can use the L command to print a list of known partition type codes, and then use it to set the type of the swap partition to that which corresponds to *Linux swap*.

In this way, the installation software will be able to automatically find your swap partitions based on type. If the installation software doesn't seem to recognize your swap partition, you might want to re-run `fdisk` and use the t command on the partition in question.

In the example above, the remaining cylinders on the disk (numbered 508 to 683) are unused. You may wish to leave unused space on the disk in case you wish to create additional partitions later.

Finally, we use the w command to write the changes to disk and exit fdisk.

```
Command (m for help): w
#
```

Keep in mind that none of the changes you make while running fdisk will take effect until you give the w command, so you can toy with different configurations and save them when you're done. Also, if you want to quit fdisk at any time without saving the changes, use the q command. Remember that you shouldn't modify partitions for operating systems other than Linux with the Linux fdisk program.

Remember that you may not be able to boot Linux from a partition using cylinders numbered over 1024. Therefore, you should try to create your Linux root partition within the sub-1024 cylinder range. Again, if this is impossible, you can simply boot Linux from floppy.

Some Linux distributions require you to reboot the system after running fdisk. This is to allow the changes to the partition table to take effect before installing the software. Newer versions of fdisk automatically update the partition information in the kernel, so rebooting isn't necessary. To be on the safe side, after running fdisk you should, as before, reboot the installation media before proceeding

Creating the Swap Space

If you are planning to use a swap partition for virtual RAM, you're ready to prepare it for use. In Chapter 4, we discuss the preparation of a swap file in case you don't want to use an individual partition.

NOTE Again, some distributions of Linux will either prepare the swap space automatically for you or via an installation menu option.

Many distributions require you to create and activate swap space before installing the software. If you have a small amount of physical RAM, the installation procedure may not be successful unless you have some amount of swap space enabled.

The command used to prepare a swap partition is mkswap, and it takes the form

```
mkswap -c <partition> <size>
```

where *<partition>* is the name of the swap partition, and *<size>* is the size of the partition, in blocks. (This is the size as reported by fdisk, using the p menu option. A block under Linux is 1024 bytes.) For example, if your swap partition is /dev/hda3 and is 10336 blocks in size, use the command

```
# mkswap -c /dev/hda3 10336
```

The -c option tells mkswap to check for bad blocks on the partition when creating the swap space.

If you are using multiple swap partitions, you will need to execute the appropriate mkswap command for each partition.

After formatting the swap space, you need to enable it for use by the system. Usually, the system automatically enables swap space at boot time. However, because you have not yet installed the Linux software, you need to enable it by hand.

The command to enable swap space is swapon, and it takes the form

```
swapon <partition>
```

In the example above, to enable the swap space on /dev/hda3, we use the command

```
# swapon /dev/hda3
```

Creating the File Systems

Before you can use your Linux partitions to store files, you must create *file systems* on them. Creating a file system is analogous to formatting a partition under MS-DOS or other operating systems. We discussed file systems briefly in "Linux Partition Requirements."

There are several types of file systems available for Linux. Each file system type has its own format and set of characteristics (such as filename length, maximum file size, and so on). Linux also supports several *third-party* file system types such as the MS-DOS file system.

The most commonly used file system type is the *Second Extended file system,* or *ext2fs.* This is one of the most efficient and flexible file systems; it allows filenames up to 256 characters and file system sizes of up to 4 terabytes. In Chapter 4, we discuss the various file system types available for Linux. Initially, however, we suggest that you use the *ext2fs* file system.

To create an `ext2fs` file system, use the command

```
mke2fs -c <partition> <size>
```

where *<partition>* is the name of the partition, and *<size>* is the size of the partition in blocks. For example, to create a 82080-block file system on `/dev/hda2`, use the command

```
# mke2fs -c /dev/hda2 82080
```

If you're using multiple file systems for Linux, you'll need to use the appropriate `mke2fs` command for each file system.

If you have encountered any problems at this point, see "Running into Trouble" at the end of this chapter.

Installing the Software

Finally, you are ready to install the software on your system. Every distribution has a different mechanism for doing this. Many distributions have a self-contained program which will step you through the installation. On other distributions, you will have to *mount* your file systems in a certain subdirectory (such as `/mnt`) and copy the software to them by hand. On CD-ROM distributions, you may be given the option to install a portion of the software on your hard drives and leave most of the software on the CD-ROM.

Some distributions offer several different ways to install the software. For example, you may be able to install the software directly from an MS-DOS partition on your hard drive, instead of from floppies. Or, you may be able to install over a TCP/IP network via ftp or NFS. See your distribution's documentation for details.

As an example, the SLS distribution of Linux uses the `doinstall` command to install the software. It takes the form

```
doinstall <rootfs> <fs1> <mount-pt1> <fs2> <mount-pt2> ... <fsN> <mount-ptN>
```

where *<rootfs>* is the name of your root file system, *<fs1>* and *<mount-pt1>* are the names of an additional file system and the mount point for that file system, and so on. For example, if you have a single file system for Linux on /dev/hda2, you would install the software with the command

```
# doinstall /dev/hda2
```

If you had an additional file system on /dev/hda4 for /usr, you would instead use the command

```
# doinstall /dev/hda2 /dev/hda4 /usr
```

Again, the above commands are meant only as examples. The exact method used to install the Linux software differs greatly with each distribution. We're hoping that installing the Linux software should be self-explanatory, as it is with most distributions.

Creating the Boot Floppy or Installing LILO

Every distribution provides some means of booting your new Linux system after you have installed the software. In many cases, the installation procedure will create a *boot floppy* which contains a Linux kernel configured to use your newly created root file system. In order to boot Linux, you would boot from this floppy and then control would be transferred to your hard drive. On other distributions, this boot floppy is the installation floppy itself.

Many distributions give you the option of installing **LILO** on your hard drive. LILO is a program that is installed on your drive's master boot record. It is able to boot a number of operating systems, including MS-DOS and Linux, and allows you to select at startup time which to boot.

In order for LILO to be installed successfully, it needs to know a good deal of information about your drive configuration—for example, which partitions contain which operating systems, how to boot each operating system, and so on. Many distributions, when installing LILO, attempt to "guess" at the appropriate parameters for your configuration. Though it doesn't happen often, the automated LILO installation provided by some distributions can fail, and leave your master boot record in shambles (although it's very doubtful that any damage to the actual data on your hard drive will take place). In particular, if you use OS/2's Boot Manager, you should not install LILO using the automated procedure—there are special instructions for using LILO with the Boot Manager, which will be covered later.

In many cases, it is best to use a boot floppy until you have a chance to configure LILO yourself, by hand. If you're feeling exceptionally trustworthy, though, you can go ahead with the automated LILO installation if it is provided with your distribution.

In Chapter 4, we cover in detail how to configure and install LILO for your particular setup.

If everything goes well, then congratulations! You have just installed Linux on your system. Go have a Diet Coke or something—you deserve it.

In case you did run into any trouble, the next section will describe the most common sticking points for Linux installations and how to get around them.

Additional Installation Procedures

Some distributions of Linux provide a number of additional installation procedures, allowing you to configure various software packages such as TCP/IP networking, the X Window System, and so on. If you are provided with these configuration options during installation, you may wish to read ahead in this book for more information on how to configure this software. Otherwise, you should put off these installation procedures until you have a complete understanding of how to configure the software.

It's up to you; if all else fails, just go with the flow and see what happens. It's very doubtful that anything you do incorrectly now cannot be undone in the future. (Knock on wood.)

Postinstallation Procedures

After you have completed installing the Linux software, there should be very little left to do before you can begin to use the system. In most cases, you should be able to reboot the system, login as root, and begin exploring the system. (Each distribution has a different method for doing this—follow the instructions given by the distribution.)

At this point it's a good idea to explain how to reboot and shut down the system as you're using it. You should never reboot or shutdown your Linux system by pressing the reset switch or with the old *Vulcan Nerve Pinch*—that is, by pressing Ctrl+Alt+Del in unison. You shouldn't simply switch off the power, either. As with most Unix systems, Linux caches disk writes in memory. Therefore, if you suddenly reboot the system without shutting down "cleanly," you can corrupt the data on your drives, causing untold damage.

The easiest way to shut down the system is with the shutdown command. As an example, to shut down and reboot the system immediately, use the following command as root:

```
# shutdown -r now
```

This will cleanly reboot your system. The main page for shutdown describes the other command-line arguments that are available.

Note, however, that many Linux distributions do not provide the shutdown command on the installation media. This means that the first time you reboot your system after installation, you may need to use the Ctrl+Alt+Del combination after all. Thereafter, you should always use the shutdown command.

After you have a chance to explore and use the system, there are several configuration chores that you should undertake. The first is to create a user account for yourself (and, optionally, for any other users that might have access to the system). Creating user accounts is described in "Managing Users" in Chapter 4.

If you created more than one file system for Linux, or if you're using a swap partition, you may need to edit the file /etc/fstab in order for those file systems to be available automatically after rebooting. (For example, if you're using a separate file system for /usr, and none of the files that should be in /usr appear to be present, you may simply need to mount that file system.) This procedure is described in "Managing File Systems" in Chapter 4.

Running into Trouble

Almost everyone runs into some kind of snag or hangup when attempting to install Linux the first time. Most of the time, the problem is caused by a simple misunderstanding. Sometimes, however, it can be something more serious, such as an oversight by one of the developers or a bug.

This section will describe some of the most common installation problems and how to solve them. If your installation appears to be successful but you received unexpected error messages during the installation, these are described here as well.

Problems with Booting the Installation Media

When attempting to boot the installation media for the first time, you may encounter a number of problems. These are listed below. Note that the following problems are *not* related to booting your newly installed Linux system. See "Problems After Installing Linux" for information on these kinds of pitfalls.

- **Floppy or media error when attempting to boot**. The most popular cause for this kind of problem is a corrupt boot floppy. Either the floppy is physically damaged, in which case you should re-create the disk with a *brand new* floppy, or the data on the floppy is bad, in which case you should verify that you downloaded and transferred the data to the floppy correctly. In many cases, simply re-creating the boot floppy will solve your problems. Retrace your steps and try again.

  If you received your boot floppy from a mail order vendor or some other distributor, instead of downloading and creating it yourself, contact the distributor and ask for a new boot floppy—but only after verifying that this is indeed the problem.

- **System *hangs* during boot or after booting.** After the installation media boots, you will see a number of messages from the kernel itself, indicating which devices were detected and configured. After this, you will usually be presented with a login prompt, allowing you to proceed with installation (some distributions instead drop you right into an installation program of some kind). The system may appear to hang during several of these steps. During all of these steps, be patient; loading software from floppy is very slow. In many cases, the system has not hung at all but is merely taking a long time. Verify that there is no drive or system activity for at least several minutes before assuming that the system is hung.

1. After booting from the LILO prompt, the system must load the kernel image from floppy. This may take several seconds; you will know that things are going well if the floppy drive light is still on.

2. While the kernel boots, SCSI devices must be probed for. If you do not have any SCSI devices installed, the system will hang for up to 15 seconds while the SCSI probe continues; this usually occurs after the line

    ```
    lp init: lp1 exists (0), using polling driver
    ```

    appears on your screen.

3. After the kernel is finished booting, control is transferred to the system bootup files on the floppy. Finally, you will be presented with a login prompt or be dropped into an installation program. If you are presented with a login prompt such as

    ```
    Linux login:
    ```

you should then login (usually as root or install—this varies with each distribution). After entering the username, the system may pause for 20 seconds or more while the installation program or shell is being loaded from floppy. Again, the floppy drive light should be on. Don't assume that the system is hung.

Any of the above items may be the source of your problem. However, it is possible that the system may actually hang while booting, which can be due to several causes. First of all, you may not have enough available RAM to boot the installation media. (See the following item for information on disabling the ramdisk to free up memory.)

The cause of many system hangs is hardware incompatibility. "Hardware Requirements" in the last chapter presented an overview of supported hardware under Linux. Even if your hardware is supported, you may run into problems with incompatible hardware configurations that are causing the system to hang. See "Hardware Problems," below, for a discussion of hardware incompatibilities.

• **System reports out of memory errors while attempting to boot or install the software.** This item deals with the amount of available RAM that you have available. On systems with 4 MB of RAM or less, you may run into trouble booting the installation media or installing the software itself. This is because many distributions use a *ramdisk*, which is a file system loaded directly into RAM, for operations while using the installation media. The entire image of the installation boot floppy, for example, may be loaded into a ramdisk, which may require more than 1 MB of RAM.

The solution to this problem is to disable the ramdisk option when booting the install media. Each release has a different procedure for doing this; on the SLS release, for example, you type `floppy` at the `LILO` prompt when booting the `a1` disk. See your distribution's documentation for details.

You may not see an *out of memory* error when attempting to boot or install the software; instead, the system may unexpectedly hang or fail to boot. If your system hangs and none of the explanations in the previous section seem to be the cause, try disabling the ramdisk.

Keep in mind that Linux itself requires at least 2 MB of RAM to run at all; some distributions of Linux require 4 MB or more.

• **The system reports an error such as `permission denied` or `file not found` while booting.** This is an indication that your installation bootup media is corrupt. If you attempt to boot from the installation media (and you're sure that you're doing everything correctly), you should not see any errors such as this. Contact the distributor of your Linux software the problem and perhaps obtain another copy of the boot media if necessary. If you downloaded the bootup disk yourself, try recreating the bootup disk and see if this solves your problem.

• **The system reports the error `VFS: Unable to mount root` when booting.** This error message means that the root file system (found on the boot media itself), could not be found. This means that either your boot media is corrupt in some way or that you are not booting the system correctly.

For example, many CD-ROM distributions require that you have the CD-ROM in the drive when booting. Also be sure that the CD-ROM drive is on, and check for any activity. It's also possible that the system is not locating your CD-ROM drive at boot time; see "Hardware Problems" for more information.

If you're sure that you are booting the system correctly, then your bootup media may indeed be corrupt. This is a very uncommon problem, so try other solutions before attempting to use another boot floppy or tape.

Hardware Problems

The most common form of problem when attempting to install or use Linux is an incompatibility with hardware. Even if all of your hardware is supported by Linux, a misconfiguration or hardware conflict can sometimes cause strange results—your devices may not be detected at boot time, or the system may hang.

It is important to isolate these hardware problems if you suspect that they may be the source of your trouble. In the following sections we will describe some common hardware problems and how to resolve them.

Isolating Hardware Problems

If you experience a problem that you believe to be hardware-related, the first thing that you should to do is attempt to isolate the problem. This means eliminating all possible variables and (usually) taking the system apart, piece-by-piece, until the offending piece of hardware is isolated.

This is not as frightening as it may sound. Basically, you should remove all nonessential hardware from your system, and then determine which device is actually causing the trouble—possibly by reinserting each device, one at a time. This means that you should remove all hardware other than the floppy and video controllers, and of course the keyboard. Even innocent-looking devices such as mouse controllers can wreak unknown havoc on your peace of mind unless you consider them nonessential.

For example, let's say that the system hangs during the Ethernet board detection sequence at boot time. You might hypothesize that there is a conflict or problem with the Ethernet board in your machine. The quick and easy way to find out is to pull the Ethernet board, and try booting again. If everything goes well, then you know that either (a) the Ethernet board is not supported by Linux (see "Hardware Requirements" in Chapter 1 for a list of compatible boards) or (b) there is an address or IRQ conflict with the board.

"Address or IRQ conflict?" What on earth does that mean? All devices in your machine use an *IRQ*, or *interrupt request line*, to tell the system that they need something done on their behalf. You can think of the IRQ as a cord that the device tugs when it needs the system to take care of some pending request. If more than one device is tugging on the same cord, the kernel won't be able to determine which device it needs to service. Instant mayhem.

Therefore, be sure that all of your installed devices are using unique IRQ lines. In general, the IRQ for a device can be set by jumpers on the card; see the documentation for the particular device for details. Some devices do not require the use of an IRQ at all, but it is suggested that you configure them to use one if possible (the Seagate ST01 and ST02 SCSI controllers being good examples).

In some cases, the kernel provided on your installation media is configured to use a certain IRQ for certain devices. For example, on some distributions of Linux, the kernel is preconfigured to use IRQ 5 for the TMC-950 SCSI controller, the Mitsumi CD-ROM controller, and the bus mouse driver. If you want to use two or more of these devices, you'll need to first install Linux with only one of these devices enabled, then recompile the kernel in order to change the default IRQ for one of them. (See Chapter 4 for information on recompiling the kernel.)

Another area where hardware conflicts can arise is with DMA (direct memory access) channels, I/O addresses, and shared memory addresses. All of these terms describe mechanisms through which the system interfaces with hardware devices. Some Ethernet boards, for example, use a shared memory address as well as an IRQ to interface with the system. If any of these are in conflict with other devices, then the system may behave unexpectedly. You should be able to change the DMA channel, I/O or shared memory addresses for your various devices with jumper settings. (Unfortunately, some devices don't allow you to change these settings.)

The documentation for your various hardware devices should specify the IRQ, DMA channel, I/O address, or shared memory address that the devices use, and how to configure them. Again, the simple way to get around these problems is just to temporarily disable the conflicting devices until you have time to determine the cause of the problem.

Table 2.2 is a list of IRQ and DMA channels used by various "standard" devices found on most systems. Almost all systems will have at least some of these devices, so you should avoid setting the IRQ or DMA of other devices in conflict with these values.

Problems Recognizing Hard Drive or Controller

When Linux boots, you should see a series of messages on your screen such as:

```
Console:  colour EGA+ 80x25, 8 virtual consoles
Serial driver version 3.96 with no serial options enabled
tty00 at 0x03f8 (irq = 4) is a 16450
```

TABLE 2.2: Linux Partition Names

Device	I/O Address	IRQ	DMA
ttyS0 (COM1)	3f8	4	n/a
ttyS1 (COM2)	2f8	3	n/a
ttyS2 (COM3)	3e8	4	n/a
ttyS3 (COM4)	2e8	3	n/a
lp0 (LPT1)	378–37f	7	n/a
lp1 (LPT2)	278–27f	5	n/a
fd0, fd1 (floppies 1 and 2)	3f0–3f7	6	2
fd2, fd3 (floppies 3 and 4)	370–377	10	3

```
tty03 at 0x02e8 (irq = 3) is a 16550A
lp init: lp1 exists (0), using polling driver
...
```

Here, the kernel is detecting the various hardware devices present on your system. At some point, you should see the line

```
Partition check:
```

followed by a list of recognized partitions, for example:

```
Partition check:
hda:  hda1 hda2
hdb:  hdb1 hdb2 hdb3
```

If, for some reason, your drives or partitions are not recognized, then you will not be able to access them in any way.

There are several things that can cause this to happen:

- **Hard drive or controller not supported**. If you are using a hard drive controller (IDE, SCSI, or otherwise) that is not supported by Linux, the kernel will not recognize your partitions at boot time.

- **Drive or controller improperly configured**. Even if your controller is supported by Linux, it may not be configured correctly. (This is particularly a problem for SCSI controllers; most non-SCSI controllers should work fine without any additional configuration).

Refer to the documentation for your hard drive and/or controller for information on solving these kinds of problems. In particular, many hard drives will need to have a jumper set if they are to be used as a *slave* drive (for example, as the second hard drive). The acid test for this kind of condition is to boot up MS-DOS, or some other operating system known to work with your drive and controller. If you can access the drive and controller from another operating system, then it is not a problem with your hardware configuration.

See "Isolating Hardware Problems," above, for information on resolving possible device conflicts, and "Problems with SCSI Controllers and Devices," below, for information on configuring SCSI devices.

- **Controller properly configured, but not detected**. Some BIOS-less SCSI controllers require the user to specify information about the controller at boot time. "Problems with SCSI Controllers and Devices," below, describes how to force hardware detection for these controllers.

- **Hard drive geometry not recognized**. Some systems, such as the IBM PS/ValuePoint, do not store hard drive geometry information in the CMOS memory, where Linux expects to find it. Also, certain SCSI controllers need to be told where to find drive geometry in order for Linux to recognize the layout of your drive.

  Most distributions provide a bootup option to specify the drive geometry. In general, when booting the installation media, you can specify the drive geometry at the LILO boot prompt with a command such as:

  ```
  boot: linux hd=<cylinders>,<heads>,<sectors>
  ```

  where *<cylinders>*, *<heads>*, and *<sectors>* correspond to the number of cylinders, heads, and sectors per track for your hard drive.

  After installing the Linux software, you will be able to install LILO, allowing you to boot from the hard drive. At that time, you can specify the drive geometry to the LILO installation procedure, making it unnecessary to enter the drive geometry each time you boot. See Chapter 4 for more about LILO.

Problems with SCSI Controllers and Devices

Presented here are some of the most common problems with SCSI controllers and devices such as CD-ROMs, hard drives, and tape drives. If you are having problems getting Linux to recognize your drive or controller, read on.

The Linux SCSI HOWTO (see Appendix A) contains much useful information on SCSI devices in addition to that listed here. SCSI can be particularly tricky to configure at times.

- **A SCSI device is detected at all possible IDs**. This is caused by strapping the device to the same address as the controller. You need to change the jumper settings so that the drive uses a different address from the controller itself.

- **Linux reports sense errors, even if the devices are known to be error-free**. This can be caused by bad cables or by bad termination. If your SCSI bus is not terminated at both ends you may have errors accessing SCSI devices. When in doubt, always check your cables.

- **SCSI devices report timeout errors**. This is usually caused by a conflict with IRQ, DMA, or device addresses. Also check that interrupts are enabled correctly on your controller.

- **SCSI controllers using BIOS are not detected**. Detection of controllers using BIOS will fail if the BIOS is disabled or if your controller's *signature* is not recognized by the kernel. See the Linux SCSI HOWTO for more information about this.

- **Controllers using memory-mapped I/O do not work**. This is caused when the memory-mapped I/O ports are incorrectly cached. Either mark the board's address space as uncacheable in the XCMOS settings or disable cache altogether.

- **When partitioning, you get a warning that** `cylinders > 1024`, **or you are unable to boot from a partition using cylinders numbered above 1023**. BIOS limits the number of cylinders to 1024, and any partition using cylinders numbered above this won't be accessible from the BIOS. As far as Linux is concerned, this only affects booting; once the system has booted, you should be able to access the partition. Your options are to either boot Linux from a boot floppy or boot from a partition using cylinders numbered below 1024. See "Creating the Boot Floppy or Installing LILO" for information on creating a boot diskette or installing LILO.

- **CD-ROM drive or other removable media devices are not recognized at boot time**. Try booting with a CD-ROM (or disk) in the drive. This is necessary for some devices.

If your SCSI controller is not recognized, you may need to force hardware detection at boot time. This is particularly important for BIOS-less SCSI controllers. Most distributions allow you to specify the controller IRQ and shared memory address when booting the installation media. For example, if you are using a TMC-8xx controller, you may be able to enter

```
boot: linux tmx8xx=<interrupt>,<memory-address>
```

at the LILO boot prompt, where *<interrupt>* is the IRQ of controller, and *<memory-address>* is the shared memory address. Whether or not you will be able to do this depends on the distribution of Linux you are using; consult your documentation for details.

Problems Installing the Software

Actually installing the Linux software should be quite trouble-free, if you're lucky. The only problems that you might experience would be related to corrupt installation media or lack of space on your Linux file systems. Here is a list of these common problems.

- **System reports `Read error, file not found` or other errors while attempting to install the software**. This is indicative of a problem with your installation media. If you are installing from floppy, keep in mind that floppies are quite susceptible to media errors of this type. Be sure to use brand-new, newly formatted floppies. If you have an MS-DOS partition on your drive, many Linux distributions allow you to install the software from the hard drive. This may be faster and more reliable than using floppies.

  If you are using a CD-ROM, be sure to check the disc for scratches, dust, or other problems which might cause media errors.

  The cause of the problem may be that the media is in the incorrect format. For example, if using floppies, many Linux distributions require that the floppies be formatted in high-density MS-DOS format. (The boot floppy is the exception; it is not in MS-DOS format in most cases.) If all else fails, either obtain a new set of floppies, or recreate the floppies (using new diskettes) if you downloaded the software yourself.

- **System reports errors such as `tar: read error` or `gzip: not in gzip format`**. This problem is usually caused by corrupt files on the installation media itself. In other words, your floppy may be error-free, but the data on the floppy is in some way corrupted. For example, if you downloaded the Linux software using text mode rather than binary mode, then your files will be corrupt and unreadable by the installation software.

- **System reports errors such as `device full` while installing**. This is a clear-cut sign that you have run out of space when installing the software. Not all Linux distributions will be able to cleanly pick up the mess; you shouldn't be able to abort the installation and expect the system to work.

  The solution is usually to recreate your file systems (with the `mke2fs` command) which will delete the partially installed software. You can then attempt to reinstall the software, this time selecting a smaller amount of software to install. In other cases, you may need to start completely from scratch and rethink your partition and file system sizes.

- **System reports errors such as `read intr: 0x10` while accessing the hard drive**. This is usually an indication of bad blocks on your drive. However, if you receive these errors while using `mkswap` or `mke2fs`, the system may be having trouble accessing your drive. This can either be a hardware problem (see "Hardware Problems") or it might be a case of poorly specified geometry. If you used the

  ```
  hd=<cylinders>,<heads>,<sectors>
  ```

  option at boot time to force detection of your drive geometry and incorrectly specified the geometry, you could be prone to this problem. This can also happen if your drive geometry is incorrectly specified in the system CMOS.

- **System reports errors such as `file not found` or `permission denied`.** This problem can occur if not all of the necessary files are present on the installation media (see the next paragraph) or if there is a permissions problem with the installation software. For example, some distributions of Linux have been known to have bugs in the installation software itself. These are usually fixed very rapidly and are quite infrequent. If you suspect that the distribution software contains bugs, and you're sure that you have not done anything wrong, contact the maintainer of the distribution to report the bug.

If you have other strange errors when installing Linux (especially if you downloaded the software yourself), be sure that you actually obtained all of the necessary files when downloading. For example, some people use the ftp command

```
mget *.*
```

when downloading the Linux software via ftp. This will download only those files that contain a "." in their filenames; if there are any files without the ".", you will miss them. The correct command to use in this case is

```
mget *
```

The best advice is to retrace your steps when something goes wrong. You may think that you have done everything correctly, when in fact you forgot a small but important step somewhere along the way. In many cases, just attempting to re-download or reinstall the Linux software can solve the problem. Don't beat your head against the wall any longer than you have to!

Also, if Linux unexpectedly hangs during installation, there may be a hardware problem of some kind. See "Hardware Problems" for hints.

Problems After Installing Linux

You've spent an entire afternoon installing Linux. In order to make space for it, you wiped your MS-DOS and OS/2 partitions, and tearfully deleted your copies of Sim-City and Wing Commander. You reboot the system, and nothing happens. Or, even worse, *something* happens, but it's not what *should* happen. What do you do?

In "Problems with Booting the Installation Media," we covered some of the most common problems that can occur when booting the Linux installation media—many of those problems may apply here. In addition, you may be victim to one of the following maladies.

Problems Booting Linux from Floppy

If you are using a floppy to boot Linux, you may need to specify the location of your Linux root partition at boot time. This is especially true if you are using the original installation floppy itself and not a custom boot floppy created during installation.

While booting the floppy, hold down Shift or Ctrl. This should present you with a boot menu; press Tab to see a list of available options. For example, many distributions allow you to type

```
boot: linux hd=<partition>
```

at the boot menu, where *<partition>* is the name of the Linux root partition, such as `/dev/hda2`. Consult the documentation for your distribution for details.

Problems Booting Linux from the Hard Drive

If you opted to install LILO, instead of creating a boot floppy, then you should be able to boot Linux from the hard drive. However, the automated LILO installation procedure used by many distributions is not always perfect. It may make incorrect assumptions about your partition layout, in which case you will need to re-install LILO to get everything right. Installing LILO is covered in Chapter 4.

- **System reports `Drive not bootable—Please insert system disk`.** You will get this error message if the hard drive's master boot record is corrupt in some way. In most cases, it's harmless, and everything else on your drive is still intact. There are several ways around this:

  1. While partitioning your drive using `fdisk`, you may have deleted the partition that was marked as *active*. MS-DOS and other operating systems attempt to boot the active partition at boot time (Linux pays no attention to whether the partition is active or not). You may be able to boot MS-DOS and run `FDISK` to set the active flag on your MS-DOS partition, and all will be well.
     Another command to try (with MS-DOS 50 and higher) is

     ```
     FDISK /MBR
     ```

     This command will attempt to rebuild the hard drive master boot record for booting MS-DOS, overwriting LILO. If you no longer have MS-DOS on your hard drive, you'll need to boot Linux from floppy and attempt to install LILO later.

  2. If you created an MS-DOS partition using Linux's version of `fdisk`, or vice versa, you may get this error. You should create MS-DOS partitions with MS-DOS's version `FDISK` only. (The same applies to operating systems other than MS-DOS.) The best solution here is either to start from scratch and repartition the drive correctly or to merely delete and recreate the offending partitions using the correct version of `fdisk`.

  3. The LILO installation procedure may have failed. In this case, you should either boot from your Linux boot floppy (if you have one) or from the original installation media. Either of these should provide options for specifying the Linux root partition to use when booting.

Hold down Shift or Ctrl at boot time, and press Tab from the boot menu for a list of options.

• **When booting the system from the hard drive, MS-DOS (or another operating system) starts instead of Linux.** First of all, be sure that you actually installed LILO when installing the Linux software. If not, then the system will still boot MS-DOS (or whatever other operating system you may have) when you attempt to boot from the hard drive. In order to boot Linux from the hard drive, you will need to install LILO (see Chapter 4).

On the other hand, if you *did* install LILO, and another operating system boots instead of Linux, then you have LILO configured to boot that other operating system by default. While the system is booting, hold down Shift or Ctrl, and press Tab at the boot prompt. This should present you with a list of possible operating systems to boot; select the appropriate option (usually just "linux") to boot Linux.

If you wish to select Linux as the default operating system to boot, you will need to re-install LILO. See Chapter 4.

It also may be possible that you attempted to install LILO, but the installation procedure failed in some way. See the previous item.

Problems Logging In

After booting Linux, you should be presented with a login prompt, like so:

```
linux login:
```

At this point, either the distribution's documentation or the system itself will tell you what to do. For many distributions, you simply login as root, with no password. Other possible usernames to try are guest or test.

Most newly installed Linux systems should not require a password for the initial login. However, if you are asked to enter a password, there may be a problem. First, try using a password equivalent to the username; that is, if you are logging in as root, use **root as the password.**

If you simply can't login, there may be a problem. First, consult your distribution's documentation; the username and password to use may be buried in there somewhere. The username and password may have been given to you during the installation procedure or they may be printed on the login banner.

One cause of this may be a problem with installing the Linux login and initialization files. If this is the case, you may need to reinstall (at least parts of) the Linux software or boot your installation media and attempt to fix the problem by hand—see Chapter 4 for hints.

Problems Using the System

If login is successful, you should be presented with a shell prompt (such as "#" or "") and can happily roam around your system. However, there are some initial problems with using the system that sometimes creep up.

The most common initial configuration problem is incorrect file or directory permissions. This can cause the error message

```
Shell-init: permission denied
```

to be printed after logging in (in fact, any time you see the message permission denied you can be fairly certain that it is a problem with file permissions).

In many cases, it's a simple matter of using the chmod command to fix the permissions of the appropriate files or directories. For example, some distributions of Linux once used the (incorrect) file mode 0644 for the root directory (/). The fix was to issue the command

```
# chmod 755 /
```

as root. However, in order to issue this command, you needed to boot from the installation media and mount your Linux root file system by hand—a hairy task for most newcomers.

As you use the system, you may run into places where file and directory permissions are incorrect or software does not work as configured. Welcome to the world of Linux! While most distributions are quite trouble-free, very few of them are perfect. We don't want to cover all of those problems here. Instead, throughout the book we help you to solve many of these configuration problems by teaching you how to find them and fix them yourself. In Chapter 1 we discussed this philosophy in some detail. In Chapter 4, we give hints for fixing many of these common configuration problems.

CHAPTER

THREE

3

Linux Tutorial

Introduction

New users of Unix and Linux may be a bit intimidated by the size and apparent complexity of the system before them. There are many good books on using Unix out there, for all levels of expertise from novice to expert. However, none of these books covers, specifically, an introduction to using Linux. While 95% of using Linux is exactly like using other Unix systems, the most straightforward way to get going on your new system is with a tutorial tailored for Linux. Herein is such a tutorial.

This chapter does not go into a large amount of detail or cover many advanced topics. Instead, it is intended to get the new Linux user running, on both feet, so that he or she may then read a more general book about Unix and understand the basic differences between other Unix systems and Linux.

Very little is assumed here, except perhaps some familiarity with personal computer systems and MS-DOS. However, even if you're not an MS-DOS user, you should be able to understand everything here. At first glance, Unix looks a lot like MS-DOS (after all, MS-DOS was modeled on the CP/M operating system, which in turn was modeled on Unix). However, only the very superficial features of Unix resemble MS-DOS in any way. Even if you're completely new to the PC world, this tutorial should be of help.

And, before we begin: *don't be afraid to experiment*. The system won't bite you. You can't destroy anything by working on the system. Unix has some amount of security built in, to prevent "normal" users (the role which you will now assume) from damaging files that are essential to the system. Even so, the absolute worst thing that can happen is that you'll delete all of your files—and you'll have to go back and reinstall the system. So, at this point, you have nothing to lose.

Basic Unix Concepts

Unix is a multitasking, multiuser operating system. This means that there can be many people using one computer at the same time, running many different applications. (This differs from MS-DOS, where only one person can use the system at any one time.) Under Unix, for users to identify themselves to the system, they must *log in*, which entails two steps: Entering your *login name* (the name which the system identifies you as), and entering your *password*, which is your personal secret key to logging into your account. Because only you know your password, no one else can log into the system under your username.

On traditional Unix systems, the system administrator will assign you a username and an initial password when you are given an account on the system. However, because you are the system administrator, you must set up your own account before you can log in—see "Creating an Account," below. For the following discussions, we'll use the imaginary username `larry`.

In addition, each Unix system has a *hostname* assigned to it. It is this hostname that gives your machine a name—gives it character and charm. The hostname is used to identify individual machines on a network, but even if your machine isn't networked, it should have a hostname. We'll cover this in "Setting the Host Name" in Chapter 4. For our examples, below, the system's hostname is `mousehouse`.

Creating an Account

Before you can use the system, you must set up a user account for yourself. This is because it's usually not a good idea to use the `root` account for normal use. The `root` account should be reserved for running privileged commands and for maintaining the system, as discussed in "About Root, Hats, and the Feeling of Power" in Chapter 4.

In order to create an account for yourself, you need to log in as `root` and use the `useradd` or `adduser` command. See "Managing Users" for information on this procedure.

Logging In

At login time, you'll see a prompt resembling the following on your screen:

```
mousehouse login:
```

Here, enter your username, and press the ↵ key. Our hero, Larry, would type the following:

```
mousehouse login: larry
Password:
```

Now, enter your password. It won't be echoed to the screen when you log in, so type carefully. If you mistype your password, you'll see the message

```
Login incorrect
```

and you'll have to try again.

Once you have correctly entered the username and password, you are officially logged into the system, and are free to roam.

Virtual Consoles

The system's console is the monitor and keyboard connected directly to the system. (Because Unix is a multiuser operating system, you may have other terminals connected to serial ports on your system, but these would not be the console.) Linux, like some other versions of Unix, provides access to *virtual consoles* (or VCs), which allow you to have more than one login session from your console at a time.

To demonstrate this, log in to your system (as demonstrated above). Now, press Alt+F2. You should see the `login:` prompt again. You're looking at the second virtual console—you logged into the first. To switch back to the first VC, press Alt+F1. Voilá! You're back to your first login session.

A newly installed Linux system will probably allow you to access the first four VCs, using Alt+F1 through Alt+F4. However, it is possible to enable up to 12 VCs—one for each function key on your keyboard. As you can see, use of VCs can be very powerful—you can be working on several different VCs at once.

While the use of VCs is somewhat limiting (after all, you can only be looking at one VC at a time), it should give you a feel for Unix's multiuser capabilities. While you're working on VC #1, you can switch over to VC #2 and start working on something else.

Shells and Commands

For most of your explorations in the world of Unix, you'll be talking to the system through the use of a *shell*. A shell is just a program which takes user input (e.g., commands that you type) and translates them into instructions. This can be compared to the COMMAND.COM program under MS-DOS, which does essentially the same thing. The shell is just one interface to Unix. There are many possible interfaces, such as the X Window System, which lets you run commands by using the mouse and keyboard in conjunction.

As soon as you log in, the system starts the shell, and you can type commands to it. Here's a quick example. Here, Larry logs in, and is left sitting at the shell *prompt*.

```
mousehouse login: larry
Password: larry's password
Welcome to Mousehouse!

/home/larry#
```

`/home/larry#` is the shell's prompt, indicating that it's ready to take commands. (More on what the prompt itself means later.) Let's try telling the system to do something interesting:

```
/home/larry# make love
make: *** No way to make target 'love'. Stop.
/home/larry#
```

Well, as it turns out `make` was the name of an actual program on the system, and the shell executed this program when given the command. (Unfortunately, the system was being unfriendly.)

This brings us to one burning question: What are commands? What happens when you type `make love`? The first word on the command line, `make`, is the name of the command to be executed. Everything else on the command line is taken as arguments to this command. Examples:

```
/home/larry# cp foo bar
```

Here, the name of the command is `cp`, and the arguments are `foo` and `bar`.

When you type a command, the shell does several things. First of all, it looks at the command name, and checks to see if it is a command that is internal to the shell. (That is, a command that the shell knows how to execute by itself. There are a number of these commands, and we'll go into them later.) The shell also checks to see if the command is an alias, or substitute name, for another command. If neither of these conditions apply, the shell looks for a program, on the disk, with the command's name. If it finds such a program, the shell runs it, giving the program the arguments specified on the command line.

In our example, the shell looks for the program called `make`, and runs it with the argument `love`. Make is a program often used to compile large programs, and it takes as arguments the name of a "target" to compile. In the case of make love, we instructed make to compile the target love. Because make can't find a target by this name, it fails with a humorous error message, and we are returned to the shell prompt.

What happens if we type a command to a shell, and the shell can't find a program with the command name to run? Well, we can try it:

```
/home/larry# eat dirt
eat: command not found
/home/larry#
```

Quite simply, if the shell can't find a program with the name given on the command line (here, eat), it prints an error message which should be self-explanatory. You'll often see this error message if you mistype a command (for example, if you had typed mkae love instead of make love).

Logging Out

Before we delve much further, we should tell you how to log out of the system. At the shell prompt, use the command

```
/home/larry# exit
```

to log out. There are other ways of logging out as well, but this is the most foolproof.

Changing Your Password

You should also be aware of how to change your password. The command passwd will prompt you for your old password and your new password. It will ask you to reenter the new password for validation. Be careful not to forget your password—if you do, you will have to ask the system administrator to reset it for you. (If you're the system administrator, see "Managing Users" in Chapter 4.)

Files and Directories

Under most operating systems (Unix included), there is the concept of a *file*, which is just a bundle of information given a name (a *filename*). Examples of files would be your history term paper, an e-mail message, or an actual program which can be executed. Essentially, anything that is saved on disk is saved in an individual file.

Files are identified by their filenames. For example, the file containing your history paper might be saved with the filename `history-paper`. These names usually identify the file and its contents in some form that is meaningful to you. There is no standard format for filenames as there is under MS-DOS and other operating systems; in general, filenames may contain any character (except /—see the discussion of pathnames, below), and are limited to 256 characters in length.

With the concept of files comes the concept of directories. A *directory* is just a collection of files. It can be thought of as a "folder" which contains many different files. Directories themselves are given names, with which you can identify them. Furthermore, directories are maintained in a tree-like structure; that is, directories may contain other directories.

A file may be referred to by its *pathname*, which is made up of the filename, preceded by the name of the directory which contains the file. For example, let's say that Larry has a directory called `papers`, which contains three files: `history-final`, `english-lit`, and `masters-thesis`. (Each of these three files contains information for three of Larry's ongoing projects.) To refer to the file `english-lit`, Larry can specify the file's pathname:

`papers/english-lit`

As you can see, the directory and filenames are separated by a single slash (/). For this reason, filenames themselves cannot contain the / character. MS-DOS users will find this convention familiar, although in the MS-DOS world, the backslash (\) is used instead.

As mentioned, directories can be nested within each other as well. For example, let's say that Larry has another directory, within `papers`, called `notes`. This directory contains the files `math-notes` and `cheat-sheet`. The pathname of the file `cheat-sheet` would be

`papers/notes/cheat-sheet`

Therefore, the pathname really is a "path" which you take to locate a certain file. The directory above a given subdirectory is known as the *parent directory*. Here, the directory `papers` is the parent of the `notes` directory.

The Directory Tree

Most Unix systems have a standard layout for files, so that system resources and programs can be easily located. This layout forms a directory tree, which starts at the / directory, also known as the root directory. Directly underneath / are some important subdirectories: /bin, /etc, /dev, and /usr, among others. These directories in turn contain other directories which contain system configuration files, programs, and so on.

In particular, each user has a *home directory,* which is the directory set aside for that user to store his or her files. In the examples above, all of Larry's files (such as cheat-sheet and history-final) were contained in Larry's home directory. Usually, user home directories are contained under /home, and are named for the user who owns that directory. Therefore, Larry's home directory is /home/larry.

In Figure 3.1 a sample directory tree is represented. It should give you some idea of how the directory tree on your system is organized.

The Current Working Directory

At any given time, commands that you type to the shell are given in terms of your *current working directory.* You can think of your working directory as the directory in which you are currently "located." When you first login, your working directory is set to your home directory—/home/larry in our case. Whenever you reference a file, you may refer to it in relationship to your current working directory instead of specifying the full pathname of the file.

Here's an example. Larry has the directory papers, and papers contains the file history-final. If Larry wants to look at this file, he can use the command

```
/home/larry# more /home/larry/papers/history-final
```

The more command simply displays a file, one screen at a time. However, because Larry's current working directory is /home/larry, he can instead refer to the file *relative* to his current location. The command would be

```
/home/larry# more papers/history-final
```

Therefore, if you begin a filename (such as papers/final) with a character other than /, the system assumes that you're referring to the file in terms relative to your current working directory. This is known as a *relative pathname.*

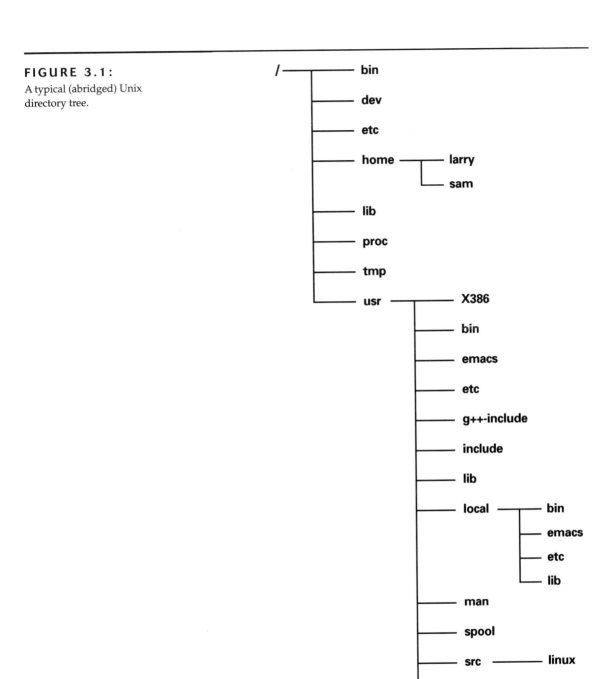

A typical (abridged) Unix
directory tree.

On the other hand, if you begin a filename with a /, the system interprets this as a full pathname—that is, a pathname including the entire path to the file, starting from the root directory, /. This is known as an *absolute pathname*.

Referring to Home Directories

Under both Tcsh and Bash on Linux, your home directory can be referred to using the tilde (~) character. For example, the command

```
/home/larry# more ~/papers/history-final
```

is equivalent to

```
/home/larry# more /home/larry/papers/history-final
```

The ~ character is simply replaced with the name of your home directory by the shell.

In addition, you can specify other user's home directories with the tilde as well. The pathname ~karl/letters translates to /home/karl/letters by the shell (if /home/karl is Karl's home directory). The use of the tilde is simply a shortcut; there is no directory named "~" —it's just syntactic sugar provided by the shell.

First Steps into Unix

Before we begin, it is important to note that all file and command names on a Unix system are case-sensitive (unlike operating systems such as MS-DOS). For example, the command make is very different than Make or MAKE. The same holds for file and directory names.

Moving Around

Now that we can login, and know how to refer to files using pathnames, how can we change our current working directory, to make life easier?

The command for moving around in the directory structure is cd, short for *change directory*. You'll notice that many often-used Unix commands are two or three letters.

The usage of the `cd` command is:

```
cd <directory>
```

where *\<directory\>* is the name of the directory you wish to change to.

As we said, when you login, you begin in your home directory. If Larry wanted to move down into the `papers` subdirectory, he'd use the command

```
/home/larry# cd papers
/home/larry/papers#
```

As you can see, Larry's prompt changes to reflect his current working directory (so he knows where he is). Now that he's in the `papers` directory, he can look at his history final with the command

```
/home/larry/papers# more history-final
```

Now, Larry is stuck in the `papers` subdirectory. To move back up to the parent directory, use the command

```
/home/larry/papers# cd ..
/home/larry#
```

(Note the space between the `cd` and the "..".) Every directory has an entry named ".." which refers to the parent directory. Similarly, every directory has an entry named "." which refers to itself. Therefore, the command

```
/home/larry/papers# cd .
```

gets us nowhere.

You can also use absolute pathnames in the `cd` command. To `cd` into Karl's home directory, we can use the command

```
/home/larry/papers# cd /home/karl
/home/karl#
```

Also, using `cd` with no argument will return you to your own home directory.

```
/home/karl# cd
/home/larry#
```

Looking at the Contents of Directories

Now that you know how to move around directories you probably think, "So what?" The basic skill of moving around directories is fairly useless, so let's introduce a new command, ls. ls prints a listing of files and directories, by default from your current directory. For example:

```
/home/larry# ls
Mail
letters
papers
/home/larry#
```

Here we can see that Larry has three entries in his current directory: Mail, letters, and papers. This doesn't tell us much—are these directories or files? We can use the -F option on the ls command to tell us more.

```
/home/larry# ls -F
Mail/
letters/
papers/
/home/larry#
```

From the / appended to each filename, we know that these three entries are in fact subdirectories.

Using ls -F may also append an * (asterisk) to the end of a filename. This indicates that the file is an *executable,* or a program which can be run. If nothing is appended to the filename using ls -F, the file is a "plain old file," that is, it's neither a directory nor an executable.

In general, each Unix command may take a number of options in addition to other arguments. These options usually begin with a - (minus sign), as demonstrated above with ls -F. The -F option tells ls to give more information about the type of the files involved—in this case, printing a / after each directory name.

If you give ls a directory name, it will print the contents of that directory.

```
/home/larry# ls -F papers
english-lit
history-final
```

```
masters-thesis
notes/
/home/larry#
```

Or, for a more interesting listing, let's see what's in the system's /etc directory.

```
/home/larry# ls /etc
Images          ftpusers        lpc             rc.new          shells
adm             getty           magic           rc0.d           startcons
bcheckrc        gettydefs       motd            rc1.d           swapoff
brc             group           mount           rc2.d           swapon
brc~            inet            mtab            rc3.d           syslog.conf
csh.cshrc       init            mtools          rc4.d           syslog.pid
csh.login       init.d          pac             rc5.d           syslogd.reload
default         initrunlvl      passwd          rmt             termcap
disktab         inittab         printcap        rpc             umount
fdprm           inittab.old     profile         rpcinfo         update
fstab           issue           psdatabase      securetty       utmp
ftpaccess       lilo            rc              services        wtmp
/home/larry#
```

(For those MS-DOS users out there, notice how the filenames can be longer than 8 characters, and can contain periods in any position. It is even possible to have more than one period in a filename.)

Let's cd up to the top of the directory tree, using cd .., and then down to another directory. /usr/bin.

```
/home/larry# cd ..
/home# cd ..
/# cd usr
/usr# cd bin
/usr/bin#
```

You can also move into directories in multiple steps, as in cd /usr/bin.

Try moving around various directories, using ls and cd. In some cases, you may run into a foreboding Permission denied error message. This is simply the concept of Unix security kicking in: in order to ls or cd into a directory, you must have permission to do so. We'll talk more about this in "File Permissions" later in this chapter.

Creating New Directories

It's time to learn how to create directories. This involves the use of the mkdir command. Try the following:

```
/home/larry# mkdir foo
/home/larry# ls -F
Mail/
foo/
letters/
papers/
/home/larry# cd foo
/home/larry/foo# ls
/home/larry/foo#
```

Congrats! You've just made a new directory and moved into it. Since there aren't any files in this new directory, let's learn how to copy files from one place to another.

Copying Files

Copying files is done with the command cp:

```
home/larry/foo# cp /etc/termcap .
/home/larry/foo# cp /etc/shells .
/home/larry/foo# ls -F
shells      termcap
/home/larry/foo# cp shells bells
/home/larry/foo# ls -F
bells      shells      termcap
/home/larry/foo#
```

The cp command copies the files listed on the command line to the file or directory given as the last argument. Notice how we use the directory "." to refer to the current directory.

Moving Files

A new command named mv moves files, instead of copying them. The syntax is very straightforward.

```
/home/larry/foo# mv termcap sells
/home/larry/foo# ls -F
```

```
bells      sells      shells
/home/larry/foo#
```

Notice how `termcap` no longer exists, but in its place is the file `sells`. This can be used to rename files, as we have just done, but also to move a file to a completely new directory.

NOTE `mv` and `cp` will overwrite the destination file (if it already exists) without asking you. Be careful when you move a file into another directory: there may already be a file with the same name in that directory, which you'll overwrite!

Deleting Files and Directories

You now have an ugly rhyme developing with the use of the `ls` command. To delete a file, use the `rm` command. (`rm` stands for *remove*).

```
/home/larry/foo# rm bells sells
/home/larry/foo# ls -F
shells
/home/larry/foo#
```

We're left with nothing but shells, but we won't complain. Note that `rm` by default won't prompt you before deleting a file—so be careful.

A related command to `rm` is `rmdir`. This command deletes a directory, but only if the directory is empty. If the directory contains any files or subdirectories, `rmdir` will complain.

Looking at Files

The commands `more` and `cat` are used for viewing the contents of files. `more` displays a file, one screenful at a time, while `cat` displays the whole file at once.

To look at the file shells, we can use the command

```
/home/larry/foo# more shells
```

In case you're interested what `shells` contains, it's a list of valid shell programs on your system. On most systems, this includes `/bin/sh`, `/bin/bash`, and `/bin/csh`.

We'll talk about these different types of shells later.

While using more, press the spacebar to display the next page of text, and b to display the previous page. There are other commands available in more as well—these are just the basics. Pressing q will quit more.

Quit more and try cat /etc/termcap. The text will probably fly by much too quickly for you to read it. The name cat actually stands for *concatenate*, which is the real use of the program. The cat command can be used to concatenate the contents of several files and save the result to another file. This will be discussed later.

Getting On-Line Help

Almost every Unix system, Linux included, provides a facility known as *manual pages*, or *man pages* for short. These man pages contain online documentation for all of the various system commands, resources, configuration files, and so on.

The command used to access man pages is man. For example, if you're interested in finding out about the other options of the ls command, you can type

```
/home/larry# man ls
```

and the man page for ls will be displayed.

Unfortunately, most of the man pages out there are written for those who already have some idea of what the command or resource does. For this reason, man pages usually only contain the hardcore technical details of the command, without a lot of tutorial. However, man pages can be an invaluable resource for jogging your memory if you forget the syntax of a command. Man pages will also tell you a lot about the commands which we won't tell you in this book.

We suggest that you try man for the commands we've already gone over, and whenever we introduce a new command. You'll notice some of these commands won't have man pages. This could be for several reasons. For one, the man pages haven't been written yet (the Linux Documentation Project is responsible for man pages under Linux as well. We are gradually accumulating most of the man pages available for the system). Secondly, the command might be an internal shell command, or an alias (as discussed in "Shells and Commands" earlier in this chapter), in which case it would not have a man page of its own. One example is cd, which is a shell internal command. The shell actually processes the cd—there is no separate program that contains this command.

Summary of Basic Commands

This section introduces some of the most useful basic commands on a Unix system, including those covered in the last section.

Note that options usually begin with a – (minus sign), and in most cases multiple one-letter options may be combined using a single –. For example, instead of using the command ls –l –F, it is adequate to use ls –lF.

Instead of listing all of the options available for each of these commands, we'll only talk about those which are useful or important at this time. In fact, most of these commands have a large number of options (most of which you'll never use). You can use man to see the manual pages for each command, which list all of the available options.

Also note that many of these commands take a list of files or directories as arguments, denoted by <file1> …<fileN>. For example, the cp command takes as arguments a list of files to copy, followed by the destination file or directory. When copying more than one file, the destination must be a directory.

cd   Change the current working directory.
Syntax: cd *<directory>*
<directory> is the directory to change to. ("." refers to the current directory, ".." the parent directory.)
Example: cd ../foo sets the current directory to ../foo.

ls   Displays information about the named files and directories.
Syntax: ls *<file1>* *<file2>* …*<fileN>*
Where *<file1>* through *<fileN>* are the filenames or directories to list. Options: There are more options than you want to think about. The most commonly used are –F (used to display some information about the type of the file), and –l (gives a "long" listing including file size, owner, permissions, and so on). This will be covered in detail later.
Example: ls –lF /home/larry will display the contents of the directory /home/larry.

cp   Copies file(s) to another file or directory.
    Syntax: cp *<file1> <file2> ...<fileN> <destination>*
    Where *<file1>* through *<fileN>* are the files to copy, and
    <destination> is the destination file or directory.
    Example: cp ../frog joe copies the file ../frog to the
    file or directory joe.

mv   Moves file(s) to another file or directory. This command
    does the equivalent of a copy followed by the deletion of
    the original. This can be used to rename files, as in the MS-
    DOS command RENAME.
    Syntax: mv *<file1> <file2> ...<fileN> <destination>*
    Where *<file1>* through *<fileN>* are the files to move, and
    <destination> is the destination file or directory.
    Example: mv ../frog joe moves the file ../frog to the
    file or directory joe.

rm   Deletes files. Note that when files are deleted under Unix,
    they are unrecoverable (unlike MS-DOS, where you can
    usually "undelete" the file).
    Syntax: rm *<file1> <file2> ...<fileN>*
    Where *<file1>* through *<fileN>* are the filenames to delete.
    Options: -i will prompt for confirmation before deleting
    the file.
    Example: rm -i /home/larry/joe /home/larry/frog
    deletes the files joe and frog in /home/larry.

mkdir Creates new directories.
    Syntax: mkdir *<dir1> <dir2> ...<dirN>*
    Where *<dir1>* through *<dirN>* are the directories to
    create.
    Example: mkdir /home/larry/test creates the directory
    test under /home/larry.

rmdir   This command deletes empty directories. When using
rmdir, your current working directory must not be
within the directory to be deleted.
Syntax: rmdir *<dir1> <dir2> ...<dirN>*
Where *<dir1>* through *<dirN>* are the directories to
delete.
Example: rmdir /home/larry/papers deletes the
directory /home/larry/papers, if it is empty.

man   Displays the manual page for the given command or
resource (that is, any system utility that isn't a command,
such as a library function).
Syntax: man *<command>*
Where *<command>* is the name of the command or
resource you wish to get help on.
Example: man ls gives help on the ls command.

more   Displays the contents of the named files, one screenful at
a time.
Syntax: more *<file1> <file2> ...<fileN>*
Where *<file1>* through *<fileN>* are the files to display.
Example: more papers/history-final displays the file
papers/history-final.

cat   Officially used to concatenate files, cat is also used to
display the entire contents of a file at once.
Syntax: cat *<file1> <file2> ...<fileN>*
Where *<file1>* through *<fileN>* are the files to display.
Example: cat letters/from-mdw displays the file
letters/from-mdw.

echo   Simply echoes the given arguments.
Syntax: echo *<arg1> <arg2> ...<argN>*
Where *<arg1>* through *<argN>* are the arguments to echo.
Example: echo "Hello world" displays the string
Hello world.

grep   Displays all of the lines in the named file(s) matching the given pattern.
Syntax: grep *<pattern> <file1> <file2> …<fileN>*
Where *<pattern>* is a regular expression pattern, and *<file1>* through *<fileN>* are the files to search.
Example: grep loomer /etc/hosts will display all lines in the file /etc/hosts which contain the pattern loomer.

Exploring the File System

The *file system* is the collection of files and the hierarchy of directories on your system. I promised before to escort you around the file system and the time has come.

You have the skills and the knowledge to make sense out of what I'm saying, and you have a roadmap. (See Figure 3.1 earlier in this chapter.)

First, change to the root directory (cd /), and do an ls -F. You'll probably see these directories: bin, dev, etc, home, install, lib, mnt, proc, root, tmp, user, usr, and var. (You may see others and you might not see any of them.)

Let's take a look at each of these directories.

/bin   /bin is short for *binaries*, or executables. This is where many essential system programs reside. Use the command ls -F /bin to list the files here. If you look down the list you may see a few commands that you recognize, such as cp, ls, and mv. These are the actual programs for these commands. When you use the cp command, you're running the program /bin/cp.

Using ls -F, you'll see that most (if not all) of the files in /bin have an *(asterisk) appended to their filenames. This indicates that the files are executables, as described in "Looking at the Contents of Directories" earlier in this chapter.

/dev   Next on our stop is /dev. Take a look, again with ls -F. The *files* in /dev are known as *device drivers*—they are used to access system devices and resources, such as disk drives, modems, memory, and so on. For example, just as you can read data from a file, you can read input from the mouse by accessing /dev/mouse. The filenames beginning with fd are floppy disk devices. fd0 is the first floppy disk drive, fd1 the second. Now, the astute among you will notice that there are more floppy disk devices then just the two I've listed above: they represent specific types of floppy disks. For example, fd1H1440 will access high-density, 3.5″ diskettes in drive

1. Here is a list of some of the most commonly used device files. Note that even though you may not have some of the devices listed below, the chances are that you'll have entries in /dev for them anyway. Don't worry. Every release of Linux differs in some respects.

- /dev/console refers to the system's console—that is, the monitor connected directly to your system.

- The various /dev/ttyS and /dev/cua devices are used for accessing serial ports. For example, /dev/ttyS0 refers to COM1 under MS-DOS. The /dev/cua devices are *callout* devices, which are used in conjunction with a modem.

- The device names beginning with hd access hard drives. /dev/hda refers to the whole first hard disk, while hda1 refers to the first partition on /dev/hda.

- The device names beginning with sd are SCSI drives. If you have a SCSI hard drive, instead of accessing it through /dev/hda, you would access /dev/sda. SCSI tapes are accessed via st devices, and SCSI CD-ROM via sr devices.

- The device names beginning with lp access parallel ports. /dev/lp0 refers to LPT1 in the MS-DOS world.

- /dev/null is used as a "black hole"—any data sent to this device is gone forever. Why is this useful? Well, if you wanted to suppress the output of a command appearing on your screen, you could send that output to /dev/null. We'll talk more about this later.

- The device names beginning with /dev/tty refer to the *virtual consoles* on your system (accessed by pressing Alt+F1, Alt+F2, and so on). /dev/tty1 refers to the first VC, /dev/tty2 refers to the second, and so on.

- The device names beginning with /dev/pty are *pseudo-terminals*. They are used to provide a "terminal" to remote login sessions. For example, if your machine is on a network, incoming telnet logins would use one of the /dev/pty devices.

/etc	/etc contains a number of miscellaneous system configuration files. These include /etc/passwd (the user database), /etc/rc (the system initialization script), and so on.
/sbin	/sbin is used for storing essential system binaries, to be used by the system administrator.
/home	/home contains user's home directories. For example, /home/larry is the home directory for the user larry. On a newly-installed system, there may not be any users in this directory.
/lib	/lib contains *shared library images*. These files contain code which many programs share in common. Instead of each program containing its own copy of these shared routines, they are all stored in one common place, in /lib. This makes executable files smaller, and saves space on your system.
/proc	/proc is a *virtual file system* . Files in /proc are stored in memory, not on the drive. They refer to the various *processes* running on the system, and allow you to get information about what programs and processes are running at any given time. We'll go into more detail in "Jobs and Processes" later in this chapter.

/tmp	Many programs have a need to generate some information and store it in a temporary file. The canonical location for these files is in /tmp.
/usr	/usr is a very important directory. It contains a number of subdirectories which in turn contain some of the most important and useful programs and configuration files used on the system.

The various directories described above are essential for the system to operate, but most of the things found in /usr are optional for the system. However, it is those optional things which make the system useful and interesting. Without /usr, you'd more or less have a boring system, only with programs like cp and ls. /usr contains most of the larger software packages and the configuration files which accompany them.

/usr/X386	/usr/X386 contains The X Window System, if you installed it. The X Window System is a large, powerful graphical environment which provides a large number of graphical utilities and programs, displayed in *windows* on your screen. If you're at all familiar with the Microsoft Windows or Macintosh environments, X Window will look very familiar. The /usr/X386 directory contains all of the X Window executables, configuration files, and support files. This will be covered in more detail in "Using the X Window System" in Chapter 5.
/usr/bin	/usr/bin is the real warehouse for software on any Unix system. It contains most of the executables for programs not found in other places, such as /bin.
/usr/etc	Just as /etc contained miscellaneous system programs and configuration files, /usr/etc contains even more of these utilities and files. In general, the files found in /usr/etc are not essential to the system, unlike those found in /etc, which are.

/usr/include	/usr/include contains *include files* for the C compiler. These files (most of which end in .h, for *header*) declare data structure names, subroutines, and constants used when writing programs in C. Those files found in /usr/include/sys are generally used when programming on the Unix system level. If you are familiar with the C programming language, here you'll find header files such as stdio.h, which declares functions such as printf().
/usr/g++ -include	/usr/g++-include contains include files for the C++ compiler (much like /usr/include).
/usr/lib	/usr/lib contains the *stub* and *static* library equivalents to the files found in /lib. When compiling a program, the program is *linked* with the libraries found in /usr/lib, which then directs the program to look in /lib when it needs the actual code in the library. In addition, various other programs store configuration files in /usr/lib.
/usr/local	/usr/local is a lot like /usr—it contains various programs and files not essential to the system, but which make the system fun and exciting. In general, those programs found in /usr/local are specialized for your system specifically—that is, /usr/local differ
	Here, you'll find large software packages such as TeX (a document formatting system) ands Emacs (a large and powerful editor), if you installed them.

/usr/man   This directory contains the actual man pages. There are two subdirectories for every man page "section" (use the command man man for details). For example, /usr/man/man1 contains the source (that is, the unformatted original) for man pages in section 1, and /usr/man/cat1 contains the formatted man pages for section 1.

/usr/src   /usr/src contains the source code (the uncompiled program) for various programs on your system. The most important thing here is /usr/src/linux, which contains the source code for the Linux kernel.

/var   /var holds directories that often change in size or tend to grow. Many of those directories used to reside in /usr, but since we are trying to keep it relatively unchangeable, the directories that change often have been moved to /var. Note that they still (seemingly) exist in /usr thanks to symbolic links there. Some of those directories are:

/var/adm   /var/adm contains various files of interest to the system administrator, specifically system logs, which record any errors or problems with the system. Other files record logins to the system, as well as failed login attempts. This will be covered in Chapter 4.

/var/spool /var/spool contains files which are to be spooled to another program For example, if your machine is connected to a network, incoming mail will be stored in /var/spool/mail, until you read it or delete it. Outgoing or incoming news articles may be found in /var/spool/news, and so on.

Types of Shells

As we have mentioned too many times before, Unix is a multitasking, multiuser operating system. Multitasking is *very* useful, and once you get used to it, you'll use it all of the time. Before long, you'll be able to run programs in the background, switch between multiple tasks, and "pipeline" programs together to achieve complicated results with a single command.

Many of the features we'll be covering in this section are features provided by the shell itself. Be careful not to confuse Unix (the actual operating system) with the shell—the shell is just an interface to the underlying system. The shell provides a great deal of functionality on top of Unix itself.

The shell is not only an interpreter for your interactive commands, which you type at the prompt. It is also a powerful programming language that allows you to write *shell scripts* to "batch" several shell commands together in a file. MS-DOS users will recognize the similarity to *batch files*. Use of shell scripts is a very powerful tool, which will allow you to automate and expand your usage of Unix. See "Shell Scripts" later in this chapter for more information.

There are several types of shells in the Unix world. The two major types are the *Bourne shell* and the *C shell*. The Bourne shell uses a command syntax like the original shell on early Unix systems, such as System III. The name of the Bourne shell on most Unix systems is /bin/sh (where sh stands for shell). The C shell (not to be confused with sea shell) uses a different syntax, somewhat like the programming language C, and on most Unix systems is named /bin/csh.

Under Linux, there are several variations of these shells available. The two most commonly used are the *Bourne Again Shell*, or *Bash* (/bin/bash), and *Tcsh* (/bin/tcsh). Bash is a form of the Bourne shell with many of the advanced features found in the C shell. Because Bash supports a superset of the Bourne shell syntax, any shell scripts written in the standard Bourne shell should work with Bash. For those who prefer to use the C shell syntax, Linux supports Tcsh, which is an expanded version of the original C shell.

The type of shell that you decide to use is mostly a religious issue. Some folks prefer the Bourne shell syntax with the advanced features of Bash, and some prefer the more structured C shell syntax. As far as normal commands, such as cp and ls, are concerned, the type of shell you're using doesn't matter—the syntax is the same. Only when you start to write shell scripts or use some of the advanced features of the shell do the differences between shell types begin to matter.

As we're discussing some of the features of the shell, below, we'll note those differences between Bourne and C shells. However, for the purposes of this manual, most of those differences are minimal. (If you're really curious at this point, read the manual pages for bash and tcsh).

Wildcards

A key feature of most Unix shells is the ability to reference more than one filename using special characters. These so-called *wildcards* allow you to refer to, say, all filenames which contain the character "n."

The wildcard * (asterisk) refers to any character or string of characters in a filename. For example, when you use the character * in a filename, the shell replaces it with all possible substitutions from filenames in the directory that you're referencing.

Here's a quick example. Let's suppose that Larry has the files frog, joe, and stuff in his current directory.

```
/home/larry# ls
frog      joe       stuff
/home/larry#
```

To access all files with the letter o in the filename, we can use the command

```
/home/larry# ls *o*
frog      joe
/home/larry#
```

As you can see, the use of the * wildcard was replaced with all substitutions which matched the wildcard from filenames in the current directory.

The use of * by itself simply matches all filenames, because all characters match the wildcard.

```
/home/larry# ls *
frog      joe       stuff
/home/larry#
```

Here are a few more examples.

```
/home/larry# ls f*
frog
/home/larry# ls *ff
stuff
/home/larry# ls *f*
frog    stuff
/home/larry# ls s*f
stuff
/home/larry#
```

The process of changing an * into filenames is called *wildcard expansion* and is done by the shell. This is important: the individual commands, such as ls, *never* see the * in their list of parameters. The shell expands the wildcard to include all of the filenames that match. So, the command

```
/home/larry# ls *o*
```

is expanded by the shell to actually be

```
/home/larry# ls frog joe
```

One important note about the * wildcard: using this wildcard will *not* match filenames that begin with a single period ("."). These files are treated as "hidden" files—while they are not really hidden, they don't show up on normal ls listings, and aren't touched by the use of the * wildcard.

Here's an example. We already mentioned that each directory has two special entries in it: "." refers to the current directory, and ".." refers to the parent directory. However, when you use ls, these two entries don't show up.

```
/home/larry# ls
frog    joe     stuff
/home/larry#
```

If you use the −a switch with ls, however, you can display filenames that begin with ".". Observe:

```
/home/larry# ls −a
.    ..      .bash_profile    .bashrc    frog    joe    stuff
/home/larry#
```

Now we can see the two special entries, "." and "..", as well as two other "hidden" files —.bash_profile and .bashrc. These two files are startup files used by bash when Larry logs in. More on them in "Shell Initialization Scripts" later in this chapter.

Note that when we use the * wildcard, none of the filenames beginning with "." are displayed.

```
/home/larry# ls *
frog      joe      stuff
/home/larry#
```

This is a safety feature: if the * wildcard matched filenames beginning with ".", it would also match the directory names "." and "..". This can be dangerous when using certain commands.

Another wildcard is ?. The ? wildcard will only expand a single character. Thus, ls ? will display all one character filenames, and ls termca? would display termcap but *not* termcap.backup. Here's another example:

```
/home/larry# ls j?e
joe
/home/larry# ls f??g
frog
/home/larry# ls ????f
stuff
/home/larry#
```

As you can see, wildcards allow you to specify many files at one time. In "Summary of Basic Commands," we said that the cp and mv commands actually can copy or move multiple files at one time. For example,

```
/home/larry# cp /etc/s* /home/larry
```

will copy all filenames in /etc beginning with s to the directory /home/larry. Therefore, the format of the cp command is really

```
cp <file1> <file2> <file3> ...<fileN> <destination>
```

where *<file1>* through *<fileN>* is a list of filenames to copy, and *<destination>* is the destination file or directory to copy them to. mv has an identical syntax.

Note that if you are copying or moving more than one file, the *<destination>* must be a directory. You can only copy or move a *single* file to another file.

Unix Plumbing

Standard Input and Output

Many Unix commands get input from what is known as *standard input* and send their output to *standard output* (often abbreviated as *stdin* and *stdout*). Your shell sets things up so that standard input is your keyboard, and standard output is the screen.

Here's an example using the command `cat`. Normally, `cat` reads data from all of the filenames given on the command line and sends this data directly to stdout. Therefore, using the command

```
/home/larry/papers# cat history-final masters-thesis
```

will display the contents of the file `history-final` followed by `masters-thesis`.

However, if no filenames are given to `cat` as parameters, it instead reads data from stdin, and sends it back to stdout. Here's an example.

```
/home/larry/papers# cat
Hello there.
Hello there.
Bye.
Bye.
Ctrl+D
/home/larry/papers#
```

As you can see, each line that the user types (displayed in italics) is immediately echoed back by the `cat` command. When reading from standard input, commands know that the input is "finished" when they receive an EOT (end-of-text) signal. In general, this is generated by pressing Ctrl+D.

Here's another example. The command `sort` reads in lines of text (again, from stdin, unless files are given on the command line), and sends the sorted output to stdout. Try the following:

```
/home/larry/papers# sort
bananas
carrots
apples
Ctrl+D
apples
```

```
bananas
carrots
/home/larry/papers#
```

Now we can alphabetize our shopping list… isn't Unix useful?

Redirecting Input and Output

Now, let's say that we wanted to send the output of sort to a file, to save our shopping list elsewhere. The shell allows us to *redirect* standard output to a filename, using the > (greater than) symbol. Here's how it works.

```
/home/larry/papers# sort > shopping-list
bananas
carrots
apples
Ctrl+D
/home/larry/papers#
```

As you can see, the result of the sort command isn't displayed; instead it's saved to the file shopping-list. Let's look at this file.

```
/home/larry/papers# cat shopping-list
apples
bananas
carrots
/home/larry/papers#
```

Now we can sort our shopping list, and save it, too! But let's suppose that we were storing our unsorted, original shopping list in the file items. One way of sorting the information and saving it to a file would be to give sort the name of the file to read, in lieu of standard input, and redirect standard output as we did above:

```
/home/larry/papers# sort items > shopping-list
/home/larry/papers# cat shopping-list
apples
bananas
carrots
/home/larry/papers#
```

However, there's another way of doing this. Not only can we redirect standard output, but we can redirect standard *input* as well, using the < (less than) symbol.

```
/home/larry/papers# sort < items
apples
```

```
bananas
carrots
/home/larry/papers#
```

Technically, `sort < items` is equivalent to `sort items`, but the former allows us to demonstrate the point: `sort < items` behaves as if the data in the file `items` was typed to standard input. The shell handles the redirection. `sort` wasn't given the name of the file (`items`) to read; as far as `sort` is concerned, it was still reading from standard input as if you had typed the data from your keyboard.

This introduces the concept of a *filter*. A filter is a program which reads data from standard input, processes it in some way, and sends the processed data to standard output. Using redirection, standard input and/or standard output can be referenced from files. `sort` is a simple filter: it sorts the incoming data and sends the result to standard output. `cat` is even simpler: it doesn't do anything with the incoming data, it simply outputs whatever was given to it.

Using Pipes

We've already demonstrated how to use `sort` as a filter. However, these examples assumed that you had data in a file somewhere, or were willing to type the data to standard input yourself. What if the data you wanted to `sort` came from the output of another command, such as `ls`? For example, using the `-r` option with `sort` sorts the data in reverse-alphabetical order. If you wanted to list the files in your current directory in reverse order, one way to do it would be:

```
/home/larry/papers# ls
english-list
history-final
masters-thesis
notes
/home/larry/papers# ls > file-list
/home/larry/papers# sort -r file-list
notes
masters-thesis
history-final
english-list
/home/larry/papers#
```

Here, we saved the output of `ls` in a file, and then ran `sort -r` on that file. But this is unwieldy and causes us to use a temporary file to save the data from `ls`.

The solution is to use *pipelining*. Pipelining is another feature of the shell which allows you to connect a string of commands in a "pipe," where the stdout of the first command is sent directly to the stdin of the second command, and so on. Here, we wish to send the stdout of `ls` to the stdin of `sort`. The | (vertical line) symbol is used to create a pipe:

```
/home/larry/papers# ls| sort -r
notes
masters-thesis
history-final
english-list
/home/larry/papers#
```

This command is much shorter, and obviously easier to type.

Another useful example—using the command

```
/home/larry/papers# ls /usr/bin
```

is going to display a long list of files, most of which will fly past the screen too quickly for you to read them. Instead, let's use `more` to display the list of files in `/usr/bin`.

```
/home/larry/papers# ls /usr/bin| more
```

Now you can page down the list of files at your own leisure.

But the fun doesn't stop here! We can pipe more than two commands together. The command `head` is a filter that displays the first lines from an input stream (here, input from a pipe). If we want to display the last filename in alphabetical order in the current directory, we can use:

```
/home/larry/papers# ls | sort -r | head -1
notes
/home/larry/papers#
```

where `head -1` simply displays the first line of input that it receives (in this case, the stream of reverse-sorted data from `ls`).

Non-Destructive Redirection

Using > to redirect output to a file is destructive. In other words, the command

```
/home/larry/papers# ls > file-list
```

overwrites the contents of the file `file-list`. If, instead, you redirect with the symbol >>, the output will be appended to the named file, instead of overwriting it.

```
/home/larry/papers# ls >> file-list
```

will append the output of the `ls` command to `file-list`.

Just keep in mind that redirection and using pipes are features provided by the shell—the shell provides this handy syntax using > and >> and |. It has nothing to do with the commands themselves, but with the shell.

File Permissions

Concepts of File Permissions

Because there are multiple users on a Unix system, in order to protect individual user's files from tampering by other users, Unix provides a mechanism known as *file permissions*. This mechanism allows files and directories to be "owned" by a particular user. As an example, because Larry created the files in his home directory, Larry owns those files, and has access to them.

Unix also allows files to be shared between users and groups of users. If Larry so desired, he could cut off access to his files, such that no other user could access them. However, on most systems the default is to allow other users to read your files, but not modify or delete them in any way.

As explained above, every file is owned by a particular user. However, files are also owned by a particular *group*, which is a system-defined group of users. Every user is placed into at least one group when that user is created. However, the system administrator may also grant the user access to more than one group.

Groups are usually defined by the type of users which access the machine. For example, on a university Unix system, users may be placed into the groups `student`, `staff`, `faculty` or `guest`. There are also a few system-defined groups (such as `bin` and `admin`) which are used by the system itself to control access to resources—very rarely do actual users belong to these system groups.

Permissions fall into three main divisions: *read*, *write*, and *execute*. These permissions may be granted to three classes of users: the owner of the file, the group to which the file belongs, and to all users, regardless of group.

Read permission allows a user to read the contents of the file, or in the case of directories, to list the contents of the directory (using ls). Write permission allows the user to write to and modify the file. For directories, write permission allows the user to create new files or delete files within that directory. Finally, execute permission allows the user to run the file as a program or shell script (if the file happens to be a program or shell script, that is). For directories, having execute permission allows the user to cd into the directory in question.

Interpreting File Permissions

Let's look at an example to demonstrate file permissions. Using the ls command with the -l option will display a "long" listing of the file, including file permissions.

```
/home/larry/foo# /home/larry/foo# ls -l stuff
-rw-r--r--   1 larry     users          505 Mar 13 19:05 stuff
/home/larry/foo#
```

The first field printed in the listing represents the file permissions. The third field is the owner of the file (larry), and the fourth field is the group to which the file belongs (users). Obviously, the last field is the name of the file (stuff), and we'll cover the other fields later.

This file is owned by larry, and belongs to the group users. Let's look at the file permissions. The string -rw-r--r-- lists, in order, the permissions granted to the file's owner, the file's group, and everybody else.

The first character of the permissions string - (minus sign) represents the type of file. A - just means that this is a regular file (as opposed to a directory or device driver). The next three letters, rw-, represent the permissions granted to the file's owner, larry. The r stands for *read* and the w stands for *write*. Thus, larry has read and write permission to the file stuff.

As we mentioned, besides read and write permission, there is also execute permission—represented by an x. However, there is a - here in place of the x, so Larry doesn't have execute permission on this file. This is fine— the file stuff isn't a program of any kind. Of course, because Larry owns the file, he may grant himself execute permission for the file if he so desires. This will be covered shortly.

The next three characters, r--, represent the group's permissions on the file. The group which owns this file is users. Because only an r appears here, any user which belongs to the group users may read this file.

The last three characters, also r--, represent the permissions granted to every other user on the system (other than the owner of the file and those in the group users). Again, because only an r is present, other users may read the file, but not write to it or execute it.

Here are some other examples of group permissions.

-rwxr-xr-x	The owner of the file may read, write, and execute the file. Users in the file's group, and all other users, may read and execute the file.
-rw-------	The owner of the file may read and write the file. No other user can access the file.
-rwxrwxrwx	All users may read, write, and execute the file.

Dependencies

It is important to note that the permissions granted to a file also depend on the permissions of the directory in which the file is located. For example, even if a file is set to -rwxrwxrwx, other users cannot access the file unless they have read and execute access to the directory in which the file is located. For example, if Larry wanted to restrict access to all of his files, he could simply set the permissions on his home directory /home/larry to -rwx------. In this way, no other user has access to his directory, and all files and directories within it. Larry doesn't need to worry about the individual permissions on each of his files.

In other words, to access a file at all, you must have execute access to all directories along the file's pathname, and read access to the file itself.

Usually, users on a Unix system are very open with their files. The usual set of permissions given to files is -rw-r--r--, which will allow other users to read the file, but not change it in any way. The usual set of permissions given to directories is -rwxr-xr-x, which allows other users to look through your directories, but not create or delete files within them.

However, many users wish to keep other users out of their files. Setting the permissions of a file to −rw−−−−−− will not allow any other user to access the file. Likewise, setting the permissions of a directory to −rwx−−−−−− will keep other users out of the directory in question.

Changing Permissions

The command chmod is used to set the permissions on a file. Only the owner of a file may change the permissions on that file. The syntax of chmod is:

```
chmod {a,u,g,o}{+,-}{r,w,x} <filenames>
```

Briefly, you supply one or more of all, user, group, or other. Then you specify whether you are adding rights (+) or taking them away (-). Finally, you specify one or more of read, write, and execute. Some examples of legal commands are:

chmod a+r stuff	Gives all users read access to the file.
chmod +r stuff	Same as above—if none of a, u, g, or o is specified, a is assumed.
chmod og-x stuff	Removes execute permission from users other than the owner.
chmod u+rwx stuff	Allows the owner of the file to read, write, and execute the file.
chmod o-rwx stuff	Removes read, write, and execute permission from users other than the owner and users in the file's group.

Managing File Links

Links allow you to give a single file multiple names. Files are actually identified to the system by their *inode number,* which is just the unique filesystem identifier for the file. (The command `ls -i` will display file inode numbers.) A directory is actually a listing of inode numbers with their corresponding filenames. Each filename in a directory is a link to a particular inode.

The `ln` command is used to create multiple links for one file. For example, let's say that you have the file `foo` in a directory. Using `ls -i`, we can look at the inode number for this file.

```
# ls -i foo
22192 foo
#
```

Here, the file `foo` has an inode number of 22192 in the file system. We can create another link to `foo`, named `bar`:

```
# ln foo bar
```

With `ls -i`, we see that the two files have the same inode.

```
# ls -i foo bar
22192 bar    22192 foo
#
```

Now, accessing either `foo` or `bar` will access the same file. If you make changes to `foo`, those changes will be made to `bar` as well. For all purposes, `foo` and `bar` are the same file.

These links are known as *hard links* because they directly create a link to an inode. Note that you can only hard-link files on the same file system; symbolic links (see below) don't have this restriction.

When you delete a file with `rm`, you are actually only deleting one link to a file. If you use the command

```
# rm foo
```

then only the link named `foo` is deleted; `bar` will still exist. A file is only actually deleted on the system when it has no links to it. Usually, files have only one link, so using the `rm` command deletes the file. However, if a file has multiple links to it, using rm will only delete a single link; in order to delete the file, you must delete all links to the file.

The command ls -l will display the number of links to a file (among other information).

```
# ls -l foo bar
-rw-r-r-   2 root      root          12 Aug 5 16:51 bar
-rw-r-r-   2 root      root          12 Aug 5 16:50 foo
#
```

The second column in the listing, 2, specifies the number of links to the file.

As it turns out, a directory is actually just a file containing information about link-to-inode translations. Also, every directory has at least two hard links in it: "." (a link pointing to itself), and ".." (a link pointing to the parent directory). The root directory (/) ".." link just points back to /.

Symbolic Links

Symbolic links are another type of link, which are somewhat different than hard links. A symbolic link allows you to give a file another name, but it doesn't link the file by inode.

The command ln -s will create a symbolic link to a file. For example, if we use the command

```
# ln -s foo bar
```

we will create the symbolic link bar pointing to the file foo. If we use ls -i, we will see that the two files have different inodes, indeed.

```
# ls -i foo bar
22195 bar   22192 foo
#
```

However, using ls -l, we see that the file bar is a symlink pointing to foo.

```
# ls -l foo bar
lrwxrwxrwx   1 root      root           3 Aug 5 16:51 bar -> foo
-rw-r--r--   1 root      root          12 Aug 5 16:50 foo
#
```

The permission bits on a symbolic link are not used (they always appear as rwxrwxrwx). Instead, the permissions on the symbolic link are determined by the permissions on the target of the symbolic link (in our example, the file foo).

Functionally, hard links and symbolic links are similar, but there are some differences. For one thing, you can create a symbolic link to a file which doesn't exist; the same is not true for hard links. Symbolic links are processed by the kernel differently than hard links are, which is just a technical difference but sometimes an important one. Symbolic links are helpful because they identify what file they point to; with hard links, there is no easy way to determine which files are linked to the same inode.

Links are used in many places on the Linux system. Symbolic links are especially important to the shared library images in /lib. See "Upgrading the Libraries" in Chapter 4 for more information.

Job Control

Jobs and Processes

Job control is a feature provided by many shells (Bash and Tcsh included) which allows you to control multiple running commands, or *jobs*, at once. Before we can delve much further, we need to talk about *processes*.

Every time you run a program, you start what is known as a *process*—which is just a fancy name for a running program. The command ps displays a list of currently running processes. Here's an example:

```
/home/larry# ps
  PID TT STAT   TIME COMMAND
   24  3 S      0:03 (bash)
  161  3 R      0:00 ps
```

```
/home/larry#
```

The PID listed in the first column is the *process ID*, a unique number given to every running process. The last column, COMMAND, is the name of the running command. Here, we're only looking at the processes which Larry is currently running. (There are many other processes running on the system as well: ps -aux lists them all.) These are bash (Larry's shell), and the ps command itself. As you can see, bash is running concurrently with the ps command. bash executed ps when Larry typed the command. After ps is finished running (after the table of processes is displayed), control is returned to the bash process, which displays the prompt, ready for another command.

A running process is known as a *job* to the shell. The terms *process* and *job* are interchangeable. However, a process is usually referred to as a job when used in conjunction with *job control*—a feature of the shell which allows you to switch between several independent jobs.

In most cases users are only running a single job at a time—that being whatever command they last typed to the shell. However, using job control, you can run several jobs at once, switching between them as needed. How might this be useful? Let's say that you're editing a text file and need to suddenly interrupt your editing and do something else. With job control, you can temporarily suspend the editor, and back at the shell prompt start to work on something else. When you're done, you can start the editor back up, and be back where you started, as if you never left the editor. This is just one example. There are many practical uses for job control.

Foreground and Background

Jobs can either be in the *foreground* or in the *background*. There can only be one job in the foreground at any one time. The foreground job is the job that you interact with—it receives input from the keyboard and sends output to your screen. (Unless, of course, you have redirected input or output, as described in "Unix Plubing.") On the other hand, jobs in the background do not receive input from the terminal—in general, they run along quietly without need for interaction.

Some jobs take a long time to finish, and don't do anything interesting while they are running. Compiling programs is one such job, as is compressing a large file. There's no reason why you should sit around being bored while these jobs complete their tasks; you can just run them in the background. While the jobs are running in the background, you are free to run other programs.

Jobs may also be *suspended.* A suspended job is a job that is not currently running, but is temporarily stopped. After you suspend a job, you can tell the job to continue in the foreground or the background as needed. Resuming a suspended job will not change the state of the job in any way—the job will continue to run where it left off.

NOTE   Suspending a job is not equal to *interrupting* a job. When you interrupt
a running process (by hitting your interrupt key, which is usually
Ctrl+C), it kills the process for good. (The interrupt key can be set
using the `stty` command. The default on most systems is Ctrl+C, but
we can't guarantee the same for your system.) Once the job is killed,
there's no hope of resuming it; you'll have to re-run the command.
Also note that some programs trap the interrupt, so that hitting Ctrl+C
won't immediately kill the job. This is to allow the program to perform
any necessary cleanup operations before exiting. In fact, some
programs simply don't allow you to kill them with an interrupt at all.

Backgrounding and Killing Jobs

Let's begin with a simple example. The command yes is a seemingly useless command which sends an endless stream of y's to standard output. (This is actually useful. If you piped the output of yes to another command which asked a series of yes
and no questions, the stream of y's would confirm all of the questions.)

Try it out.

```
/home/larry# yes
y
y
y
y
y
```

The y's will continue *ad infinitum*. You can kill the process by hitting your interrupt
key, which is usually Ctrl+C. So that we don't have to put up with the annoying
stream of y's, let's redirect the standard output of yes to /dev/null. As you may
remember, /dev/null acts as a "black hole" for data. Any data sent to it will disap-
pear. This is a very effective method of quieting an otherwise verbose program.

```
/home/larry# yes > /dev/null
```

Ah, much better. Nothing is printed, but the shell prompt doesn't come back. This
is because yes is still running, and is sending those inane y's to /dev/null. Again,
to kill the job, hit the interrupt key.

Let's suppose that we wanted the yes command to continue to run, but wanted to get our shell prompt back to work on other things. We can put yes into the background, which will allow it to run, but without need for interaction.

One way to put a process in the background is to append an & (ampersand) character to the end of the command.

```
/home/larry# yes > /dev/null &
[1] 164
/home/larry#
```

As you can see, we have our shell prompt back. But what is this [1] 164? And is the yes command really running?

The [1] represents the *job number* for the yes process. The shell assigns a job number to every running job. Because yes is the one and only job that we're currently running, it is assigned job number 1. The 164 is the process ID, or PID, number given by the system to the job. Either number may be used to refer to the job, as we'll see later.

You now have the yes process running in the background, continuously sending a stream of y's to /dev/null. To check on the status of this process, use the shell internal command jobs.

```
/home/larry# jobs
[1]+  Running                      yes >/dev/null &
/home/larry#
```

Sure enough, there it is. You could also use the ps command as demonstrated above to check on the status of the job.

To terminate the job, use the command kill. This command takes either a job number or a process ID number as an argument. This was job number 1, so using the command

```
/home/larry# kill %1
```

will kill the job. When identifying the job with the job number, you must prefix the number with a % (percent sign).

Now that we've killed the job, we can use jobs again to check on it:

```
/home/larry# jobs
```

```
[1]+  Terminated              yes >/dev/null
```

```
/home/larry#
```

The job is in fact dead, and if we use the jobs command again nothing should be printed.

You can also kill the job using the process ID (PID) number, which is printed along with the job ID when you start the job. In our example, the process ID is 164, so the command

```
/home/larry# kill 164
```

is equivalent to

```
/home/larry# kill %1
```

You don't need to use the % when referring to a job by its process ID.

Stopping and Restarting Jobs

There is another way to put a job into the background. You can start the job normally (in the foreground), *stop* the job, and then restart it in the background.

First, start the yes process in the foreground, as you normally would:

```
/home/larry# yes > /dev/null
```

Again, because yes is running in the foreground, you shouldn't get your shell prompt back.

Now, instead of interrupting the job with Ctrl+C, we'll *suspend* the job. Suspending a job doesn't kill it: it only temporarily stops the job until you restart it. To do this, you hit the suspend key, which is usually Ctrl+Z.

```
/home/larry# yes > /dev/null
Ctrl+Z
[1]+  Stopped                 yes >/dev/null
/home/larry#
```

While the job is suspended, it's simply not running. No CPU time is used for the job. However, you can restart the job, which will cause the job to run again as if nothing had ever happened. It will continue to run where it left off.

To restart the job in the foreground, use the command fg (for "foreground").

```
/home/larry# fg yes >/dev/null
```

The shell prints the name of the command again so you're aware of which job you just put into the foreground. Stop the job again, with Ctrl+Z. This time, use the command bg to put the job into the background. This will cause the command to run just as if you started the command with & as in the last section.

```
/home/larry# bg
[1]+ yes >/dev/null &
/home/larry#
```

And we have our prompt back. jobs should report that yes is indeed running, and we can kill the job with kill as we did before.

How can we stop the job again? Using Ctrl+Z won't work, because the job is in the background. The answer is to put the job in the foreground, with fg, and then stop it. As it turns out you can use fg on either stopped jobs or jobs in the background.

There is a big difference between a job in the background and a job that is stopped. A stopped job is not running—it's not using any CPU time, and it's not doing any work (the job still occupies system memory, although it may be swapped out to disk). A job in the background is running, and using memory, as well as completing some task while you do other work. However, a job in the background may try to display text onto your terminal, which can be annoying if you're trying to work on something else. For example, if you used the command

```
/home/larry# yes &
```

without redirecting stdout to /dev/null, a stream of y's would be printed to your screen, without any way of interrupting it (you can't use Ctrl+C to interrupt jobs in the background). In order to stop the endless y's, you'd have to use the kill command (without being able to see what you're typing).

Another note: The fg and bg commands normally foreground or background the job that was last stopped, indicated by a + (plus sign) next to the job number when you use the command jobs. If you are running multiple jobs at once, you can foreground or background a specific job by giving the job ID as an argument to fg or bg, as in

```
/home/larry# fg %2
```

(to foreground job number 2), or

```
/home/larry# bg %3
```

(to background job number 3). You can't use process ID numbers with `fg` or `bg`.

Furthermore, using the job number alone, as in

```
/home/larry# %2
```

is equivalent to

```
/home/larry# fg %2
```

Just remember that using job control is a feature of the shell. The commands `fg`, `bg` and `jobs` are internal to the shell. If for some reason you use a shell which does not support job control, don't expect to find these commands available.

In addition, there are some aspects of job control which differ between Bash and Tcsh. In fact, some shells don't provide job control at all—however, most shells available for Linux do support it.

Using the vi Editor

A *text editor* is simply a program used to edit files which contain text, such as a letter, C program, or a system configuration file. While there are many such editors available for Linux, the only editor that you are guaranteed to find on any Unix system is `vi`— the *visual editor*. `vi` is not the easiest editor to use, nor is it very self-explanatory. However, because it is so common in the Unix world, and at times you may be required to use it, it deserves some documentation here.

Your choice of an editor is mostly a question of personal taste and style. Many users prefer the baroque, self-explanatory and powerful `emacs`—an editor with more features than any other single program in the Unix world. For example, `emacs` has its own built-in dialect of the LISP programming language, and has many extensions (one of which is an "Eliza"-like AI program). However, because `emacs` and all of its support files are relatively large, you may not have access to it on many systems. `vi`, on the other hand, is small and powerful, but more difficult to use. However, once you know your way around `vi`, it's actually very easy. It's just the learning curve which is sometimes difficult to cross.

This section is a coherent introduction to `vi`—we won't discuss all of its features, just the ones you need to know to get you started. You can refer to the manual page for vi if you're interested in learning more about this editor's features. Or, you can read the book *Learning the vi Editor* from O'Reilly and Associates. See Appendix A for information.

Concepts

While using vi, at any one time you are in one of three modes of operation. These modes are known as *command mode, insert mode,* and *last line mode.*

When you start up vi, you are in *command mode.* This mode allows you to use certain commands to edit files or to change to other modes. For example, typing x while in command mode deletes the character underneath the cursor. The arrow keys move the cursor around the file you're editing. Generally, the commands used in command mode are one or two characters long.

You actually insert or edit text within *insert mode.* When using vi, you'll probably spend most of your time within this mode. You start insert mode by using a command such as i (for "insert") from command mode. While in insert mode, you are inserting text into the document from your current cursor location. To end insert mode and return to command mode, press Esc.

Last line mode is a special mode used to give certain extended commands to vi. While typing these commands, they appear on the last line of the screen (hence the name). For example, when you type :(colon) from command mode, you jump into last line mode, and can use commands such as wq (to write the file and quit vi), or q! (to quit vi without saving changes). Last line mode is generally used for vi commands which are longer than one character.

Starting vi

The best way to understand these concepts is to actually fire up vi and edit a file. In the example "screens" below, we're only going to show a few lines of text, as if the screen was only six lines high (instead of twenty-five).

The syntax for vi is

```
vi <filename>
```

where *<filename>* is the name of the file that you wish to edit.

Start up vi by typing

```
/home/larry# vi test
```

which will edit the file test. You should see something like

```
~
~
~
~
~
~
~
~
"test" [New file]
```

The column of ~ characters indicates that you are at the end of the file.

Inserting Text

You are now in command mode; in order to insert text in the file, press i (which will place you into insert mode), and begin typing.

```
Now is the time for all good men to come to the aid of the party.
~
~
~
~
```

While inserting text, you may type as many lines as you wish (pressing ↵ after each, of course), and you may correct mistakes using the backspace key.

To end insert mode and return to command mode, press Esc.

While in command mode, you can use the arrow keys to move around the file. Here, because we only have one line of text, trying to use the up- or down-arrow keys will probably cause vi to beep at you.

There are several ways to insert text other than using the i command. For example, the a command inserts text beginning *after* the current cursor position, instead of on the current cursor position. For example, use the left arrow key to move the cursor between the words good and men.

```
Now is the time for all good_men to come to the aid of the party.
~
~
~
~
```

Press a to start edit mode, type wo, and then hit Esc to return to command mode.

```
Now is the time for all good women to come to the aid of the party.
~
~
~
~
~
```

To begin inserting text at the line below the current one, use the o command. For example, press o and type another line or two:

```
Now is the time for all good women to come to the aid of the party.
Afterwards, we'll go out for pizza and beer.
~
~
~
~
```

Just remember that at any time you're either in command mode (where commands such as i, a, or o are valid), or in insert mode (where you're inserting text, followed by Esc to return to command mode), or last line mode (where you're entering extended commands, as discussed below).

Deleting Text

From command mode, the x command deletes the character under the cursor. If you press x five times, you'll end up with:

```
Now is the time for all good women to come to the aid of the
party.
Afterwards, we'll go out for pizza and_
~
~
~
```

Now press a, insert some text, followed by Esc:

```
Now is the time for all good women to come to the aid of the
party.
Afterwards, we'll go out for pizza and Diet Coke.
~
~
~
```

You can delete entire lines using the command dd (that is, press d twice in a row). If your cursor is on the second line, and you type dd,

```
Now is the time for all good women to come to the aid of the party.
~
~
~
~
~
```

To delete the word that the cursor is on, use the dw command. Place the cursor on the word good, and type dw.

```
Now is the time for all women to come to the aid of the party.
~
~
~
~
~
```

Changing Text

You can replace sections of text using the R command. Place the cursor on the first letter in party, press R, and type the word hungry.

```
Now is the time for all women to come to the aid of the hungry.
~
~
~
~
~
```

Using R to edit text is much like the i and a commands, but R overwrites text, instead of inserting it.

The r command replaces the single character under the cursor. For example, move the cursor to the beginning of the word Now, and type r followed by C. You'll have:

```
Cow is the time for all women to come to the aid of the hungry.
~
~
~
~
~
```

The ~ command changes the case of the letter under the cursor from upper- to lower-case, and vise versa. For example, if you place the cursor on the o in Cow, above, and repeatedly press ~, you'll end up with:

```
COW IS THE TIME FOR ALL WOMEN TO COME TO THE AID OF THE HUNGRY.
~
~
~
~
~
```

Moving Commands

You already know how to use the arrow keys to move around the document. In addition, you can use the h, j, k, and 1 commands to move the cursor left, down, up, and right, respectively. This comes in handy when (for some reason) your arrow keys aren't working correctly.

The w command moves the cursor to the beginning of the next word; the b moves it to the beginning of the previous word.

The 0 (that's a zero) command moves the cursor to the beginning of the current line, and the $ command moves it to the end of the line.

When editing large files, you'll want to move forwards or backwards through the file one screen at a time. Pressing Ctrl+F moves the cursor one screen forward, and Ctrl+B moves it a screen back.

In order to move the cursor to the end of the file, type G. You can also move to an arbitrary line; for example, typing the command 10G would move the cursor to line 10 in the file. To move to the beginning of the file, use 1G.

You can couple moving commands with other commands, such as deletion. For example, the command d$ will delete everything from the cursor to the end of the line; dG will delete everything from the cursor to the end of the file, and so on.

Saving Files and Quitting vi

To quit vi without making changes to the file, use the command :q!. When you type the :, the cursor will move to the last line on the screen; you'll be in last line mode.

```
COW IS THE TIME FOR ALL WOMEN TO COME TO THE AID OF THE HUNGRY.
~
~
~
~
:_
```

In last line mode, certain extended commands are available. One of them is q!, which quits vi without saving. The command :wq saves the file and then exits vi. The command ZZ (from command mode, without the :) is equivalent to :wq.

To save the file without quitting vi, just use :w.

Editing Another File

To edit another file, use the :e command. For example, to stop editing test, and edit the file foo instead, use the command

```
COW IS THE TIME FOR ALL WOMEN TO COME TO THE AID OF THE HUNGRY.
~
~
~
~
:e foo_
```

If you use :e without saving the file first, you'll get the error message

```
No write since last change (":edit| overrides)
```

which simply means that `vi` doesn't want to edit another file until you save the first one. At this point, you can use `:w` to save the original file, and then use `:e`, or you can use the command

```
COW IS THE TIME FOR ALL WOMEN TO COME TO THE AID OF THE HUNGRY.
~
~
~
~
:e foo_
```

The `!` tells `vi` that you really mean it—edit the new file without saving changes to the first.

Including Other Files

If you use the `:r` command, you can include the contents of another file in the current file. For example, the command

```
:r foo.txt
```

would insert the contents of the file `foo.txt` in the text at the current cursor location.

Running Shell Commands

You can also run shell commands from within `vi`. The `:r!` command works like `:r`, but instead of reading a file, it inserts the output of the given command into the buffer at the current cursor location. For example, if you use the command

```
:r! ls -F
```

you'll end up with

```
COW IS THE TIME FOR ALL WOMEN TO COME TO THE AID OF THE HUNGRY.
letters/
misc/
papers/
~
~
```

You can also *shell out* of `vi`; in other words, run a command from within `vi`, and return to the editor when you're done. For example, if you use the command

```
:! ls -F
```

the `ls -F` command will be executed, and the results displayed on the screen, but not inserted into the file that you're editing. If you use the command

```
:shell
```

`vi` will start an instance of the shell, allowing you to temporarily put `vi` "on hold" while you execute other commands. Just logout of the shell (using the `exit` command) to return to `vi`.

Getting Help

`vi` doesn't provide much in the way of interactive help (most Unix programs don't), but you can always read the manual page for `vi`. `vi` is a visual front-end to the `ex` editor; it is `ex` which handles many of the last-line mode commands in `vi`. So, in addition to reading the manual page for `vi`, see `ex` as well.

Customizing Your Environment

The shell provides many mechanisms to customize your work environment. As we've mentioned before, the shell is more than a command interpreter—it is also a powerful programming language. While writing shell scripts is an extensive subject, we'd like to introduce you to some of the ways that you can simplify your work on a Unix system by using these advanced features of the shell.

As we have mentioned before, different shells use different syntaxes when executing shell scripts. For example, Tcsh uses a C-like syntax, while Bourne shells use another type of syntax. In this section, we won't be running into many of the differences between the two, but we will assume that shell scripts are executed using the Bourne shell syntax.

Shell Scripts

Let's say that you use a series of commands often, and would like to shorten the amount of required typing by grouping all of them together into a single "command." For example, the commands

```
/home/larry# cat chapter1 chapter2 chapter3 > book
/home/larry# wc -l book
/home/larry# lp book
```

would concatenate the files chapter1, chapter2, and chapter3 and place the result in the file book. Then, a count of the number of lines in book would be displayed, and finally book would be printed with the lp command.

Instead of typing all of these commands, you could group them into a *shell script*. We described shell scripts briefly in "Shell Scripts" earlier in this chapter. The shell script used to run all of these commands would look like

```
#!/bin/sh
# A shell script to create and print the book

cat chapter1 chapter2 chapter3 > book
wc -l book
lp book
```

If this script were saved in the file makebook, you could simply use the command

```
/home/larry# makebook
```

to run all of the commands in the script. Shell scripts are just plain text files; you can create them with an editor such as emacs or vi (vi is covered in "Using the vi Editor" earlier in this chapter).

Let's look at this shell script. The first line, #!/bin/sh, identifies the file as a shell script, and tells the shell how to execute the script. It instructs the shell to pass the script to /bin/sh for execution, where /bin/sh is the shell program itself. Why is this important? On most Unix systems, /bin/sh is a Bourne-type shell, such as Bash. By forcing the shell script to run using /bin/sh, we are ensuring that the script will run under a Bourne-syntax shell (instead of, say, a C shell). This will cause your script to run using the Bourne syntax even if you use Tcsh (or another C shell) as your login shell.

The second line is a *comment*. Comments begin with the character # (pound sign) and continue to the end of the line. Comments are ignored by the shell—they are commonly used to identify the shell script to the programmer.

The rest of the lines in the script are just commands, as you would type them to the shell directly. In effect, the shell reads each line of the script and runs that line as if you had typed it at the shell prompt.

Permissions are important for shell scripts. If you create a shell script, you must make sure that you have execute permission on the script in order to run it. (When you create text files, the default permissions usually don't include execute permissions.) The command

```
/home/larry# chmod u+x makebook
```

can be used to give yourself execute permission on the shell script `makebook`.

Shell Variables and the Environment

The shell allows you to define *variables*, as most programming languages do. A variable is just a piece of data that is given a name.

NOTE Tcsh, as well as other C-type shells, uses a different mechanism for setting variables than is described here. This discussion assumes the use of a Bourne shell, such as Bash (which you're probably using). See the Tcsh manual page for details.

When you use the = (equal sign) operator to assign a value to a variable, you can access the variable by prepending a $ (dollar sign) to the variable name, as demonstrated below.

```
/home/larry# foo="hello there"
```

The variable `foo` is given the value `hello there`. You can now refer to this value by the variable name, prefixed with a $ character. The command

```
/home/larry# echo $foo
hello there
/home/larry#
```

produces the same results as

```
/home/larry# echo "hello there"
hello there
/home/larry#
```

These variables are internal to the shell. This means that only the shell can access them. This can be useful in shell scripts; if you need to keep track of a filename, for example, you can store it in a variable, as above. Using the command set will display a list of all defined shell variables.

However, the shell allows you to *export* variables to the *environment*. The environment is the set of variables to which all commands that you execute have access. Once you define a variable inside the shell, exporting it makes that variable part of the environment as well. The export command is used to export a variable to the environment.

> **NOTE**   Again, here we differ between Bash and Tcsh. If you're using Tcsh, another syntax is used for setting environment variables (the setenv command is used). See the Tcsh manual page for more information.

The environment is very important to the Unix system. It allows you to configure certain commands just by setting variables that the commands know about.

Here's a quick example. The environment variable PAGER is used by the man command. It specifies the command to use to display manual pages one screenful at a time. If you set PAGER to be the name of a command, it will use that command to display the manual pages, instead of more (which is the default).

Set PAGER to cat. This will cause output from man to be displayed to the screen all at once, without breaking it up into pages.

```
/home/larry# PAGER="cat"
```

Now, export PAGER to the environment.

```
/home/larry# export PAGER
```

Try the command man ls. The manual page should fly past your screen without pausing for you.

Now, if we set PAGER to more, the more command will be used to display the manual page.

```
/home/larry# PAGER="more"
```

Note that we don't have to use the export command after we change the value of PAGER. We only need to export a variable once; any changes made to it thereafter will automatically be propagated to the environment.

The manual pages for a particular command will tell you if the command uses any environment variables; for example, the man manual page explains that PAGER is used to specify the pager command. Some commands share environment variables; for example, many commands use the EDITOR environment variable to specify the default editor to use when one is needed.

The environment is also used to keep track of important information about your login session. An example is the HOME environment variable, which contains the name of your home directory.

```
/home/larry/papers# echo $HOME
/home/larry
```

Another interesting environment variable is *PS1*, which defines the main shell prompt. For example,

```
/home/larry# PS1="Your command, please: "
Your command, please:
```

To set the prompt back to our usual (which contains the current working directory followed by a # symbol),

```
Your command, please: PS1="\w# "
/home/larry#
```

The bash manual page describes the syntax used for setting the prompt.

The PATH Environment Variable

When you use the ls command, how does the shell find the ls executable itself? In fact, ls is found in /bin/ls on most systems. The shell uses the environment variable PATH to locate executable files for commands which you type.

For example, your PATH variable may be set to:

```
/bin:/usr/bin:/usr/local/bin:.
```

This is a list of directories for the shell to search, each directory separated by a `:`. When you use the command `ls`, the shell first looks for `/bin/ls`, then `/usr/bin/ls`, and so on.

Note that the PATH has nothing to do with finding regular files. For example, if you use the command

```
/home/larry# cp foo bar
```

The shell does not use PATH to locate the files `foo` and `bar`—those filenames are assumed to be complete. The shell only uses PATH to locate the `cp` executable.

This saves you a lot of time; it means that you don't have to remember where all of the command executables are stored. On many systems, executables are scattered about in many places, such as `/usr/bin`, `/bin`, or `/usr/local/bin`. Instead of giving the command's full pathname (such as `/usr/bin/cp`), you can simply set PATH to the list of directories that you want the shell to search automatically.

Notice that PATH contains ".", which is the current working directory. This allows you to create a shell script or program and run it as a command from your current directory, without having to specify it directly (as in `./makebook`). If a directory isn't on your PATH, then the shell will not search it for commands to run—this includes the current directory.

Shell Initialization Scripts

In addition to shell scripts that you create, there are a number of scripts that the shell itself uses for certain purposes. The most important of these are your *initialization scripts*, scripts automatically executed by the shell when you login.

The initialization scripts themselves are simply shell scripts, as described above. However, they are very useful in setting up your environment by executing commands automatically when you login. For example, if you always use the `mail` command to check your mail when you login, you place the command in your initialization script so it will be executed automatically.

Both Bash and Tcsh distinguish between a *login shell* and other invocations of the shell. A login shell is a shell invoked at login time; usually, it's the only shell which you'll use. However, if you "shell out" of another program, such as `vi`, you start another instance of the shell, which isn't your login shell. In addition, whenever you run a shell script, you automatically start another instance of the shell to execute the script.

The initialization files used by Bash are: `/etc/profile` (set up by the system administrator, executed by all Bash users at login time), `$HOME/.bash_profile` (executed by a login Bash session), and `$HOME/.bashrc` (executed by all non-login instances of Bash). If `.bash_profile` is not present, `.profile` is used instead.

Tcsh uses the following initialization scripts: `/etc/csh.login` (executed by all Tcsh users at login time), `$HOME/.tcshrc` (executed a login time and by all new instances of Tcsh), and `$HOME/.login` (executed at login time, following `.tcshrc`). If `.tcshrc` is not present, `.cshrc` is used instead.

To fully understand the function of these files, you'll need to learn more about the shell itself. Shell programming is a complicated subject, far beyond the scope of this book. See the manual pages for `bash` and/or `tcsh` to learn more about customizing your shell environment.

So You Want to Strike Out on Your Own?

Hopefully we have provided enough information to give you a basic idea of how to use the system. Keep in mind that most of the interesting and important aspects of Linux aren't covered here—these are the very basics. With this foundation, before long you'll be up and running complicated applications and fulfilling the potential of your system. If things don't seem exciting at first, don't despair—there is much to be learned.

One indispensable tool for learning about the system is to read the manual pages. While many of the manual pages may appear confusing at first, if you dig beneath the surface there is a wealth of information contained therein.

We also suggest reading a complete book on using a Unix system. There is much more to Unix than meets the eye—unfortunately, most of it is beyond the scope of this book. Some good Unix books are listed in Appendix A.

CHAPTER

FOUR

System Administration

4

This chapter is an overview of Linux system administration, including a number of advanced features which aren't necessarily for system administrators only. Just as every dog has its day, every system has its administrator, and running the system is a very important and sometimes time-consuming job, even if you're the only user on your system.

We have tried to cover the most important things about Linux system administration in sufficient detail to get you comfortably started. In order to keep it short and sweet, we have only covered the very basics, and have skipped many an important detail. You should read the *Linux System Administrator's Guide* if you are serious about running Linux. It will help you understand better how things work, and how they hang together. At least skim through it so that you know what it contains and know what kind of help you can expect from it.

About Root, Hats, and the Feeling of Power

As you know, Unix differentiates between users, so that what they do to each other and to the system can be regulated (one wouldn't want anybody to be able to read one's love letters, for instance). Each user is given an *account*, which includes a username, home directory, and so on. In addition to accounts given to real people, there are special system-defined accounts which have special privileges. The most important of these is the *root account*, for the username root.

The Root Account

Ordinary users are generally restricted so that they can't do harm to anybody else on the system, just to themselves. File permissions on the system are arranged such that normal users aren't allowed to delete or modify files in directories shared by all users (such as /bin and /usr/bin). Most users also protect their own files with the appropriate file permissions so that other users can't access or modify those files.

There are no such restrictions on root. The user root can read, modify, or delete any file on the system, change permissions and ownerships on any file, and run special programs, such as those which partition the drive or create file systems. The basic idea is that the person or persons who run and take care of the system logs in as root whenever it is necessary to perform tasks that cannot be executed as a normal user. Because root can do anything, it is easy to make mistakes that have catastrophic consequences when logged in using this account.

For example, as a normal user, if you inadvertently attempt to delete all of the files in /etc, the system will not permit you to do so. However, when logged in as root, the system won't complain at all. It is very easy to trash your system when using root. The best way to prevent accidents is to:

- Sit on your hands before you press ⏎ on a command which may cause damage. For example, if you're about to clean out a directory, re-read the entire command and make sure that it is correct before hitting ⏎.

- Don't get accustomed to using root. The more comfortable you are in the role of the root user, the more likely you are to confuse your privileges with those of a normal user. For example, you might *think* that you're logged in as larry, when you're really logged in as root.

- Use a different prompt for the root account. You should change root's .bashrc or .login file to set the shell prompt to something other than your regular user prompt. For example, many people use the character $ in prompts for regular users, and reserve the character # for the root user prompt.

- Only login as root when absolutely necessary. And, as soon as you're finished with your work as root, log out. The less you use the root account, the less likely you'll be to do damage on your system.

Of course, there is a breed of Unix hackers out there who use root for virtually everything. But every one of them has, at some point, made a silly mistake as root and trashed the system. The general rule is, until you're familiar with the lack of restrictions on root, and are comfortable using the system without such restrictions, login as root sparingly.

Of course, everyone makes mistakes. Linus Torvalds himself once accidentally deleted the entire kernel directory tree on his system. Hours of work were lost forever. Fortunately, however, because of his knowledge of the file system code, he was able to reboot the system and reconstruct the directory tree by hand on disk.

Put another way, if you picture using the root account as wearing a special magic hat that gives you lots of power, so that you can, by waving your hand, destroy entire cities, it is a good idea to be a bit careful about what you do with your hands. Since it is easy to move your hand in a destructive way by accident, it is not a good idea to wear the magic hat when it is not needed, despite the wonderful feeling.

Abusing the System

Along with the feeling of power comes the tendency to do harm. This is one of the grey areas of Unix system administration, but everyone goes through it at some point in time. Most users of Unix systems never have the ability to wield this power—on university and business Unix systems, only the highly-paid and highly-qualified system administrators ever login as root. In fact, at many such institutions, the root password is a highly guarded secret: it is treated as the Holy Grail of the institution. A large amount of hubbub is made about logging in as root; it is portrayed as a wise and fearsome power, given only to an exclusive cabal.

This kind of attitude towards the root account is, quite simply, the kind of thing that breeds malice and contempt. Because root is so fluffed-up, when some users have their first opportunity to login as root (either on a Linux system or elsewhere), the tendency is to use root's privileges in a harmful manner. I have known so-called "system administrators" who read other users' mail, delete users' files without warning, and generally behave like children when given such a powerful "toy."

Because root has such privilege on the system, it takes a certain amount of maturity and self-control to use the account as it was intended—to run the system. There is an unspoken code of honor that exists between the system administrator and the users on the system. How would you feel if your system administrator was reading your e-mail or looking over your files? There is still no strong legal precedent for electronic privacy on time-sharing computer systems. On Unix systems, the root user has the ability to forego all security and privacy mechanisms on the system. It is important that the system administrator develop a trusting relationship with the users on the system. I can't stress that enough.

Dealing with Users

Unix security is rather lax by design. Security on the system was an afterthought—the system was originally developed in an environment where users intruding upon other users was simply unheard of. Because of this, even with security measures, there is still the ability for normal users to do harm.

System administrators can take two stances when dealing with abusive users: they can be either paranoid or trusting. The paranoid system administrator usually causes more harm than he or she prevents. One of my favorite sayings is, "Never attribute to malice anything which can be attributed to stupidity." Put another way, most users don't have the ability or knowledge to do real harm on the system. 90% of the time, when a user is causing trouble on the system (by, for instance, filling up the user partition with large files, or running multiple instances of a large program), the user is simply unaware that what he or she is doing is a problem. I have come down on users who were causing a great deal of trouble, but they were simply acting out of ignorance—not malice.

When you deal with users who are causing potential trouble, don't be accusative. The old rule of "innocent until proven guilty" still holds. It is best to simply talk to the user, and question about the trouble, instead of causing a confrontation. The last thing you want to do is be on the user's bad side. This will raise a lot of suspicion about you—the system administrator—running the system correctly. If a user believes that you distrust or dislike them, they might accuse you of deleting files or breaching privacy on the system. This is certainly not the kind of position that you want to be in.

If you do find that a user has been attempting to "crack" the system, or was intentionally doing harm to the system, don't return the malicious behavior with malice of your own. Instead, simply provide a warning—but be flexible. In many cases, you may catch a user "in the act" of doing harm to the system—give them a warning. Tell them not to let it happen again. However, if you *do* catch them causing harm again, be absolutely sure that it is intentional. I can't even begin to describe the number of cases where it appeared as though a user was causing trouble, when in fact it was either an accident or a fault of my own.

Setting the Rules

The best way to run a system is not with an iron fist. That may be how you run the military, but Unix was not designed for such discipline. It makes sense to lay down a simple and flexible set of guidelines for users—but remember, the fewer rules you have, the less chance there is of breaking them. Even if your rules for using the system are perfectly reasonable and clear, users will at times break these rules without intending to. This is especially true in the case of new Unix users, who are just learning the ropes of the system. It's not patently obvious, for example, that you shouldn't download a gigabyte of files and mail them to everyone on the system. Users need help understanding the rules, and why they are there.

If you do specify usage guidelines for your system, make sure that the reason behind a particular guideline is made clear. If you don't, then users will find all sorts of creative ways to get around the rule, and not know that they are in fact breaking it.

What it All Means

We can't tell you how to run your system to the last detail. Most of the philosophy depends on how you're using the system. If you have many users, things are much different than if you only have a few users, or if you're the only user on the system. However, it's always a good idea—in any situation—to understand what being the system administrator really means.

Being the system administrator doesn't make you a Unix wizard. There are many system admins out there who know very little about Unix. Likewise, there are many "normal" users out there who know more about Unix than any system administrator could. Also, being the system administrator does not allow you to use malice against your users. Just because the system gives you the privilege to mess with user files does not mean that you have any right to do so.

Lastly, being the system administrator is really not a big deal. It doesn't matter if your system is a little 386 or a Cray supercomputer. Running the system is the same, regardless. Knowing the root password isn't going to earn you money or fame. It will allow you to maintain the system, and keep it running. That's it.

Booting the System

There are several ways to boot the system, either from floppy or from the hard drive.

Using a Boot Floppy

Many people boot Linux using a *boot floppy* which contains a copy of the Linux kernel. This kernel has the Linux root partition coded into it, so it will know where to look on the hard drive for the root file system. (The `rdev` command can be used to set the root partition in the kernel image; see below.) This is the type of floppy created by SLS during installation, for example.

To create your own boot floppy, first locate the kernel image on your hard disk. It should be in the file `/Image` or `/etc/Image`. Some installations use the file `/vmlinux` for the kernel.

You may instead have a compressed kernel. A compressed kernel uncompresses itself into memory at boot time, and takes up much less space on the hard drive. If you have a compressed kernel, it may be found in the file `/zImage` or `/etc/zImage`.

Once you know where the kernel is, set the root device in the kernel image to the name of your Linux root partition with the `rdev` command. The format of the command is

`rdev <kernel-name> <root-device>`

where *<kernel-name>* is the name of the kernel image, and *<root-device>* is the name of the Linux root partition. For example, to set the root device in the kernel `/etc/Image` to `/dev/hda2`, use the command

`# rdev /etc/Image /dev/hda2`

`rdev` can set other options in the kernel as well, such as the default SVGA mode to use at boot time. Just use `rdev -?` to get a help message.

After setting the root device, you can simply copy the kernel image to the floppy. Whenever copying data to a floppy, it's a good idea to format the floppy as MS-DOS first. This lays down the sector and track information on the floppy, so it can be detected as either high or low density.

For example, to copy the kernel in the file `/etc/Image` to the floppy in `/etc/fd0`, use the command

`# cp /etc/Image /dev/fd0`

This floppy should now boot Linux.

Using LILO

Another method of booting is to use LILO, a program which resides in the boot sector of your hard disk. This program is executed when the system is booted from the hard disk, and can automatically boot up Linux from a kernel image stored on the hard drive itself.

LILO can also be used as a first-stage boot loader for several operating systems, allowing you to select at boot time which operating system (such as Linux or MS-DOS) to boot. When you boot using LILO, the default operating system is booted unless you press Ctrl, Alt, or Shift during the bootup sequence. If you press any of these keys, you will be provided with a boot prompt, at which point you type the name of the operating system to boot (such as linux or msdos). If you press Tab at the boot prompt, a listing of available operating systems will be provided.

LILO is located in the directory /etc/lilo (if you have it). The easy way to install LILO is to edit the configuration file, /etc/lilo/config, and then run the command

```
# /etc/lilo/lilo
```

The LILO configuration file contains a *stanza* for each operating system that you want to boot. The best way to demonstrate this is with an example LILO configuration file. The setup below is for a system that has a Linux root partition on /dev/hda1, and an MS-DOS partition on /dev/hda2.

```
# Tell LILO to modify the boot record on /dev/hda (the first
# non-SCSI hard drive). If you boot from a drive other than /dev/hda,
# change the following line.
boot = /dev/hda

# Name of the boot loader. No reason to modify this unless you're doing
# some serious hacking on LILO.
install = /etc/lilo/boot.b

# Have LILO perform some optimization.
compact

# Stanza for Linux root partition on /dev/hda1.
image = /etc/Image    # Location of kernel
   label = linux      # Name of OS (for the LILO boot menu)
   root = /dev/hda1   # Location of root partition
   vga = ask          # Tell kernel to ask for SVGA modes at boot time
# Stanza for MSDOS partition on /dev/hda2.
```

```
other = /dev/hda2     # Location of partition
  table = /dev/hda   # Location of partition table for /dev/hda2
  label = msdos      # Name of OS (for boot menu)
```

The first operating system stanza in the configuration file will be the default OS for LILO to boot. You can select another OS to boot at the LILO boot prompt, as discussed above.

The program `/etc/lilo/QuickInst` will ask you questions about your setup and generate a LILO configuration file for you.

Remember that every time you update the kernel image on disk, you should rerun `/etc/lilo/lilo` in order for the changes to be reflected on the boot sector of your drive.

Also note that if you use the `root` = line, above, there's no reason to use `rdev` to set the root partition in the kernel image. LILO sets it for you at boot time.

The Linux FAQ (see Appendix A) provides more information on LILO, including how to use LILO to boot with OS/2's Boot Manager.

Shutting Down

Shutting down a Linux system is a bit tricky. Remember that you should never just turn off the power or hit the reset switch while the system is running. The kernel keeps track of disk I/O in memory buffers. If you reboot the system without giving the kernel the chance to write its buffers to disk, you can corrupt your file systems.

Other precautions are taken at shutdown time as well. All processes are sent a signal, which allows them to die gracefully (writing and closing all files, and so on). file systems are unmounted for safety. If you wish, the system can also alert users that the system is going down and give them a chance to log off.

The easiest way to shut down is with the `shutdown` command. The format of the command is

```
shutdown <time> <warning-message>
```

The `<time>` argument is the time to shutdown the system (in the format *hh*:*mm*:*ss*), and `<warning-message>` is a message displayed on all user's terminals before shutdown. Alternately, you can specify the <time> as "now", to shutdown immediately. The -r option may be given to shutdown to reboot the system after shutting down.

For example, to shutdown the system at 8:00pm, use the command

```
# shutdown -r 20:00
```

The command halt may be used to force an immediate shutdown, without any warning messages or grace period. halt is useful if you're the only one using the system, and want to shut down the system and turn it off.

> **WARNING** Don't turn off the power or reboot the system until you see the message: The system is halted. It is very important that you shutdown the system "cleanly" using the shutdown or halt commands. On some systems, pressing Ctrl-Alt-Del will be trapped and cause a shutdown; on other systems, however, using the "Vulcan nerve pinch" will reboot the system immediately and may cause disaster.

Managing Users

Whether or not you have many users on your system, it's important to understand the aspects of user management under Linux. Even if you're the only user, you should presumably have a separate account for yourself (an account other than root to do most of your work).

Each person using the system should have his or her own account. It is seldom a good idea to have several people share the same account. Not only is security an issue, but accounts are used to uniquely identify users to the system. You need to be able to keep track of who is doing what.

User Management Concepts

The system keeps track of a number of pieces of information about each user. They are summarized below.

username	The username is the unique identifier given to every user on the system. Examples of usernames are larry, karl, and mdw. Letters and digits may be used, as well as the characters _ (underscore) and . (period). Usernames are usually limited to eight characters in length.
user ID	The user ID, or UID, is a unique number given to every user on the system. The system usually keeps track of information by UID, not username.
group ID	The group ID, or GID, is the ID of the user's default group. In "File Permissions" in Chapter 3, we discussed group permissions; each user belongs to one or more groups defined by the system administrator. More about this below.
password	The system also stores the user's encrypted password. The passwd command is used to set and change user passwords.
full name	The user's "real name" or "full name" is stored along with the username. For example, the user schmoj may have the name "Joe Schmo" in real life.
login shell	The user's login shell is the shell which is started for the user at login time. Examples are /bin/bash and /bin/tcsh.
home directory	The home directory is the directory in which the user is initially placed at login time. Every user should have his or her own home directory, usually found under /home.

The file `/etc/passwd` contains this information about users. Each line in the file contains information about a single user; the format of each line is

```
username:encrypted password:UID:GID:full name:home directory:login shell
```

An example might be:

```
kiwi:Xv8Q981g71oKK:102:100:Laura Poole:/home/kiwi:/bin/bash
```

As we can see, the first field, `kiwi`, is the username.

The next field, `Xv8Q981g71oKK`, is the encrypted password. Passwords are not stored on the system in any human-readable format. The password is encrypted, using itself as the secret key. In other words, you need to know the password to decrypt it. This form of encryption is fairly secure.

Some systems use *shadow password* in which password information is relegated to the file `/etc/shadow`. Because `/etc/passwd` is world-readable, `/etc/shadow` provides some degree of extra security because it is not. Shadow password provides some other features such as password expiration and so on; we will not go into these features here.

The third field, `102`, is the UID. This must be unique for each user. The fourth field, `100`, is the GID. This user belongs to the group numbered 100. Group information, like user information, is stored in the file `/etc/group`. (See "Groups" later in this chapter for more information.)

The fifth field is the user's full name, `Laura Poole`. The last two fields are the user's home directory (`/home/kiwi`) and login shell (`/bin/bash`), respectively. It is not required that the user's home directory be given the same name as the username. It does help identify the directory, however.

Adding Users

When adding a user, there are several steps to be taken. First, the user must be given an entry in `/etc/passwd`, with a unique username and UID. The GID, fullname, and other information must be specified. The user's home directory must be created, and the permissions on the directory set so that the user owns the directory. Shell initialization files must be provided in the new home directory and other system-wide configuration must be done (for example, setting up a spool for incoming e-mail for the new user).

While it is not difficult to add users by hand (I do), when you are running a system with many users it is easy to forget something. The easiest way to add users is to use an interactive program that asks you for the required information and updates all of the system files automatically. The name of this program is useradd or adduser, depending on what software was installed. The man pages for these commands should be fairly self-explanatory.

use command

Deleting Users   *cd etc/Jobe passwd*

Similarly, deleting users can be accomplished with the commands userdel or deluser depending on what software was installed on the system.

If you'd like to temporarily "disable" a user from logging into the system (without deleting the user's account), you can simply prepend an *(asterisk) to the password field in /etc/passwd. For example, changing kiwi's /etc/passwd entry to

```
kiwi:*Xv8Q981g71oKK:102:100:Laura Poole:/home/kiwi:/bin/bash
```

will restrict kiwi from logging in.

Setting User Attributes

After you have created a user, you may need to change attributes for that user, such as home directory or password. The easiest way to do this is to change the values directly in /etc/passwd. To set a user's password, use the passwd command. For example,

```
# passwd larry
```

will change larry's password. Only root may change another user's password in this manner. Users can change their own passwords with passwd as well.

On some systems, the commands chfn and chsh will be available to allow users to set their own fullname and login shell attributes. If not, they will have to ask the system administrator to change these attributes for them.

Groups

As we have mentioned, each user belongs to one or more groups. The only real importance of group relationships pertains to file permissions. As you'll recall from "File Permissions" in Chapter 3, each file has a *group ownership* and a set of group permissions which defines how users in that group may access the file.

There are several system-defined groups such as `bin`, `mail`, and `sys`. Users should not belong to any of these groups; they are used for system file permissions. Instead, users should belong to an individual group such as `users`. If you want to be cute, you can maintain several groups of users such as `student`, `staff`, and `faculty`.

The file `/etc/group` contains information about groups. The format of each line is

```
group name:password:GID:other members
```

Some example groups might be:

```
root:*:0:
users:*:100:mdw,larry
guest:*:200:
other:*:250:kiwi
```

The first group, `root`, is a special system group reserved for the `root` account. The next group, `users`, is for regular users. It has a GID of 100. The users `mdw` and `larry` are given access to this group. Remember that in `/etc/passwd` each user was given a default GID. However, `users` may belong to more than one group by adding their usernames to other group lines in `/etc/group`. The `groups` command lists what groups you are given access to.

The third group, `guest`, is for guest users, and `other` is for "other" users. The user `kiwi` is given access to this group as well.

As you can see, the "password" field of `/etc/group` is rarely used. It is sometimes used to set a password on group access. This is seldom necessary. To protect users from changing into privileged groups (with the `newgroup` command), set the password field to `*`.

The commands `addgroup` or `groupadd` may be used to add groups to your system. Usually, it's easier just to add entries in `/etc/group` yourself, as no other configuration needs to be done to add a group. To delete a group, simply delete its entry in `/etc/group`.

Archiving and Compressing Files

Before we can talk about backups, we need to introduce the tools used to archive software on Unix systems.

Using tar

The `tar` command is most often used to archive software.

The format of the `tar` command is

```
tar <options> <file1> <file2> ... <fileN>
```

where *<options>* is the list of commands and options for `tar`, and *<file1>* through *<fileN>* is the list of files to add or extract from the archive.

For example, the command

```
# tar cvf backup.tar /etc
```

would pack all of the files in `/etc` into the `tar` archive `backup.tar`. The first argument to `tar`—`cvf`—is the `tar` "command". `c` tells `tar` to create a new archive file. The `v` option forces `tar` into verbose mode—printing each filename as it is archived. The `f` option tells `tar` that the next argument—`backup.tar`—is the name of the archive to create. The rest of the arguments to `tar` are the file and directory names to add to the archive.

The command

```
# tar xvf backup.tar
```

will extract the tar file `backup.tar` in the current directory. This can sometimes be dangerous—when extracting files from a tar file, old files are overwritten.

Furthermore, before extracting tar files it is important to know where the files should be unpacked. For example, let's say you archived the following files: `/etc/hosts`, `/etc/group`, and `/etc/passwd`. If you use the command

```
# tar cvf backup.tar /etc/hosts /etc/group /etc/passwd
```

the directory name /etc/ is added to the beginning of each filename. In order to extract the files to the correct location, you would need to use the following commands

```
# cd /
# tar xvf backup.tar
```

because files are extracted with the pathname saved in the archive file.

If, however, you archived the files with the command

```
# cd /etc
# tar cvf hosts group passwd
```

the directory name is not saved in the archive file. Therefore, you would need to cd /etc before extracting the files. As you can see, how the tar file is created makes a large difference in where you extract it. The command

```
# tar tvf backup.tar
```

may be used to display an "index" of the tar file before unpacking it. In this way you can see what directory the filenames in the archive are stored relative to, and can extract the archive from the correct location.

gzip and compress

Unlike archiving programs for MS-DOS, tar does not automatically compress files as it archives them. Therefore, if you are archiving two 1 MB files, the resulting tar file will be 2 MBs in size. The gzip command may be used to compress a file (the file to compress need not be a tar file). The command

```
# gzip -9 backup.tar
```

will compress backup.tar and leave you with backup.tar.gz, the compressed version of the file. The -9 switch tells gzip to use the highest compression factor.

The gunzip command may be used to uncompress a gzipped file. Equivalently, you may use gzip -d.

gzip is a relatively new tool in the Unix community. For many years, the compress command was used instead. However, because of several factors, compress is being phased out. (These factors include a software patent dispute against the compress algorithm and the fact that gzip is much more efficient than compress.)

compressed files end in the extension `.Z`. For example, `backup.tar.Z` is the compressed version of `backup.tar`, while `backup.tar.gz` is the gzipped version. (To add further confusion, for some time the extension `.z` was used for gzipped files. The official gzip extension is now `.gz`.) The `uncompress` command is used to expand a `compressed` file; `gunzip` knows how to handle `compressed` files as well.

Putting Them Together

Therefore, to archive a group of files and compress the result, you can use the commands

```
# tar cvf backup.tar /etc
# gzip -9 backup.tar
```

The result will be `backup.tar.gz`. To unpack this file, use the reverse set of commands

```
# gunzip backup.tar.gz
# tar xvf backup.tar
```

Of course always make sure that you are in the correct directory before unpacking a tar file.

You can use some Unix cleverness to do all of this on one command line, as in the following:

```
# tar cvf - /etc | gzip -9c > backup.tar.gz
```

Here, we are sending the tar file to -, which stands for `tar`'s standard output. This is piped to `gzip`, which compresses the incoming tar file, and the result is saved in `backup.tar.gz`. The –c option to `gzip` tells `gzip` to send its output to stdout, which is redirected to `backup.tar.gz`.

A single command used to unpack this archive would be:

```
# gunzip -c backup.tar.gz | tar xvf -
```

Again, `gunzip` uncompresses the contents of `backup.tar.gz` and sends the resulting tar file to stdout. This is piped to `tar`, which reads -, this time referring to `tar`'s standard input.

Happily, the `tar` command also includes the `-z` option to automatically compress/uncompress files on the fly. However, it does this as per the `compress` algorithm—it does not use `gzip`.

NOTE The newest versions of GNU `tar` does in fact use `gzip` when using the `-z` option. However, if you use a `tar` binary from the Stone Age, like me, then don't expect `-z` to use `gzip` compression.

For example, the command

```
# tar cvfz backup.tar.Z /etc
```

is equivalent to

```
# tar cvf backup.tar /etc
# compress backup.tar
```

Just as the command

```
# tar xvfz backup.tar.Z
```

may be used instead of

```
# uncompress backup.tar.Z
# tar xvf backup.tar
```

Refer to the manual pages for `tar` and `gzip` for more information.

Using Floppies and Making Backups

Floppies are usually used as backup media. If you don't have a tape drive connected to your system, floppy disks can be used (although they are slower and somewhat less reliable).

You may also use floppies to hold individual file systems—in this way, you can *mount* the floppy to access the data on it.

Using Floppies for Backups

The easiest way to make a backup using floppies is with `tar`. The command

```
# tar cvfzM /dev/fd0 /
```

will make a complete backup of your system using the floppy drive /dev/fd0. The M option to tar allows the backup to be a multivolume backup; that is, when one floppy is full, tar will prompt for the next. The command

```
# tar xvfzM /dev/fd0
```

can be used to restore the complete backup. This method can also be used if you have a tape drive (/dev/rmt0) connected to your system.

> **NOTE**
>
> In using this method, you must settle for the compress algorithm; tar doesn't use gzip with the z option. Several other programs exist for making multiple-volume backups; the backflops program on tsx-11.mit.edu may come in handy.

Making a complete backup of the system can be time- and resource-consuming. Most system administrators use an incremental backup policy, in which every month a complete backup is taken, and every week only those files which have been modified in the last week are backed up. In this case, if you trash your system in the middle of the month, you can simply restore the last full monthly backup, and then restore the last weekly backups as needed.

The find command can be useful in locating files which have changed since a certain date. Several scripts for managing incremental backups can be found on sunsite.unc.edu.

Using Floppies as File Systems

You can create a file system on a floppy just as you would on a hard drive partition. For example,

```
# mke2fs /dev/fd0 1440
```

creates a file system on the floppy in /dev/fd0. The size of the file system must correspond to the size of the floppy. High-density 3½" disks are 1.44 MBs, or 1440 blocks, in size. High-density 5¼" disks are 1200 blocks.

In order to access the floppy, you must mount the file system contained on it. The command

```
# mount -t ext2 /dev/fd0 /mnt
```

will mount the floppy in /dev/fd0 on the directory /mnt. Now, all of the files on the floppy will appear under /mnt on your drive. The -t ext2 specifies an ext2fs file system type. If you created another type of file system on the floppy, you'll need to specify its type to the mount command.

The *mount point* (the directory where you're mounting the file system) needs to exist when you use the mount command. If it doesn't exist, simply create it with mkdir. "Managing File Systems" later in this chapter for more information on file systems, mounting, and mount points.

> **NOTE** Any I/O to the floppy is buffered just as hard disk I/O is. If you change data on the floppy, you may not see the drive light come on until the kernel flushes its I/O buffers. It's important that you not remove a floppy before you unmount it; this can be done with the command *# umount /dev/fd0.* Do not simply switch floppies as you would on an MS-DOS system; whenever you change floppies, umount the first one and then mount the next.

Upgrading and Installing New Software

Another duty of the system administrator is upgrading and installing new software.

The Linux community is very dynamic. New kernel releases come out every few weeks, and other software is updated almost as often. Because of this, new Linux users often feel the need to upgrade their systems constantly to keep up with the rapidly changing pace. Not only is this unnecessary, it's a waste of time: to keep up with all of the changes in the Linux world, you would be spending all of your time upgrading and none of your time using the system.

So, when should you upgrade? Some people feel that you should upgrade when a new distribution release is made—for example, when SLS comes out with a new version. Many Linux users completely reinstall their system with the newest SLS release every time. This is also a waste of time. In general, changes to SLS releases are small. Downloading and reinstalling 30 disks when only 10% of the software has actually been modified is, of course, pointless.

The best way to upgrade your system is to do it by hand: only upgrade those software packages that you know you should upgrade. This scares a lot of people: they want to know what to upgrade, and how, and what will break if they don't . In order to be successful with Linux, it's important to overcome your fears of "doing it yourself"— which is what Linux is all about. In fact, once you have your system working and all software correctly configured, reinstalling with the newest SLS release will no doubt wipe all of your configuration and things will be broken again, just as they were when you first installed your system. Setting yourself back in this manner is unnecessary—all that is needed is some know-how about upgrading your system, and how to do it right.

You'll find that when you upgrade one component of your system, other things should not break. For example, most of the software on my system is left over from an ancient 0.96 MCC Interim installation. Yet, I run the newest version of the kernel and libraries with this software and have no problems. For the most part, senselessly upgrading to "keep up with the trend" is not important at all. This isn't MS-DOS or Microsoft Windows. There is no important reason to run the newest version of all of the software. If you find that you would like or need features in a new version, then upgrade. If not, then don't. In other words, only upgrade what you have to, and when you have to. Don't just upgrade for the sake of upgrading. That will waste a lot of time and effort trying to keep up.

The most important software to upgrade on your system are the kernel, the libraries, and the gcc compiler. These are the three essential parts of your system, and in some cases they all depend on each other for everything to work successfully. Most of the other software on your system does not need to be upgraded periodically.

Upgrading the Kernel

Upgrading the kernel is simply a matter of getting the sources and compiling them yourself. You must compile the kernel yourself in order to enable or disable certain features, as well as to ensure that the kernel will be optimized to run on your machine. The process is quite painless.

The kernel sources may be retrieved from any of the Linux ftp sites (*see* Appendix C for a list). On sunsite.unc.edu, for instance, the kernel sources are found in /pub/linux/kernel. Kernel versions are numbered using a version number and a patchlevel. For example, kernel version 0.99 patchlevel 11 is usually written as 0.99.pl11, or just 0.99.11.

The kernel sources are released as a gzipped tar file. For example, the file containing the 0.99.pl11 kernel sources is linux-0.99.11.tar.gz.

NOTE
Often, a patch file is also released for the current kernal version, which allows you to patch your current kernel sources from the last patchlevel to the current one (using the program patch). In most cases, however, it's usually easier to install the entire new verison of the kernel sources.

Unpack this tar file from the directory /usr/src; it creates the directory /usr/src/linux, which contains the kernel sources. You should delete or rename your existing /usr/src/linux before unpacking the new version.

Once the sources are unpacked, you need to make sure that two symbolic links in /usr/include are correct. To create these links, use the commands

```
# ln -sf /usr/src/linux/include/linux /usr/include/linux
# ln -sf /usr/src/linux/include/asm /usr/include/asm
```

Once you have created these links, there is no reason to create them again when you install the next version of the kernel sources. (See "Managing File Links" in Chapter 3 for more about symbolic links.)

Note that in order to compile the kernel, you must have the gcc and g++ C and C++ compilers installed on your system. You may need to have the most recent versions of these compilers (See "Upgrading gcc" below for more information).

To compile the kernel, first cd to /usr/src/linux. Run the command make config. This command will prompt you for a number of configuration options, such as what file system types you wish to include in the new kernel.

Next, edit /usr/src/linux/Makefile. Be sure that the definition for ROOT_DEV is correct—it defines the device used as the root file system at boot time. The usual definition is

```
ROOT_DEV = CURRENT
```

Unless you are changing your root file system device, there is no reason to change this.

Next, run the command make dep to fix all of the source dependencies. This is a very important step.

Finally, you're ready to compile the kernel. The command make Image will compile the kernel and leave the new kernel image in the file /usr/src/linux/Image. Alternately, the command make zImage will compile a compressed kernel image, which uncompresses itself at boot time and uses less drive space.

Once you have the kernel compiled, you need to either copy it to a boot floppy (with a command such as cp Image /dev/fd0) or install it using LILO to boot from your hard drive. (See "Using LILO" earlier in this chapter for more information.)

Upgrading the Libraries

As mentioned before, most of the software on the system is compiled to use shared libraries, which contain common subroutines shared among different programs.

If you see the message

```
Incompatible library version
```

when attempting to run a program, then you need to upgrade to the version of the libraries that the program requires. Libraries are back-compatible; that is, a program compiled to use an older version of the libraries should work with the new version of the libraries installed. However, the reverse is not true.

The newest version of the libraries can be found on the Linux ftp sites. On sunsite.unc.edu, they are located in /pub/Linux/GCC. The "release" files there should explain what files you need to download and how to install them. Briefly, you should get the files image-*version*.tar.gz and inc-*version*.tar.gz where *version* is the version of the libraries to install, such as 4.4.1. These are gzipped tar files; the image file contains the library images to install in /lib and /usr/lib. The inc file contents include files to install in /usr/include.

The release-*version*.tar.gz should explain the installation procedure in detail (the exact instructions vary for each release). In general, you need to install the library .a and .sa files in /usr/lib. These are the libraries used at compilation time.

In addition, the shared library image files, libc.so.*version*, are installed in /lib. These are the shared library images loaded at runtime by programs using the libraries. Each library has a symbolic link using the major version number of the library in /lib.

For example, the libc library version 4.4.1 has a major version number of 4. The file containing the library is libc.so.4.4.1. In addition to containing the file iibc.so.4.4.1, the directory contains a symbolic link from the name to the file libc.so.4.4.1. You need to change this symbolic link when upgrading the libraries. For example, when upgrading from libc.so.4.4 to libc.so.4.4.1, you need to change the symbolic link to point to the new version.

NOTE It is very important that you change the symbolic link in one step, as given below. If you somehow delete the symbolic link libc.so.4, then programs that depend on the link (including basic utilities like ls and cat) will stop working. Use the following command to update the symbolic link libc.so.4 to point to the file libc.so.4.4.1:

```
# ln -sf /lib/libc.so.4.4.1 /lib/libc.so.4
```

You also need to change the symbolic link libm.so.*version* in the same manner. If you are upgrading to a different version of the libraries, substitute the appropriate filenames above. The library release notice should explain the details. (See "Managing File Links" in Chapter 3 for more information about symbolic links.)

Upgrading gcc

The gcc C and C++ compiler is used to compile software on your system, most importantly the kernel. The newest version of gcc is found on the Linux ftp sites. On sunsite.unc.edu, it is found in the directory /pub/Linux/GCC (along with the libraries). There should be a release file for the gcc distribution detailing what files you need to download and how to install them.

Upgrading Other Software

Upgrading other software is usually just a matter of downloading the appropriate files and installing them. Most software for Linux is distributed at gzipped tar files, including either sources or binaries or both. If binaries are not included in the release, you may need to compile them yourself; usually, this means typing `make` in the directory where the sources are held.

Reading the Usenet newsgroup `comp.os.linux.announce` for announcements of new software releases is the easiest way to find out about new software. Whenever you are looking for software on an ftp site, downloading the `ls-lR` index file from the ftp site and using `grep` to find the files in question is the easiest way to locate software. If you have `archie` available to you, it can be of assistance as well. If you don't have `archie`, you can `telnet` to an `archie` server such as `archie.rutgers.edu`, login as "archie" and use the command `help`. (See Appendix A for more details.)

One handy source of Linux software is the SLS distribution disk images. Each disk contains a number of `.tgz` files, which are simply gzipped tar files. Instead of downloading the disks, you can download the desired `.tgz` files from the SLS directories on the ftp site and install them directly. If you run the SLS distribution, the `sysinstall` command can be used to automatically load and install a complete series of disks. For example, the command

```
# sysinstall -series t
```

will install the entire SLS t series of disks. Of course, most of the time you may not wish to download and install an entire series, in which case you'll need to unpack the `.tgz` files by hand.

Again, it's usually not a good idea to upgrade by reinstalling with the newest version of SLS, or another distribution. SLS in particular was not designed to be upgradeable. If you reinstall in this way, you will no doubt wreck your current installation, including user directories and all of your customized configuration. The best way to upgrade software is piece by piece; that is, if there is a program that you use often that has a new version, upgrade it. Otherwise, don't bother. If it ain't broke, don't fix it. If your current software works, there's no reason to upgrade.

Managing File Systems

Another task of the system administrator is to maintain file systems. Most of this job entails periodically checking the file systems for damage or corrupted files; many systems automatically check the file systems at boot time.

Mounting File Systems

First, a few concepts about file systems. Before a file system is accessible to the system, it must be *mounted* on some directory. For example, if you have a file system on a floppy, you must mount it under some directory, say /mnt, in order to access the files on it. (See "Using Floppies as file systems" earlier in this chapter.) After mounting the file system on that directory, all of the files in the file system appear in that directory. The files on the floppy will appear in the directory /mnt. After un-mounting the floppy, the directory /mnt will be empty.

The same is true of file systems on the hard drive. The system automatically mounts file systems on your hard drive for you at bootup time. The *root file system* is mounted on the directory /. If you have a separate file system for /usr, for example, it is mounted on /usr. If you only have a root file system, all files (including those in /usr) exist on that file system.

The command mount is used to mount a file system. The command

```
mount -av
```

is executed from the file /etc/rc (which is the system initialization file executed at boot time; see "System Startup Files" later in this chapter). The mount -av command obtains information on file systems and mount points from the file /etc/fstab. An example fstab file appears below.

```
# device      directory    type     options
/dev/hda2     /            ext2     defaults
/dev/hda3     /usr         ext2     defaults
/dev/hda4     none         swap     sw
/proc         /proc        proc     none
```

The first field is the device—the name of the partition to mount. The second field is the mount point. The third field is the file system type—such as ext2 (for ext2fs) or minix (for Minix file systems). The last field contains mount options—usually, this is set to defaults.

As you can see, swap partitions are included in /etc/fstab as well. They have a mount directory of none, and type swap. The swapon -a command, executed from /etc/rc as well, is used to enable swapping on all swap devices listed in /etc/fstab.

The fstab file contains one special entry—for the /proc file system. As mentioned in "Jobs and Processes" in Chapter 3, the /proc file system is used to store information about system processes, available memory, and so on. If /proc is not mounted, commands such as ps will not work.

NOTE The mount command may only be used by root. This is to ensure security on the system; you wouldn't want regular users mounting and unmounting file systems on a whim. There are several software packages available which allow regular users to mount and unmount file systems (floppies in particular) without compromising system security.

The mount -av command actually mounts all file systems other than the root file system (in the table above, /dev/hda2). The root file system is automatically mounted at boot time by the kernel.

Instead of using mount -av, you can mount a file system by hand. The command

```
# mount -t ext2 /dev/hda3 /usr
```

is equivalent to mounting the file system with the entry /dev/hda3 in the fstab example file above.

In general, you should never have to mount or unmount file systems by hand. The mount -av command in /etc/rc takes care of mounting the file systems at boot time. file systems are automatically unmounted by the shutdown or halt commands before bringing the system down.

Checking File Systems

It is usually a good idea to check your file systems for damage or corrupt files every now and then. Some systems automatically check their file systems at boot time (with the appropriate commands in /etc/rc).

The command used to check a file system depends on the type of the file system in question. For ext2fs file systems (the most commonly used type), this command is e2fsck. For example, the command

```
# e2fsck -av /dev/hda2
```

will check the ext2fs file system on /dev/hda2 and automatically correct any errors.

It is usually a good idea to unmount a file system before checking it. For example, the command

```
# umount /dev/hda2
```

will unmount the file system on /dev/hda2, after which you can check it. The one exception is that you cannot unmount the root file system. In order to check the root file system when it's unmounted, you should use a maintenance boot/root diskette. (See "Recovering Using a Maintenance Diskette" later in this chapter.) You also cannot unmount a file system if any of the files in it are "busy"—that is, being used by a running process. For example, you cannot unmount a file system if any user's current working directory is on that file system. You will receive a `Device busy` error if you attempt to unmount a file system that is in use.

Other file system types use different forms of the e2fsck command, such as efsck and xsfck. On some systems, you can simply use the command fsck, which will determine the file system type and execute the appropriate command.

NOTE
It is important that you reboot your system immediately after checking a file system if any corrections were made to that file system. For example, if e2fsck reports that it corrected any errors with the file system, you should immediately shutdown -r in order to reboot the system. This is to allow the system to re-sync its information about the file system when e2fsck modifies it.

The /proc file system never needs to be checked in this manner. /proc is a memory file system, managed directly by the kernel.

Using a Swap File

Instead of reserving an individual partition for swap space, you can use a file. However, to do so you'll need to install the Linux software and get everything going *before* you create the swap file.

If you have a Linux system installed, you can use the following commands to create a swap file. Below, we're going to create a 8208=block (about 8 MB) swap file .

```
# dd if=/dev/zero of=/swap bs=1024 count=8208
```

This command creates the swap file itself. Replace the `count=` with the size of the swap file in blocks.

```
# mkswap /swap 8208
```

This command will initialize the swapfile; again, replace the name and size of the swapfile with the appropriate values.

```
# /etc/sync
# swapon /swap
```

Now we are swapping on the file /swap that we created, after *syncing*, which ensures that the swap file has been written to disk.

The one major drawback to using a swapfile in this manner is that all access to the swap file is through the file system. This means that the blocks that make up the swap file may not be contiguous. Therefore, performance may not be as great as when using a swap partition, for which blocks are always contiguous and I/O requests are done directly to the device.

Another drawback to using a swapfile is the chance that you may corrupt your file system data when using large swap files. Keeping your file systems and swap partitions separate will prevent this from happening.

Using a swap file can be very useful if you have a temporary need for more swap space. For example, if you're compiling a large program and would like to speed things up somewhat, you can temporarily create a swap file and use it in addition to your regular swap space.

To get rid of a swap file, first use `swapoff`, as in

```
# swapoff /swap
```

And you can safely delete the file.

```
# rm /swap
```

Remember that each swap file (or partition) may be as large as 16 MB, but you may use up to 8 swap files or partitions on your system.

Miscellaneous Tasks

Believe it or not, there are a number of housekeeping tasks for the system administrator that don't fall into any major category.

System Startup Files

When the system boots, a number of scripts are executed automatically by the system before any user logs in. Here is a description of what happens.

At bootup time, the kernel spawns the process /etc/init. init is a program which reads its configuration file, /etc/inittab, and spawns other processes based on the contents of this file. One of the important processes started from inittab is the /etc/getty process started on each virtual console. The getty process grabs the VC for use, and starts a login process on the VC. This allows you to login on each VC; if /etc/inittab does not contain a getty process for a certain VC, you will not be able to login on that VC.

Another process executed from /etc/inittab is /etc/rc the main system initialization file. This file is a simple shell script that executes any initialization commands needed at boot time, such as mounting the file systems (see "Managing File Systems" earlier in this chapter) and initializing swap space.

Your system may execute other initialization scripts as well, such as /etc/rc.local. /etc/rc.local usually contains initialization commands specific to your own system, such as setting the hostname (see the next section). rc.local may be started from /etc/rc or from /etc/inittab directly.

Setting the Hostname

In a networked environment, the hostname is used to uniquely identify a particular machine, while in a stand-alone environment the host name just gives the system personality and charm. It's like naming a pet: you can always address your dog as "the dog," but it's much more interesting to assign the dog a name such as Spot or Woofie.

Setting the system's host name is a simple matter of using the `host name` command. If you are on a network, your host name should be the full host name of your machine, such as `goober.norelco.com`. If you are not on a network of any kind, you can choose an arbitrary host and domain name, such as `loomer.vpizza.com`, `shoop.nowhere.edu`, or `floof.org`.

When setting the host name, the host name must appear in the file `/etc/hosts`, which assigns an IP address to each host. Even if your machine is not on a network, you should include your own host name in `/etc/hosts`.

For example, if you are not on a TCP/IP network, and your host name is `floof.org`, simply include the following line in `/etc/hosts`:

```
127.0.0.1        floof.org localhost
```

This assigns your host name, `floof.org`, to the loopback address 127.0.0.1 (used if you're not on a network). The `localhost` alias is also assigned to this address.

If you are on a TCP/IP network, however, your real IP address and host name should appear in `/etc/hosts`. For example, if your host name is `goober.norelco.com`, and your IP address is 128.253.154.32, add the following line to `/etc/hosts`:

```
128.253.154.32        goober.norelco.com
```

If your host name does not appear in `/etc/hosts`, you will not be able to set it.

To set your host name, simply use the `host name` command. For example, the command

```
# hostname -S goober.norelco.com
```

sets the hostname to `goober.norelco.com`. In most cases, the `hostname` command is executed from one of the system startup files, such as `/etc/rc` or `/etc/rc.local`. Edit these two files and change the `hostname` command found there to set your own hostname; upon rebooting the system the hostname will be set to the new value.

What to Do in an Emergency

On some occasions, the system administrator will be faced with the problem of recovering from a complete disaster, such as forgetting the root password or trashing file systems. The best advice is, *don't panic*. Everyone makes stupid mistakes—that's the best way to learn about system administration: the hard way.

Linux is not an unstable version of Unix. In fact, I have had fewer problems with system hangs than with commercial versions of Unix on many platforms. Linux also benefits from a strong complement of wizards who can help you get out of a bind.

The first step in investigating any problem is to attempt to fix it yourself. Poke around, see how things work. Too much of the time, a system administrator will post a desperate plea for help before looking into the problem at all. Most of the time, you'll find that fixing problems yourself is actually very easy. It is also the path to guruhood.

There are very few cases where reinstalling the system from scratch is necessary. Many new users accidentally delete some essential system file, and immediately reach for the installation disks. This is not a good idea. Before taking such drastic measures, investigate the problem and ask others to help fix things up. In almost all cases, you can recover your system from a maintenance diskette.

Recovering Using a Maintenance Diskette

One indispensable tool for the system administrator is the *boot/root disk*—a floppy which can be booted for a complete Linux system, independent of your hard drive. Boot/root disks are actually very simple—you create a root file system on the floppy, place all of the necessary utilities on it, and install LILO and a bootable kernel on the floppy. Another technique is to use one floppy for the kernel and another for the root file system. In any case, the result is the same: you are running a Linux system completely from floppy.

The Slackware boot disks are the canonical examples of boot/root disk is . (See "Getting Linux from the Internet" in Chapter 2 for information on downloading these from the Internet. For this procedure, you don't need to download the entire

Slackware release—only the boot and root diskettes.) These diskettes contain a bootable kernel and a root file system, all on floppy. They are intended to be used to install the Slackware distribution, but come in very handy when doing system maintenance.

The H.J Lu boot/root disk, available from `/pub/Linux/GCC` on `sunsite.unc.edu`, is another example of such a maintenance disk. Or, if you're ambitious, you can create your own. In most cases, however, using a premade boot/root disk is much easier and will probably be more complete.

Using a boot/root disk is very simple. Just boot the disk on your system, and login as `root` (usually no password). In order to access the files on your hard drive, you will need to mount your file systems by hand. For example, the command

```
# mount -t ext2 /dev/hda2 /mnt
```

will mount an ext2fs file system on `/dev/hda2` under `/mnt`. Remember that `/` is now on the boot/root disk itself; you need to mount your hard drive file systems under some directory in order to access the files. Therefore, `/etc/passwd` on your hard drive is now `/mnt/etc/passwd` if you mount your root file system on `/mnt`.

Fixing the Root Password

If you forget your root password, no problem. Just boot the boot/root disk, mount your root file system on `/mnt`, and blank out the password field for `root` in `/mnt/etc/passwd`, as so

```
root::0:0:root:/:/bin/sh
```

Now `root` has no password; when you reboot from the hard drive you should be able to login as `root` and reset the password using `passwd`.

Aren't you glad you learned how to use `vi`? On your boot/root disk, other editors such as Emacs probably aren't available, but `vi` should be.

Fixing Trashed File Systems

If you somehow trash your file systems, you can run `e2fsck` (if you use the ext2fs file system type, that is) to correct any damaged data on the file systems from floppy. Other file system types use different forms of the `fsck` command; see "Managing file systems" earlier in this chapter for details.

When checking your file systems from floppy, it's best for the file systems not to be mounted.

One common cause of file system damage is *superblock* corruption. The superblock is the "header" of the file system that contains information on the file system status, size, free blocks, and so forth. If you corrupt your superblock (for example, by accidentally writing data directly to the file system's partition), the system may not recognize the file system at all. Any attempt to mount the file system could fail, and e2fsck won't be able to fix the problem.

Happily, the ext2fs file system type saves copies of the superblock at "block group" boundaries on the drive—usually, every 8 K blocks.

In order to tell e2fsck to use a copy of the superblock, you can use a command such as

```
# e2fsck -b 8193 <partition>
```

where *<partition>* is the partition on which the file system resides. The −b 8193 option tells e2fsck to use the copy of the superblock stored at block 8193 in the file system.

Recovering Lost Files

If you accidentally delete important files on your system, there's no way to "undelete" them. However, you can copy the relevant files from the floppy to your hard drive. For example, if you deleted /bin/login on your system (which allows you to login), simply boot the boot/root floppy, mount the root file system on /mnt, and use the command

```
# cp -a /bin/login /mnt/bin/login
```

The −a option tells cp to preserve the permissions on the file(s) being copied.

Of course, if the files you deleted weren't essential system files that have counterparts on the boot/root floppy, you're out of luck. If you made backups, you can always restore from them.

Fixing Trashed Libraries

If you accidentally trash your libraries or symbolic links in /lib, more than likely commands which depended on those libraries will no longer run. (See "Upgrading the Libraries" earlier in this chapter.) The easiest solution is to boot your boot/root floppy, mount your root file system, and fix the libraries in /mnt/lib.

CHAPTER

FIVE

Advanced Features

5

This chapter will introduce you to some of the more interesting features of Linux. We assume that you have at least basic Unix experience, and understand the information contained in the previous chapters.

The most important aspect of Linux that distinguishes it from other implementations of Unix is its open design and philosophy. Linux was not developed by a small team of programmers headed by a marketing committee with a single goal in mind. It was developed by an ever-increasing group of hackers, putting what they wanted into a homebrew Unix system. The types of software and diversity of design in the Linux world is large. Some people dislike this lack of uniformity and conformity— however, some call it one of Linux's strongest qualities.

The X Window System

The X Window System is a large and powerful (and somewhat complex) graphics environment for Unix systems. The original X Window code was developed at MIT; commercial vendors have since made X the industry standard for Unix platforms. Virtually every workstation in the world runs some variant of X Window.

A free port of the MIT X Window Version 11, Release 5 (X11R5) for 80386/80486 Unix systems has been developed by a team of programmers headed by David Wexelblat. (David may be reached on the Internet at dwex@mtgzfs3.att.com.) The release, known as XFree86, is available for System V/386, 386BSD, and other i386 Unix implementations, including Linux. It includes all of the required binaries, support files, libraries, and tools.

Configuring and using the X Window System is far beyond the scope of this book. You are encouraged to read *The X Window System User's Guide,* by Valerie Quercia and Tim O'Reilly. (See Appendix A for information on this book.) In this section, we'll give a general overview of installing and configuring X Window for Linux, but it is far from complete. The man pages and README files included with the Linux X Window distribution should be very helpful.

The Linux XFree86 HOWTO (see Appendix A for details) contains a complete discussion of installation and configuration of X Window for Linux. We refer all interested readers to this document.

Hardware Requirements

As of XFree86 version 2.1, the following video chipsets are supported. The documentation included with your video adaptor should specify the chipset used.

- Tseng ET3000, ET4000AX, ET4000/W32
- Western Digital/Paradise PVGA1
- Western Digital WD90C00, WD90C10, WD90C11, WD90C24, WD90C30, WD90C31
- Genoa GVGA
- Trident TVGA8800CS, TVGA8900B, TVGA8900C, TVGA8900CL, TVGA9000, TVGA9000i, TVGA9100B, TVGA9200CX, TVGA9320, TVGA9400CX, TVGA9420
- ATI 28800-4, 28800-5, 28800-a
- NCR 77C22, 77C22E, 77C22E+
- Cirrus Logic CLGD5420, CLGD5422, CLGD5424, CLGD5426, CLGD5428
- CLGD6205, CLGD6215, CLGD6225, CLGD6235
- Compaq AVGA
- OAK OTI067, OTI077

The following accelerated chipsets are supported:

- 8514/A (and true clones)
- ATI Mach8, Mach32
- Cirrus CLGD5420, CLGD5422, CLGD5424, CLGD5426, CLGD5428
- S3 86C911, 86C924, 86C801, 86C805, 86C805i, 86C928
- Western Digital WD90C31.

All of these, except for the ATI and Cirrus chipsets, are supported in both 256-color or monochrome mode. ATI and Cirrus are supported only in color. There is also a monochrome server that supports generic VGA, Hercules, Sigma LaserView, Hyundai HGC1280, and Visa cards.

This list will undoubtedly expand as time passes. The release notes for the current version of XFree86 should contain the complete list of supported video chipsets.

One problem faced by the XFree86 developers is that some video card manufacturers use non-standard mechanisms for determining clock frequencies used to drive the card. Some of these manufacturers either don't release specifications describing how to program the card, or they require developers to sign a non-disclosure statement to obtain the information. This would obviously restrict the free distribution of the XFree86 software, something that the XFree86 development team is not willing to do. Specifically, the Diamond Speedstar 24/Speedstar+, and Diamond's S3-based cards are not supported for this reason.

Local bus cards are supported as well. The suggested setup for XFree86 under Linux is a 486 machine with at least 8 MB of RAM, and a video card with a chipset listed above. For optimal performance, we suggest using an S3-chipset card. You should check the documentation for XFree86 and verify that your particular card is supported before taking the plunge and purchasing expensive hardware.

I have run XFree86 on a 486/50 MHz machine with 8 MB of RAM, and it's as fast or faster than many color workstations running proprietary versions of Unix and X. 16 MB of RAM or more is certainly a plus.

You will need at least 4 MB of physical RAM, and 16 MB of virtual RAM (for example, 8 MB physical and 8 MB swap). Remember that physical RAM is speed! A system with 4 MB of physical RAM will run *much* (up to 10 times) more slowly than one with 8 MB or more. Furthermore, swapping is too slow to compensate for lack of physical RAM. It is strongly suggested that you have at least 8 MB of physical RAM.

Installing XFree86

The Linux binary distribution of XFree86 can be found on a number of Linux ftp sites. On sunsite.unc.edu, it is found in the directory /pub/Linux/X11. (As of the time of this writing, the current version is 2.1.1; newer versions are released periodically). The binary distribution consists of a number of gzipped tar files, all of which unpack from /.

It's quite likely that you obtained XFree86 as part of a Linux distribution, in which case downloading the software separately is not necessary.

The XFree86 directory should contain README files and installation notes for the current version. Installation is covered in the XFree86-HOWTO; essentially you need to unpack the tar files (as root) from /.

After unpacking the files, you first need to link the file /usr/bin/X11/X to the server that you're using. For example, if you wish to use the SVGA color server, /usr/bin/X11/X should be linked to /usr/bin/X11/XF86_SVGA. If you wish to use the monochrome server instead, relink this file to XF86_MONO with the command

```
# ln -sf /usr/bin/X11/XF86_MONO /usr/bin/X11/X
```

The same holds true if you are using one of the other servers.

Configuring XFree86

Setting up XFree86 is not difficult in most cases. Only when you have non-standard hardware will XFree86 configuration give you any problems. However, XFree86 configuration is beyond the scope of this document; here, we'll give you a brief overview of how it works.

A complete discussion of XFree86 configuration can be found in the file /usr/lib/X11/etc/README.Config included with XFree86. Please read this file for complete information on setting up the system. You should also read the manual pages for Xconfig, XFree86, and the server that you are using (such as XF86_SVGA). These manual pages describe all of the options that are available for the configuration files.

The main XFree86 configuration file is /usr/lib/X11/Xconfig. This file contains information on your mouse, video card parameters, and so on. The file Xconfig.sample is provided with the XFree86 distribution as an example. The XFree86 man page explains the format of this file in detail.

As an overview: your video card uses a number of "driving clock frequencies" (or "dot clocks") which specify the maximum rates at which the card can send video information to the monitor. Each dot clock has a resolution mode associated with it, such as 640 x 480 or 1024 x 768. (Although you are not restrained to using "standard" resolutions, as we will see). In the Xconfig file there exist stanzas for configuring your mouse, keyboard, and so on. There also exist stanzas for each server, headed by keywords such as vga256 for the color SVGA server, and vga2 for the monochrome server.

Within each server stanza are lines to set the virtual resolution, chipset type, and other parameters for your video card. There is also a Modes line which specifies which resolution modes are available. Modes are usually named after their resolution. For example,

```
Modes "640x480" "800x600" "1024x768"
```

Each mode on this line is an index into the modeDB stanza at the end of the Xconfig file. It is this section of the file that determines the actual video parameters for each mode.

There is also an optional Clocks line which you can use to set the available dot clocks for your card. By default, XFree86 will determine the clocks at startup time; however, because clock timing can be thrown off by other programs running on your system, it is usually more accurate to set the clocks explicitly in the Xconfig file.

The modeDB section of the Xconfig file is the important part. Each video card and monitor has its own set of timing and sync frequencies for different resolutions. The file /usr/lib/X11/etc/modeDB.txt contains a database of known timing numbers for several types of monitors and video cards. Many cards and monitors use the VESA standard timings included in the sample Xconfig file.

There are various other documents in /usr/lib/X11/etc that you should read. The file VideoModes.txt is a tutorial on hacking your own monitor frequency timings if you simply can't get any of the numbers in modeDB.txt to work. There is also a collection of sample Xconfig files on sunsite.unc.edu in the file /pub/Linux/X11/Xconfig.tgz. See the XFree86 man pages for more information.

WARNING Be careful when setting up your Xconfig file. If you select a clock frequency higher (or lower) than your monitor can support, you may very well damage the monitor. Check the documentation for your monitor before hacking your video timings.

If you are not sure what kind of video hardware you have, you can run the program /usr/bin/X11/SuperProbe, which is fairly good at detecting video hardware. However, SuperProbe is not always correct, so rely on your manuals and common sense before trusting it completely. Also note that SuperProbe will detect more hardware than XFree86-2.0 supports.

Again, we refer you to the Linux XFree86-HOWTO for complete information on setting up this beast.

Starting Up X

After configuring the Xconfig file, you can start the server with the startx command. There are a few things to take into consideration first, however.

Make sure that the directory /usr/bin/X11 is on your path. This directory contains all of the X binaries and the server itself.

Secondly, the X server requires a free VC to enable VC switching. In other words, you must have one of your VCs available with no login process running on it. The easiest way to ensure this is to edit /etc/inittab and delete one of the getty lines, which starts up a login process on each VC. In my inittab, for example, I run getty on /dev/tty1 through /dev/tty7 (that is, VCs 1 through 7), but not on /dev/tty8.

When running startx, the file $HOME/.xinitrc is read. This file is a shell script that contains commands to run after the X server is started. If this file doesn't exist, the file /usr/lib/X11/Xinit/xinitrc is used as a system-wide default instead. You can use this default file as a sample .xinitrc file.

Using X Window is a large topic, and we won't try to cover it here. Read *The X Window System User's Guide*, or another book on using X, for details. (See Appendix A for information on this book.)

Exiting X

Usually, the last client started in .xinitrc is the one used to shut down X cleanly. For example, if the last command in .xinitrc is

```
exec twm
```

then killing the twm process will result in X shutting down.

However, if you need to immediately kill the X server for some reason, you can use the key combination Ctrl+Alt+Backspace.

Accessing MS-DOS Files

If, for some twisted and bizarre reason, you would have need to access files from MS-DOS, it's quite easily done under Linux.

The usual way to access MS-DOS files is to mount an MS-DOS partition or floppy under Linux, allowing you to access the files directly through the file system. For example, if you have an MS-DOS floppy in /dev/fd0, the command

```
# mount -t msdos /dev/fd0 /mnt
```

will mount it under /mnt. See "Using Floppies as File Systems" in Chapter 4 for more information on mounting floppies.

You can also mount an MS-DOS partition of your hard drive for access under Linux. If you have an MS-DOS partition on /dev/hda1, the command

```
# mount -t msdos /dev/hda1 /mnt
```

will mount it. Be sure to umount the partition when you're done using it. You can have your MS-DOS partitions automatically mounted at boot time if you include entries for them in /etc/fstab. (See "Managing File systems" in Chapter 4 for details.) For example, the following line in /etc/fstab will mount an MS-DOS partition on /dev/hda1 on the directory /dos.

```
/dev/hda1      /dos      msdos      defaults
```

The Mtools software may also be used to access MS-DOS files. For example, the commands mcd, mdir, and mcopy all behave as their MS-DOS counterparts. If you installed Mtools, there should be manual pages available for these commands.

Accessing MS-DOS files is one thing; running MS-DOS programs from Linux is another. There is an MS-DOS Emulator under development for Linux; it is widely available, and even distributed with SLS. It can be retrieved from a number of locations, including the various Linux ftp sites (see Appendix C for details). The MS-DOS Emulator is reportedly powerful enough to run a number of applications, including Wordperfect, from Linux. However, Linux and MS-DOS are vastly different operating systems. The power of any MS-DOS emulator under Unix is somewhat limited.

In addition, work is underway on a Microsoft Windows emulator to run under X Window. Watch the newsgroups and ftp sites for more information.

Networking with TCP/IP

Linux supports a full implementation of the TCP/IP (Transport Control Protocol/Internet Protocol) networking protocols. TCP/IP has become the most successful mechanism for networking computers worldwide. With Linux and an Ethernet card, you can network your machine to a local area network, or (with the proper network connections), to the Internet—the worldwide TCP/IP network.

Hooking up a small LAN of Unix machines is easy. It simply requires an Ethernet controller in each machine and the appropriate Ethernet cables and other hardware. Or, if your business or university provides access to the Internet, you can easily add your Linux machine to this network.

The current implementation of TCP/IP and related protocols for Linux is called *NET-2*. This has no relationship to the so-called NET-2 release of BSD Unix; instead, *NET-2* in this context means the second implementation of TCP/IP for Linux.

Linux NET-2 also supports SLIP—Serial Line Internet Protocol. SLIP allows you to have dial-up Internet access using a modem. If your business or university provides SLIP access, you can dial in to the SLIP server and put your machine on the Internet over the phone line. Alternatively, if your Linux machine also has Ethernet access to the Internet, you can set up your Linux box as a SLIP server.

For complete information on setting up TCP/IP under Linux, we encourage you to read the Linux NET-2 HOWTO, available via anonymous ftp from `sunsite.unc.edu`. The NET-2 HOWTO is a complete guide to configuring TCP/IP, including Ethernet and SLIP connections, under Linux. The Linux Ethernet HOWTO is a related document that describes configuration of various Ethernet card drivers for Linux. The *Linux Network Administrator's Guide*, from the Linux Documentation Project, is also available. See Appendix A for more information on these documents.

Also of interest is the book *TCP/IP Network Administration*, by Craig Hunt. It contains complete information on using and configuring TCP/IP on Unix systems.

Hardware Requirements

You can use Linux TCP/IP without any networking hardware at all—configuring "loopback" mode (loopback is simply a way in which a machine can send network data to itself) allows you to talk to yourself. This is necessary for some applications and games that use the "loopback" network device.

However, if you want to use Linux with an Ethernet TCP/IP network, you need one of the following Ethernet cards:

- 3com 3c503, 3c503/16
- Novell NE1000, NE2000
- Western Digital WD8003, WD8013
- Hewlett Packard HP27245, HP27247, HP27250.

The following clones are reported to work:

- WD-80x3 clones: LANNET LEC-45
- NE2000 clones: Alta Combo, Artisoft LANtastic AE-2, Asante Etherpak 2001/2003, D-Link Ethernet II, LTC E-NET/16 P/N 8300-200-002, Network Solutions HE-203, SVEC 4 Dimension Ethernet, 4-Dimension FD0490 Ether-Board 16, D-Link DE-600, SMC Elite 16.

See the Linux Ethernet HOWTO for a more complete discussion of Linux Ethernet hardware compatibility.

Linux also supports SLIP, which allows you to use a modem to access the Internet over the phone line. In this case, you'll need a modem compatible with your SLIP server—most servers require a 14.4bps V.32bis modem.

Configuring TCP/IP on Your System

In this section we're going to discuss how to configure an Ethernet TCP/IP connection on your system. Note that this method should work for many systems, but certainly not all. This discussion should be enough to get you on the right path to configuring the network parameters of your machine, but there are numerous caveats and fine details not mentioned here. We direct you to the *Linux Network Administrators' Guide* and the NET-2-HOWTO for more information. (Some of the information in this section is adapted from the NET-2-HOWTO by Terry Dawson and Matt Welsh.) First of all, we assume that you have a Linux system that has the TCP/IP software installed. This includes basic clients such as `telnet` and `ftp`, system administration commands such as `ifconfig` and `route` (information found only in /etc), and networking configuration files (such as /etc/hosts). The other Linux-related networking documents described above explain how to go about installing the Linux networking software if you do not have it already.

We also assume that your kernel has been configured and compiled with TCP/IP support enabled. (See "Upgrading and Installing New Software" in Chapter 4. for information on compiling your kernel.) To enable networking, you must answer "yes" to the appropriate questions during the make config step, and rebuild the kernel.

Once this has been done, you must modify a number of configuration files used by NET-2. For the most part this is a simple procedure. Unfortunately, however, there is wide disagreement between Linux distributions as to where the various TCP/IP configuration files and support programs should go. Much of the time, they can be found in /etc, but in other cases may be found in /usr/etc, /usr/etc/inet, or other bizarre locations. In the worst case, you'll have to use the find command to locate the files on your system. Also note that not all distributions keep the NET-2 configuration files and software in the same location—they may be spread across several directories.

The following information applies primarily to Ethernet connections. If you're planning to use SLIP, read this section to understand the concepts, and follow the SLIP-specific instructions in the following section.

Your Network Configuration

Before you can configure TCP/IP, you need to determine the following information about your network setup. In most cases, your local network administrator can provide you with this information.

IP address.   This is the unique machine address in dotted-decimal format. An example is 128.253.153.54. Your network admins will provide you with this number.

If you're only configuring loopback mode (i.e. no SLIP, no Ethernet card, just TCP/IP connections to your own machine), then your IP address is 127.0.0.1.

Your network mask ("netmask").   This is a dotted quad, similar to the IP address, which determines that portion of the IP address specifies the subnetwork number, and which portion specifies the host on that subnet. (If you're shaky on these TCP/IP networking terms, we suggest reading some introductory material on network administration.) The network mask is a pattern of bits, which when overlayed onto an address on your network, will tell you which subnet that address lives on. This is very important for routing, and if you find, for example, that you can happily talk to people outside your network, but not to some people within your network, there is a good chance that you have an incorrect mask specified.

Your network administrators will have chosen the netmask when the network was designed, and therefore they should be able to supply you with the correct mask to use. Most networks are Class C subnetworks which use 255.255.255.0 as their netmask. Other Class B networks use 255.255.0.0. The NET-2 code will automatically select a mask that assumes no subnetting as a default if you do not specify one.

This applies as well to the loopback port. Since the loopback port's address is always 127.0.0.1, the netmask for this port is always 255.0.0.0. You can either specify this explicitly or rely on the default mask.

Your network address.   This is your IP address bitwise-ANDed the netmask. For example, if your netmask is 255.255.255.0, and your IP address is 128.253.154.32, your network address is 128.253.154.0. With a netmask of 255.255.0.0, this would be 128.253.0.0.

If you're only using loopback, you don't have a network address.

Your broadcast address.   The broadcast address is used to broadcast packets to every machine on your subnet. Therefore, if the host number of machines on your subnet is given by the last byte of the IP address (netmask 255.255.255.0), your broadcast address will be your network address ORed with 0.0.0.255.

For example, if your IP address is 128.253.154.32, and your netmask is 255.255.255.0, your broadcast address is 128.253.154.255.

Note that for historical reasons, some networks are set up to use the network address as the broadcast address. If you have any doubt, check with your network administrators. (In many cases, it will suffice to duplicate the network configuration of other machines on your subnet, substituting your own IP address, of course.) If you're only using loopback, you don't have a broadcast address.

Your gateway address.   This is the address of the machine that is your "gateway" to the outside world (i.e. machines not on your subnet). In many cases, the gateway machine has an IP address identical to yours but with a `.1` as its host address (e.g., if your IP address is `128.253.154.32`, your gateway might be `128.253.154.1`). Your network admins will provide you with the IP address of your gateway.

In fact, you may have multiple gateways. A gateway is simply a machine that lives on two different networks (has IP addresses on different subnets), and routes packets between them. Many networks have a single gateway to "the outside world" (the network directly adjacent to your own), but in some cases you will have multiple gateways—one for each adjacent network.

If you're only using loopback, you don't have a gateway address. The same is true if your network is isolated from all others.

Your name server address.   Most machines on the net have a name server that translates hostnames into IP addresses for them. Your network admins will tell you the address of your name server. You can also run a server on your own machine by running `named`, in which case the name server address is `127.0.0.1`. Unless you absolutely must run your own name server, we suggest using the one provided to you on the network (if any). Configuration of `named` is another issue altogether; our priority at this point is to get you talking to the network. You can deal with name resolution issues later. If you're only using loopback, you don't have a name server address.

SLIP users: You may or may not require any of the above information, except for a name server address. When using SLIP, your IP address is usually determined in one of two ways: Either (a) you have a "static" IP address, which is the same every time you connect to the network, or (b) you have a "dynamic" IP address, which is allocated from a pool of available addresses when you connect to the server. This is covered in more detail in the following section on SLIP configuration.

NET-2 supports full routing, multiple routes, subnetworking (at this stage on byte boundaries only)—the whole nine yards. The above describes most basic TCP/IP configurations. Yours may be quite different: when in doubt, consult your local network gurus and check out the man pages for `route` and `ifconfig`. Configuring TCP/IP networks is very much beyond the scope of this book; the above should be enough to get most people started.

The Networking rc Files

rc files are system-wide configuration scripts, executed at boot time by init, which start up all of the basic system daemons (such as sendmail, cron, etc.) and configure things such as the network parameters, system hostname, and so on. rc files are usually found in the directory /etc/rc.d but on other systems may be in /etc.

Here, we're going to describe the rc files used to configure TCP/IP. There are two of them: rc.inet1 and rc.inet2. rc.inet1 is used to configure the basic network parameters (such as IP addresses and routing information) and rc.inet2 fires up the TCP/IP daemons (telnetd, ftpd, and so forth).

Many systems combine these two files into one, usually called rc.inet or rc.net. The names given to your rc files don't matter, as long as they perform the correct functions and are executed at boot time by init. To ensure this, you may need to edit /etc/inittab and uncomment lines to execute the appropriate rc file(s). In the worst case, you will have to create the rc.inet1 and rc.inet2 files from scratch and add entries for them to /etc/inittab.

As we said, rc.inet1 configures the basic network interface. This includes your IP and network address, and the routing table information for your network. The routing tables are used to route outgoing (and incoming) network datagrams to other machines. On most simple configurations, you have three routes: one for sending packets to your own machine, another for sending packets to other machines on your network, and another for sending packets to machines outside of your network (through the gateway machine). Two programs are used to configure these parameters: ifconfig and route. Both of these are usually found in /etc.

ifconfig is used for configuring the network device interface with the parameters that it requires to function, such as the IP address, network mask, broadcast address and the like. route is used to create and modify entries in the routing table.

For most configurations, an rc.inet1 file that looks like the following should work. You will, of course, have to edit this for your own system. Do not use the sample IP and network addresses listed here for your own system; they correspond to an actual machine on the Internet.

```
#!/bin/sh
# This is /etc/rc.d/rc.inet1 - Configure the TCP/IP interfaces

# First, configure the loopback device
```

```
HOSTNAME='hostname'

/etc/ifconfig lo 127.0.0.1        # uses default netmask 255.0.0.0
/etc/route add 127.0.0.1          # a route to point to the loopback device

# Next, configure the ethernet device. If you're only using loopback or
# SLIP, comment out the rest of these lines.

# Edit for your setup.
IPADDR="128.253.154.32"           # REPLACE with YOUR IP address
NETMASK="255.255.255.0"           # REPLACE with YOUR netmask
NETWORK="128.253.154.0"           # REPLACE with YOUR network address
BROADCAST="128.253.154.255"       # REPLACE with YOUR broadcast address, if
# you have one. If not, leave blank and
# edit below.
GATEWAY="128.253.154.1"           # REPLACE with YOUR gateway address!

/etc/ifconfig eth0 ${IPADDR} netmask ${NETMASK} broadcast ${BROADCAST}

# If you don't have a broadcast address, change the above line to just:
# /etc/ifconfig eth0 ${IPADDR} netmask ${NETMASK}

/etc/route add ${NETWORK}

# The following is only necessary if you have a gateway; that is, your
# network is connected to the outside world.
/etc/route add default gw ${GATEWAY} metric 1

# End of Ethernet Configuration
```

Again, you may have to tweak this file somewhat to get it to work. The above should be sufficient for the majority of simple network configurations, but certainly not all.

rc.inet2 starts up various servers used by the TCP/IP suite. The most important of these is inetd. It sits in the background and listens to various network ports. When a machine tries to make a connection to a certain port (for example, the incoming telnet port), inetd forks off a copy of the appropriate daemon for that port (in the case of the telnet port, inetd starts in.telnetd). This is simpler than running many separate, standalone daemons (e.g., individual copies of telnetd, ftpd, and so forth)—inetd starts up the daemons only when they are needed.

syslogd is the system logging daemon—it accumulates log messages from various applications and stores them in log files based on the configuration information in

`/etc/syslogd.conf. routed` is a server used to maintain dynamic routing information. When your system attempts to send packets to another network, it may require additional routing table entries in order to do so. `routed` takes care of manipulating the routing table without the need for user intervention.

Our example `rc.inet2`, below, only starts up the bare minimum of servers. There are many other servers as well—many of which have to do with NFS configuration. When attempting to setup TCP/IP on your system, it's usually best to start with a minimal configuration and add more complex pieces (such as NFS) when you have things working.

Note that in the below file, we assume that all of the network daemons are held in `/etc`. As usual, edit this for your own configuration.

```
#! /bin/sh
# Sample /etc/rc.d/rc.inet2

# Start syslogd
if [ -f /etc/syslogd ]
then
      /etc/syslogd
fi

# Start inetd
if [ -f /etc/inetd ]
then
      /etc/inetd
fi

# Start routed
if [ -f /etc/routed ]
then
      /etc/routed -q
fi

# Done!
```

Among the various additional servers that you may want to start in `rc.inet2` is `named`. `named` is a nameserver—it is responsible for translating (local) IP addresses to names, and vice versa. If you don't have a nameserver elsewhere on the network, or want to provide local machine names to other machines in your domain, it may be necessary to run `named`. (For most configurations it is not necessary, however.)

named configuration is somewhat complex and requires planning; we refer interested readers to a good book on TCP/IP network administration.

/etc/hosts

/etc/hosts contains a list of IP addresses and the hostnames that they correspond to. In general, /etc/hosts only contains entries for your local machine, and perhaps other "important" machines (such as your nameserver or gateway). Your local name server will provide address-to-name mappings for other machines on the network, transparently.

For example, if your machine is loomer.vpizza.com with the IP address 128.253.154.32, your /etc/hosts would look like:

```
127.0.0.1               localhost
128.253.154.32          loomer.vpizza.com loomer
```

If you're only using loopback, the only line in /etc/hosts should be for 127.0.0.1, with both localhost and your hostname after it.

/etc/networks

The /etc/networks file lists the names and addresses of your own, and other, networks. It is used by the route command, and allows you to specify a network by name, should you so desire.

Every network you wish to add a route to using the route command (generally called from rc.inet1—see above) must have an entry in /etc/networks.

example,

```
default 0.0.0.0 # default route - mandatory
loopnet 127.0.0.0 # loopback network - mandatory
mynet 128.253.154.0 # Modify for your own network address
```

/etc/host.conf

This file is used to specify how your system will resolve hostnames.

It should contain the two lines:

```
order hosts,bind
multi on
```

These lines tell the resolve libraries to first check the `/etc/hosts` file for any names to look up, and then ask the name server (if one is present). The `multi` entry allows you to have multiple IP addresses for a given machine name in `/etc/hosts`.

/etc/resolv.conf

This file configures the name resolver, specifying the address of your name server (if any) and your domain name. Your domain name is your fully-qualified hostname (if you're a registered machine on the Internet, for example), with the hostname chopped off. That is, if your full hostname is `loomer.vpizza.com`, your domain name is just `vpizza.com`.

For example, if your machine is `goober.norelco.com`, and has a name server at the address `128.253.154.5`, your `/etc/resolv.conf` would look like:

```
domain      norelco.com
nameserver  127.253.154.5
```

You can specify more than one nameserver—each must have a `name server` line of its own in `resolv.conf`.

Setting Your Hostname

You should set your system hostname with the `hostname` command. This is usually called from `/etc/rc` or `/etc/rc.local`; simply search your system `rc` files to determine where it is invoked. For example, if your (full) hostname is `loomer.vpizza.com`, edit the appropriate `rc` file to execute the command:

```
/bin/hostname loomer.vpizza.com
```

Note that the hostname executable may not be found in `/bin` on your system.

Trying It Out

Once you have all of these files set up, you should be able to reboot your new kernel and attempt to use the network. There are many places where things can go wrong, so it's a good idea to test individual aspects of the network configuration (e.g., it's probably not a good idea to test your network configuration by firing up Mosaic over a network-based X connection).

You can use the `netstat` command to display your routing tables; this is usually the source of the most trouble. The `netstat` manual page describes the exact syntax of this command in detail. In order to test network connectivity, we suggest using a client such as `telnet` to connect to machines both on your local subnetwork and external networks. This will help to narrow down the source of the problem. (For example, if you're unable to connect to local machines, but can connect to machines on other networks, more than likely there is a problem with your netmask and routing table configuration). You can also invoke the `route` command directly (as `root`) to play with the entries in your routing table.

You should also test network connectivity by specifying IP addresses directly, instead of hostnames. For example, if you have problems with the command

```
$ telnet shoop.vpizza.com
```

the cause may be incorrect name server configuration. Try using the actual IP address of the machine in question; if that works, then you know that your basic network setup is (more than likely) correct, and the problem lies in your specification of the name server address.

Debugging network configurations can be a difficult task, and we can't begin to cover it here. If you are unable to get help from a local guru we strongly suggest reading the *Linux Network Administrators' Guide* from the Linux Documentation Project.

SLIP Configuration

SLIP (Serial Line Internet Protocol) allows you to use TCP/IP over a serial line, be that a phone line, with a dialup modem, or a leased asynchronous line of some sort. Of course, to use SLIP you'll need access to a dial-in SLIP server in your area. Many universities and businesses provide SLIP access for a modest fee.

There are two major SLIP-related programs available—`dip` and `slattach`. Both of these programs are used to initiate a SLIP connection over a serial device. It is necessary to use one of these programs in order to enable SLIP—it will not suffice to dial up the SLIP server (with a communications program such as `kermit`) and issue `ifconfig` and `route` commands. This is because `dip` and `slattach` issue a special `ioctl()` system call to seize control of the serial device to be used as a SLIP interface.

dip can be used to dial up a SLIP server, do some handshaking to log in to the server (exchanging your username and password, for example) and then initiate the SLIP connection over the open serial line. slat tach, on the other hand, does very little other than grab the serial device for use by SLIP. It is useful if you have a permanent line to your SLIP server and no modem dialup or handshaking is necessary to initiate the connection. Most dial-up SLIP users should use dip, on the other hand.

dip can also be used to configure your Linux system as a SLIP server, where other machines can dial into your own and connect to the network through a secondary Ethernet connection on your machine. See the documentation and manual pages for dip for more information on this procedure.

SLIP is quite unlike Ethernet, in that there are only two machines on the "network"—the SLIP host (that's you) and the SLIP server. For this reason, SLIP is often referred to as a "point-to-point" connection. A generalization of this idea, known as PPP (Point to Point Protocol) has also been implemented for Linux.

When you initiate a connection to a SLIP server, the SLIP server will give you an IP address based on (usually) one of two methods. Some SLIP servers allocate "static" IP addresses—in which case your IP address will be the same every time you connect to the server. However, many SLIP servers allocate IP addresses dynamically—in which case you receive a different IP address each time you connect. In general, the SLIP server will print the values of your IP and gateway addresses when you connect. dip is capable of reading these values from the output of the SLIP server login session and using them to configure the SLIP device.

Essentially, configuring a SLIP connection is just like configuring for loopback or Ethernet. The main differences are discussed below. Read the previous section on configuring the basic TCP/IP files, and apply the changes described below.

Static IP Address SLIP Connections Using dip

If you are using a static-allocation SLIP server, you may want to include entries for your IP address and hostname in /etc/hosts. Also, configure these files listed in the above section: rc.inet2, host.conf, and resolv.conf.

Also, configure rc.inet1, as described above. However, you only want to execute ifconfig and route commands for the loopback device. If you use dip to connect to the SLIP server, it will execute the appropriate ifconfig and route commands for the SLIP device for you. (If you're using slattach, on the other hand, you will need to include ifconfig/route commands in rc.inet1 for the SLIP device—see below.)

dip should onfigure your routing tables appropriately for the SLIP connection when you connect. In some cases, however, dip's behavior may not be correct for your configuration, and you'll have to run ifconfig or route commands by hand after connecting to the server with dip (this is most easily done from within a shell script that runs dip and immediately executes the appropriate configuration commands). Your gateway is, in most cases, the address of the SLIP server. You may know this address before hand, or the gateway address will be printed by the SLIP server when you connect. Your dip chat script (described below) can obtain this information from the SLIP server.

ifconfig may require use of the pointopoint argument, if dip doesn't configure the interface correctly. For example, if your SLIP server address is 128.253.154.2, and your IP address is 128.253.154.32, you may need to run the command

```
ifconfig sl0 128.253.154.32 pointopoint 128.253.154.2
```

as root, after connecting with dip. The manual pages for ifconfig will come in handy.

Note that SLIP device names used with the ifconfig and route commands are sl0, sl1 and so on (as opposed to eth0, eth1, etc. for Ethernet devices).

In "Using dip," below, we explain how to configure dip to connect to the SLIP server.

Static IP Address SLIP Connections Using slattach

If you have a leased line or cable running directly to your SLIP server, then there is no need to use dip to initiate a connection. slattach can be used to configure the SLIP device instead. In this case, your /etc/rc.inet1 file should look something like the following:

```
#!/bin/sh
IPADDR="128.253.154.32"
# Replace with your IP address REMADDR="128.253.154.2"
# Replace with your SLIP server address
# Modify the following for the appropriate serial device for the SLIP
# connection:
slattach -p cslip -s 19200 /dev/ttyS0
/etc/ifconfig sl0 $IPADDR pointopoint $REMADDR up
/etc/route add default gw $REMADDR
```

slattach allocates the first unallocated SLIP device (sl0, sl1, etc.) to the serial line specified.

Note that the first parameter to slattach -p cslip is the SLIP protocol to use. At present, the only valid values are slip and cslip. slip is regular SLIP, as you would expect, and cslip is SLIP with datagram header compression. In most cases you should use cslip; however, if you seem to be having problems with this, try slip.

If you have more than one SLIP interface then you will have routing considerations to make. You will have to decide what routes to add, and those decisions can only be made on the basis of the actual layout of your network connections. A book on TCP/IP network configuration, as well as the man pages to route, will be of use.

Dynamic IP Address SLIP Connections Using dip

If your SLIP server allocates an IP address dynamically, then you certainly don't know your address in advance—therefore, you can't include an entry for it in /etc/hosts. (You should, however, include an entry for your host with the loopback address, 127.0.0.1.) Many SLIP servers print your IP address (as well as the server's address) when you connect. For example, one type of SLIP server prints a string such as

```
Your IP address is 128.253.154.44.
Server address is 128.253.154.2.
```

dip can capture these numbers from the output of the server and use them to configure the SLIP device.

See "SLIP Configuration," above, for information on configuring your various TCP/IP files for use with SLIP. Below, we explain how to configure dip to connect to the SLIP server.

Using dip

dip can simplify the process of connecting to a SLIP server, logging in, and configuring the SLIP device. Unless you have a leased line running to your SLIP server, dip is the way to go.

To use dip, you'll need to write a *chat script* that contains a list of commands used to communicate with the SLIP server at login time. These commands can automatically send your username/password to the server, as well as get information on your IP address from the server.

Here is an example dip chat script, for use with a dynamic IP address server. For static servers, you will need to set the variables $local and $remote to the values of your local IP address and server IP address, respectively, at the top of the script. See the dip manual page for details.

```
main:
    # Set Maximum Transfer Unit. This is the maximum size of packets
    # transmitted on the SLIP device. Many SLIP servers use either 1500 or
    # 1006; check with your network admins when in doubt.
    get $mtu 1500

    # Make the SLIP route the default route on your system.
    default

    # Set the desired serial port and speed.
    port cua03
    speed 38400

    # Reset the modem and terminal line. If this causes trouble for you,
    # comment it out.
    reset

    # Prepare for dialing. Replace the following with your
    # modem initialization string.
    send ATT&C1&D2\\N3&Q5%M3%C1N1W1L1S48=7\r
    wait OK 2
    if $errlvl != 0 goto error
    # Dial the SLIP server
    dial 2546000
    if $errlvl != 0 goto error
    wait CONNECT 60
    if $errlvl != 0 goto error

    # We are connected. Login to the system.
login:
    sleep 3
    send \r\n\r\n
    # Wait for the login prompt
    wait login: 10
    if $errlvl != 0 goto error
```

```
    # Send your username
    send USERNAME\n

    # Wait for password prompt
    wait ord: 5
    if $errlvl != 0 goto error

    # Send password.
    send PASSWORD\n

    # Wait for SLIP server ready prompt
    wait annex: 30
    if $errlvl != 0 goto error

    # Send commands to SLIP server to initiate connection.
    send slip\n
    wait Annex 30

    # Get the remote IP address from the SLIP server. The 'get... remote'
    # command reads text in the form xxx.xxx.xxx.xxx, and assigns it
    # to the variable given as the second argument (here, $remote).
    get $remote remote
    if $errlvl != 0 goto error
    wait Your 30

    # Get local IP address from SLIP server, assign to variable $local.
    get $local remote
    if $errlvl != 0 goto error

    # Fire up the SLIP connection
done:
    print CONNECTED to $remote at $rmtip
    print GATEWAY address $rmtip
    print LOCAL address $local
    mode SLIP
    goto exit
error:
    print SLIP to $remote failed.

exit:
```

dip automatically executes ifconfig and route commands based on the values of
the variables $local and $remote. Here, those variables are assigned using the
get... remote command, which obtains text from the SLIP server and assigns it to
the named variable.

If the `ifconfig` and `route` commands that `dip` runs for you don't work, you can either run the correct commands in a shell script after executing `dip`, or modify the source for `dip` itself. Running `dip` with the –v option will print debugging information while the connection is being set up, which should help you to determine where things might be going awry.

Now, in order to run `dip` and open the SLIP connection, you can use a command such as

```
/etc/dip/dip -v /etc/dip/mychat 2>&1
```

Where the various `dip` files, and the chat script (`mychat.dip`), are stored in `/etc/dip`.

The above discussion should be enough to get you well on your way to talking to the network, either via Ethernet or SLIP. Again, we strongly suggest looking into a book on TCP/IP network configuration, especially if your network has any special routing considerations other than those mentioned here.

Networking with UUCP

UUCP (Unix-to-Unix Copy) is an older mechanism used to transfer information between Unix systems. Using UUCP, Unix systems dial each other up (using a modem) and transfer mail messages, news articles, files, and so on. If you don't have TCP/IP or SLIP access, you can use UUCP to communicate with the world. Most of the mail and news software (see"Electronic Mail" and "News and Usenet" later in this chapter) can be configured to use UUCP to transfer information to other machines. In fact, if there is an Internet site nearby, you can arrange to have Internet mail sent to your Linux machine via UUCP from that site.

The *Linux Network Administrator's Guide* contains complete information on configuring and using UUCP under Linux. Also, the Linux UUCP HOWTO, available via anonymous ftp from `sunsite.unc.edu`, should be of help. Another source of information on UUCP is the book *Managing UUCP and USENET*, by Tim O'Reilly and Grace Todino. (See Appendix A for more information.)

Electronic Mail

Like most Unix systems, Linux provides a number of software packages for using electronic mail. E-mail on your system can either be local (that is, you only mail other users on your system) or networked (that is, you mail, using either TCP/IP or UUCP, users on other machines on a network). E-mail software usually consists of two parts: a *mailer* and a *transport*. The mailer is the user-level software which is used to actually compose and read e-mail messages. Popular mailers include `elm` and `mailx`. The transport is the low-level software which actually takes care of delivering the mail, either locally or remotely. The user never sees the transport software; they only interact with the mailer. However, as the system administrator, it is important to understand the concepts behind the transport software and how to configure it.

The most popular transport software for Linux is `Smail`. This software is easy to configure, and is able to send both local and remote TCP/IP e-mail. The more powerful `sendmail` transport is used on most Unix systems; however, because of its complicated setup mechanism, most Linux systems don't use it.

The Linux Mail HOWTO gives more information on the available mail software for Linux and how to configure it on your system. If you plan to send mail remotely, you'll need to understand either TCP/IP or UUCP, depending on how your machine is networked (see "Networking with TCP/IP" and "Networking with UUCP" earlier in this chapter). The UUCP and TCP/IP documents listed in Appendix A should be of help there.

Most of the Linux mail software can be retrieved via anonymous ftp from sun-site.unc.edu in the directory /pub/Linux/system/Mail.

News and Usenet

Linux also provides a number of facilities for managing electronic news. You may choose to set up a local news server on your system, which will allow users to post "articles" to various "newsgroups" on the system...a lively form of discussion. However, if you have access to a TCP/IP or UUCP network, then you will be able to participate in Usenet—a worldwide network news service.

There are two parts to news software—the *server* and the *client*. The news server is the software that controls the newsgroups and handles delivering articles to other machines (if you are on a network). The news client, or *newsreader*, is the software that connects to the server to allow users to read and post news.

There are several forms of news servers available for Linux. They all follow the same basic protocols and design. The two primary versions are "C News" and "INN." There are many types of newsreaders, as well, such as rn and tin. The choice of newsreader is more or less a matter of taste; all newsreaders should work equally well with different versions of the server software. That is, the newsreader is independent of the server software, and vice versa.

If you only want to run news locally (that is, not as part of Usenet), then you will need to run a server on your system, as well as install a newsreader for the users. The news server will store the articles in a directory such as /usr/spool/news, and the newsreader will be compiled to look in this directory for news articles.

However, if you wish to run news over the network, there are several options open to you. TCP/IP network-based news uses a protocol known as NNTP (Network News Transmission Protocol). NNTP allows a newsreader to read news over the network, on a remote machine. NNTP also allows news *servers* to send articles to each other over the network—this is the software upon which Usenet is based. Most businesses and universities have one or more NNTP servers set up to handle all of the Usenet news for that site. Every other machine at the site runs an NNTP-based newsreader to read and post news over the network via the NNTP server. This means that only the NNTP server actually stores the news articles on disk.

Here are some possible scenarios for news configuration.

- You run news locally. That is, you have no network connection, or no desire to run news over the network. In this case, you need to run C News or INN on your machine, and install a newsreader to read the news locally.

- You have access to a TCP/IP network and an NNTP server. If your organization has an NNTP news server set up, you can read and post news from your Linux machine by simply installing an NNTP-based newsreader. (Most newsreaders available can be configured to run locally or use NNTP). In this case, you do not need to install a news server or store news articles on your system. The newsreader will take care of reading and posting news over the network.

Of course, you will need to have TCP/IP configured and have access to the network (see "Networking with TCP/IP" earlier in this chapter).

- You have access to a TCP/IP network but have no NNTP server. In this case, you can run an NNTP news server on your Linux system. You can install either a local or an NNTP-based newsreader, and the server will store news articles on your system. In addition, you can configure the server to communicate with other NNTP news servers to transfer news articles.

- You want to transfer news using UUCP. If you have UUCP access (see "Networking with UUCP" earlier in this chapter), you can participate in Usenet as well. You will need to install a (local) news server and a newsreader. In addition, you will need to configure your UUCP software to periodically transfer news articles to another nearby UUCP machine (known as your "news feed"). UUCP does not use NNTP to transfer news; simply, UUCP provides its own mechanism for transferring news articles.

The one downside to most news server and newsreader software is that it must be compiled by hand. Most of the news software does not use configuration files; instead, configuration options are determined at compile time.

Most of the "standard" news software (available via anonymous ftp from `ftp.uu.net` in the directory `/news`) will compile out-of-the-box on Linux. Necessary patches can be found on `sunsite.unc.edu` in `/pub/Linux/system/Mail` (which is, incidentally, also where mail software for Linux is found). Other news binaries for Linux may be found in this directory as well.

For more information, refer to the Linux News HOWTO from `sunsite.unc.edu` in `/pub/Linux/docs/HOWTO`. Also, the Linux Documentation Project's *Linux Network Administrator's Guide* contains complete information on configuring news software for Linux. The book *Managing UUCP and Usenet*, by Tim O'Reilly and Grace Todino, is an excellent guide to setting up UUCP and news software. Also of interest is the Usenet document "How to become a Usenet site," available from `ftp.uu.net`, in the directory `/Usenet/news.announce.newusers`.

APPENDIX

A

Sources of Linux Information

A

This appendix contains information on various sources of Linux information, such as on-line documents, books, and more. Many of these documents are available either in printed form, or electronically from the Internet or BBS systems. Many Linux distributions also include much of this documentation in the distribution itself, so after you have installed Linux these files may be present on your system.

On-Line Documents

These documents should be available on any of the Linux ftp archive sites (see Appendix C for a list). If you do not have direct access to ftp, you may be able to locate these documents on other on-line services (such as CompuServe, local BBSs, and so on). If you have access to Internet mail, you can use the `ftpmail` service to receive these documents. See Appendix C for more information.

In particular, the following documents may be found on `sunsite.unc.edu` in the directory `/pub/Linux/docs`. Many sites mirror this directory; however, if you're unable to locate a mirror site near you, this is a good one to fall back on.

You can also access Linux files and documentation using `gopher`. Just point your `gopher` client to port 70 on `sunsite.unc.edu`, and follow the menus to the Linux archive. This is a good way to browse Linux documentation interactively.

The Linux Frequently Asked Questions List   (or *FAQ*) is a list of common questions and answers about Linux. This document is meant to provide a general source of information about Linux, common problems and solutions, and a list of other sources of information. Every new Linux user should read this document. It is available in a number of formats, including plain ASCII, PostScript, and Lout typesetter format. The Linux FAQ is maintained by Ian Jackson, `ijackson@nyx.cs.du.edu`.

The Linux META-FAQ   is a collection of *metaquestions* about Linux; that is, sources of information about the Linux system, and other general topics. It is a good starting place for the Internet user wishing to find more information about the system. It is maintained by Michael K. Johnson, `johnsonm@sunsite.unc.edu`.

The Linux INFO-SHEET is a technical introduction to the Linux system. It gives an overview of the system's features and available software, and also provides a list of other sources of Linux information. The format and content is similar in nature to the META-FAQ; incidentally, it is also maintained by Michael K. Johnson.

The Linux Software Map is a list of many applications available for Linux, where to get them, who maintains them, and so forth. It is far from complete—to compile a complete list of Linux software would be nearly impossible. However, it does include many of the most popular Linux software packages. If you can't find a particular application to suit your needs, the LSM is a good place to start. It is maintained by Jeff Kopmanis, jeffk@msen.com.

The Linux HOWTO Index is a collection of "how to" documents, each describing in detail a certain aspect of the Linux system. They are maintained by Matt Welsh, mdw@sunsite.unc.edu. The HOWTO Index lists the HOWTO documents which are available (several of which are listed below).

The Linux Installation HOWTO describes how to obtain and install a distribution of Linux. The information is similar to that presented in Chapter 2.

The Linux Distribution HOWTO is a list of Linux distributions available via mail order and anonymous ftp. It also includes information on other Linux-related goodies and services. Appendix B is a condensed version of the list in the Distribution HOWTO.

The Linux XFree86 HOWTO describes how to install and configure the X Window System software for Linux. See "The X Window System" in Chapter 5 for more information.

The Linux Mail, News, and UUCP HOWTOs describe configuration and setup of electronic mail, news, and UUCP communications on a Linux system. Because these three subjects are often intertwined, you may wish to read all three of these HOWTOs together.

The Linux Hardware HOWTO   contains an extensive list of hardware supported by Linux. While this list is far from complete, it should give you a general picture of which hardware devices should be supported by the system.

The Linux SCSI HOWTO   is a complete guide to configuration and usage of SCSI devices under Linux, such as hard drives, tape drives and CD-ROM.

The Linux NET-2-HOWTO   describes installation, setup, and configuration of the "NET-2" TCP/IP software under Linux, including SLIP. If you want to use TCP/IP on your Linux system, this document is a must read.

The Linux Ethernet HOWTO   (closely related to the NET-2-HOWTO) describes the various Ethernet devices supported by Linux, and explains how to configure each of them for use by the Linux TCP/IP software.

The Linux Printing HOWTO   describes how to configure printing software under Linux, such as `lpr`. Configuration of printers and printing software under Unix can be very confusing at times; this document sheds some light on the subject.

Other On-Line documents   If you browse the `docs` subdirectory of any Linux ftp site, you'll see many other documents that are not listed here: a slew of FAQ's, interesting tidbits, and other important information. This miscellany is difficult to categorize here; if you don't see what you're looking for on the list above, just take a look at one of the Linux archive sites listed in Appendix C.

Linux Documentation Project Manuals

The Linux Documentation Project is working on developing a set of manuals and other documentation for Linux, including man pages. These manuals are in various stages of development, and any help revising and updating them is greatly appreciated. If you have questions about the LDP, please contact Matt Welsh (`mdw@sunsite.unc.edu`).

The following books are available via anonymous ftp from a number of Linux archive sites, including `sunsite.unc.edu` in the directory `/pub/Linux/docs/LDP`. A number of commercial distributors are selling printed copies of these books; in the future, you may be able to find the LDP manuals on the shelves of your local bookstore.

Linux Installation and Getting Started, by Matt Welsh   A new user's guide for Linux covering everything the new user needs to know to get started. You hold this book in your hands.

The Linux System Administrators' Guide, by Lars Wirzenius   This is a complete guide to running and configuring a Linux system. There are many issues relating to systems administration that are specific to Linux, such as needs for supporting a user community, filesystem maintenance, backups, and more. This guide covers them all.

The Linux Network Administrators' Guide, by Olaf Kirch   An extensive and complete guide to networking under Linux, including TCP/IP, UUCP, SLIP, and more. This book is a very good read; it contains a wealth of information on many subjects, clarifying the many confusing aspects of network configuration.

The Linux Kernel Hackers' Guide, by Michael Johnson   The gritty details of kernel hacking and development under Linux. Linux is unique in that the complete kernel source is available. This book opens the doors to developers who wish to add or modify features within the kernel. This guide also contains comprehensive coverage of kernel concepts and conventions used by Linux.

Books and Other Published Works

The *Linux Journal* is a monthly magazine for and about the Linux community. It is distributed worldwide, and is an excellent way to keep in touch with the dynamics of the Linux world, especially if you don't have access to Usenet news. See Appendix B for information on subscribing to the *Linux Journal*.

As we have said, not many books have been published dealing with Linux specifically. However, if you are new to the world of Unix, or want more information than is presented here, we suggest that you take a look at the following books.

Using Unix

Title:	*Learning the UNIX Operating System*
Author:	Grace Todino & John Strang
Publisher:	O'Reilly and Associates, 1987
ISBN:	0-937175-16-1

A good introductory book on learning the Unix operating system. Most of the information should be applicable to Linux as well. I suggest reading this book if you're new to Unix and really want to get started with using your new system.

Title:	*Learning the* **vi** *Editor*
Author:	Linda Lamb
Publisher:	O'Reilly and Associates, 1990
ISBN:	0-937175-67-6

This is a book about the vi editor, a powerful text editor found on every Unix system in the world. It's often important to know and be able to use vi, because you won't always have access to a "real" editor such as Emacs.

Systems Administration

Title:	*Essential System Administration*
Author:	Æleen Frisch

Title:	*Essential System Administration*
Publisher:	O'Reilly and Associates, 1991
ISBN:	0-937175-80-3

From the O'Reilly and Associates catalog: "Like any other multi-user system, Unix requires some care and feeding. *Essential System Administration* tells you how. This book strips away the myth and confusion surrounding this important topic and provides a compact, manageable introduction to the tasks faced by anyone responsible for a Unix system." I couldn't have said it better myself.

Title:	*TCP/IP Network Administration*
Author:	Craig Hunt
Publisher:	O'Reilly and Associates, 1990
ISBN:	0-937175-82-X

This is a complete guide to setting up and running a TCP/IP network. While this book is not Linux-specific, roughly 90% of it is applicable to Linux. Along with the *Linux NET 2 HOWTO* and *Linux Network Administrator's Guide*, this is a great book on the concepts and technical details of managing TCP/IP.

Title:	*Managing UUCP and Usenet*
Author:	Tim O'Reilly and Grace Todino
Publisher:	O'Reilly and Associates, 1991
ISBN:	0-937175-93-5

This book covers how to install and configure UUCP networking software, including configuration for Usenet news. If you're at all interested in using UUCP or accessing Usenet news on your system, this book is a mustread.

The X Window System

Title:	*The X Window System: A User's Guide*
Author:	Niall Mansfield
Publisher:	Addison-Wesley
ISBN:	0-201-51341-2

This is a complete tutorial and reference guide to using the X Window System. If you installed X Window on your Linux system, and want to know how to get the most out of it, you should read this book. Unlike some windowing systems, a lot of the power provided by X is not obvious at first sight.

Programming

Title:	*The C Programming Language*
Author:	Brian Kernighan and Dennis Ritchie
Publisher:	Prentice-Hall, 1988
ISBN:	0-13-110362-8

This book is a must have for anyone wishing to do C programming on a Unix system (or any system, for that matter). While this book is not ostensibly Unix-specific, it is quite applicable to programming C under Unix.

Title:	*The Unix Programming Environment*
Author:	Brian Kernighan and Bob Pike
Publisher:	Prentice-Hall, 1984
ISBN:	0-13-937681-X

An overview to programming under the Unix system, this book covers all of the tools of the trade; a good read to get acquainted with the somewhat amorphous Unix programming world.

Title:	*Advanced Programming in the UNIX Environment*
Author:	W. Richard Stevens
Publisher:	Addison-Wesley
ISBN:	0-201-56317-7

This mighty tome contains everything that you need to know to program Unix at the system level—file I/O, process control, interprocess communication, signals, terminal I/O…the works. This book focuses on various Unix standards, including POSIX.1, which Linux mostly adheres to.

Kernel Hacking

Title:	*The Design of the UNIX Operating System*
Author:	Maurice J. Bach
Publisher:	Prentice-Hall, 1986
ISBN:	0-13-201799-7

This book covers the algorithms and internals of the Unix kernel. It is not specific to any particular kernel, although it does lean towards System V-isms. This is the best place to start if you want to understand the inner tickings of the Linux system.

Author:	Berny Goodheart and James Cox
Publisher:	Prentice-Hall, 1994
ISBN:	0-13-098138-9

This recently published book describes the System V R4 kernel in detail. Unlike Bach's book, which concentrates heavily on the algorithms that make the kernel tick, this book presents the SVR4 implementation on a more technical level. Although Linux and SVR4 are distant cousins, this book can give you much insight into the workings of an actual Unix kernel implementation.

APPENDIX

B

Linux Distribution and Mail Order List

This appendix lists a number of the distributions of Linux that are available via anonymous ftp, from BBS systems, and via mail order. It also lists various services available for Linux. If you would like your service or distribution included in this list, please mail the author at mdw@sunsite.unc.edu.

Disclaimer: The author makes no guarantee as to the accuracy of any of the information listed in this appendix. All information is included nearly verbatim from the distributors themselves; it has been edited only for clarity. In addition, the author is not affiliated in any way with any of the distributors listed in this appendix, except for the Debian Linux Association. Inclusion in this appendix does not indicate that the author endorses or supports any of the products or services listed here. This information is included here only as a service to the Linux community, not as an advertisement for any particular organization.

Please note that it is very likely that some of this information will be out of date by the time you read this document. For this reason, the date of the last modification for each entry is given. If an entry appears to be dated, please get in touch with the distributor to receive the latest information.

Linux Software Distributions

Slackware Linux Distribution

Distributor

Patrick Volkerding, volkerdi@mhd1.moorhead.msus.edu.

Description

Slackware Linux is a full-featured distribution of the Linux operating system designed for 386/486 computers with a 3½" floppy. Slackware changes rapidly, but here's a current (partial) feature list:

- **A series (14 disks):** Base Linux 1.0 kernel OS and utilities. Networking, UUCP, gcc/g++ 2.5.8, libc 4.5.24, and more.

- **E series (5 disks):** emacs 19.22.

- **F series (1 disk):** FAQs, HOWTOs, and other documentation.
- **OI series (3 disks):** ObjectBuilder 2.0 for X.
- **X series (5 disks):** Base XFree86 2.1 X Window system with fvwm.
- **XAP series (2 disks):** windows applications such as seyon and ghostview.
- **XD series (3 disks):** X Window program/server development.
- **XV series (2 disks):** XView 3.2 Release 5, Open Look Window Manager.
- **Y series (1 disk):** Games from BSD, such as "hunt."

Availability

The home site is `ftp.cdrom.com`, where the latest distribution can be found in `/pub/linux/slackware`. To make it easy to download, the disks can also be found pre-zooed in `/pub/linux/zooed_slackware`. (Zoo is just a compression utility for MS-DOS).

Ordering

ftp only, although various independent distributors provide it on disk, floppy, and CD.

Entry Last Modified

November 5, 1993.

NOTE

From the Editor: Slackware is the distribution of Linux on the CD that comes with The Complete Linux Kit (Sybex, 1995). This distribution of Slackware is current as of March, 1995.

MCC Interim Linux

The current MCC-Interim release is based on 0.99.pl10, which is quite robust. If you are one of those people who demands to be on top of the current release, you'll need to upgrade your kernel (this is easy to do) and possibly your version of `gcc` and libraries. However, I see no reason why 0.99.pl10 shouldn't be good enough, at least to get you started.

Distributor

Dr. A. V. Le Blanc, `LeBlanc@mcc.ac.uk`.

Description

Base Linux installation. Complete sources and patches for all included software are available. Full details vary from release to release; see `/pub/linux/mcc-interim/*/Acknowledegments` at `ftp.mcc.ac.uk`. Roughly, this includes the kernel (with source), C, C++, `groff`, man pages, basic utilities, and networking. The binaries fit on six or seven floppies. It is also possible to have them on a DOS or Linux partition on a hard drive (plus one floppy) or on an NFS-mountable partition (plus two floppies). New versions appear at two to three month intervals, depending on various factors.

Availability

By anonymous ftp from `ftp.mcc.ac.uk`; mirrored at `tsx-11.mit.edu`, `nic.funet.fi`, and elsewhere. At `ftp.mcc.ac.uk`, in `/pub/linux/mcc-interim`.

Miscellaneous

Suggestions and contributions are welcome.

Entry Last Modified

October 31, 1993.

TAMU Linux Distribution

Distributor

Dave Safford, Texas A&M University, `dave.safford@net.tamu.edu`.

Description

TAMU.99p12+ is the latest release in the TAMU Linux series. Unlike previous releases, this one includes both integrated source and binary sets, with the entire binary set created from a single top level source make. This ensures that all programs are compiled and linked with the same current tools and libraries, and guarantees availability of working source for every program in the binary set. In addition, the new boot diskette fully automates the installation process, including partitioning, lilo bootstrapping, and network configuration. Installation requires no rebooting, and requires the user to know only the host's name and IP address. At every step of installation, the program provides intelligent defaults, making it a snap for novices, while allowing experts full flexibility in setting installation parameters. Reliability has been improved over past TAMU installation by the use of labels on all disk images, so that the program can detect and recover from bad or misordered diskettes.

This release is a full-featured package, including XFree86-1.3, `emacs`-19.18, net-2, bootutils, and sources for all installation programs (without any use restrictions :-).

Availability

The most recent TAMU release is available by anonymous ftp from `net.tamu.edu:pub/linux`.

Entry Last Modified

October 31, 1993.

Linux Support Team Erlangen Distribution (LST)

Distributor

The Linux Support Team Erlangen, a small group of students at the University of Erlangen-Nuernberg. Contact Stefan Probst, `snprobst@cip.informatik.uni-erlangen.de`, or Ralf Flaxa, `rfflaxa@informatik.uni-erlangen.de`. There will probably be a collective address soon.

Description

The LST distribution's goal is to provide a solid, reliable, easy to install (even for beginners), and well-documented system. We are not hunting for the newest kernel or `gcc` versions. We do updates when they are necessary or provide really new functionality, and when they are well tested, integrated in the system, and working smoothly with the rest of the system. The distribution consists of a base system and additional packages. Currently, the following packages are available: doku , (doc), text, tex, develop, xdevelop, xbasis, xappl, xemacs, tinyx, network, grafik, src, misc.

The complete system consists of 50 high-density disks and 1500 pages of printed documentation, including the LDP guides (IGS, KHG, NAG), HOWTOs, FAQs, the German *Linuxhandbuch*, installation guide, and many other useful documents we've collected over time.

Our distribution is preconfigured for German users and comes with a 50-page step-by-step installation guide that leads you through the menu-driven installation scripts (both in German). We started this distribution to help newcomers with their first steps into Linux. Therefore, our scripts are smart enough to handle all of the "dirty work" like setting up system configuration (including LILO, modem, mouse, mounts, mtools, access to DOS, users, X11) and network configuration (TCP/IP, Routing, Mail, News, UUCP, SLIP).

Historically, most of the documentation for this distribution is written in German. We are planning to translate these documents into English, but at the moment we don't have time for this. Any volunteers are welcome! Our scripts also accept to install SLS and Slackware packages, but with no warranty if they work well together with the rest of the system.

Availability

Via anonymous ftp: ftp.uni-erlangen.de under pub/Linux/LST.Distribution, or on 3½" disks (also on one QIC-80 tape).

Ordering

Order from the following address:

>Stefan Probst
>In der Reuth 200
>91056 Erlangen
>Germany

Complete documentation (IGS, LHB, KHG, GDB, NAG, HOWTOs, FAQs, installation Guide) is over 1500 pages altogether for DM 139 (plus shipping).

Complete documentation plus complete distribution on QIC-80 tape (about 65 MB) for DM 199 (including shipping in Germany).

Complete documentation plus complete distribution on about 50 3½" disks for DM 269 (including shipping in Germany).

Entry Last Modified

February 21, 1993

S.u.S.E. GmbH German Linux CD-ROM

Distributor

S.u.S.E. GmbH
Gebhardtstr. 2
90762 Fuerth
Germany

Description

This is a CD especially for German users. It contains a German version of the Slackware distribution and two additional German distributions based on Slackware and SLS. It contains additional software, such as the Postgres system, the pbm-Tools and lots of other tools and utilities (ctwm window manager, GREAT environment, andrew toolkit, the POV-ray raytracer, and so on). The source code for the complete system is included, too, as is a live system to enable using software without the need to install everything on the hard drive. The current version of the CD contains version 1.2.0 of the Slackware distribution containing Version 1.0 of the Linux kernel, version 2.5.8 of the GNU-Compiler, and XFree86tm 2.1.

A German installation guide will help new users to successfully install the system.

The CD is updated every three months.

Ordering

You can order by mail, by phone (49-911-74053-31), by fax (49-911-7417755), or by sending e-mail to `bestellung@suse.de`.

Price The price for a single CD is DM 89 for new customers. If you are already an S.u.S.E.customer, you will get the CD for an update-price of DM 78. You may also subscribe for one year to receive four CDs for the price of DM 230.

Disks The German version of the Slackware distribution on 3½" disks. You can get either a basic version of the distribution (about 28 disks) for DM 89, the "standard" version (about 38 disks) for DM 119, or the "full" version (about 59 disks) for DM 159. The update prices are DM 69, DM 94, and DM 139, respectively.

Documentation S.u.S.E. is selling high-quality printed issues of the books from the Linux Documentation Project (LDP) for people who would like to have a real book rather than printed loose papers. The prices are DM 24 for Matt Welsh's *Linux Installation and Getting Started*, DM 39 for Olaf Kirch's *Network Administrators' Guide* and DM 29 for Michael K. Johnson's *Kernel Hackers' Guide*. S.u.S.E. also offers the complete O'Reilly series, which is the best documentation available for Unix in general. You can also order these well-known German Linux books: *Deutsches Anwenderhandbuch* (for DM 49) and *Linux-vom PC zur Workstation* (for DM 38).

Motif Metrolink Motif for Linux is available for DM 169 for the run-time system only. For DM 288, you can get the run-time and development system.

Miscellaneous

Service and support for our customers via e-mail, fax, snail mail and phone (hot line Monday and Thursday from 13:00–17:00).

Free information and catalogues of CD-ROMs and books. (All Infomagic Unix CDs are available.)

Commercial software for Linux.

Individual software for Linux and other Unix systems.

Almost anything concerning Linux—just ask!

Entry Last Modified

May 23, 1994

Debian Linux Distribution

Distributor

Ian A. Murdock, `imurdock@gnu.ai.mit.edu`.

Description

For those of you who are not familiar with Debian, it is an effort to create a well thought-out, powerful, flexible yet complete Linux distribution. The motivations behind Debian are detailed in the Debian Manifesto.

For up-to-date information, please look at the files in the directory `/pub/Linux/distributions/debian/info` at `sunsite.unc.edu`. If you do not have access to the Internet or ftp, you may obtain printed copies by sending a self-addressed, stamped envelope to:

> The Debian Linux Association
> Station 11
> P.O. Box 3121
> West Lafayette, IN 47906
> USA

This information includes how Debian can be obtained (via ftp or mail order), why Debian is being constructed (the Manifesto) and other general information, including how to join the Debian mailing lists.

Availability

Debian has not yet been "officially" released, but beta releases are available to the general public at `sunsite.unc.edu` in the directory `/pub/Linux/distributions/debian`.

Entry Last Modified

February 21, 1994.

Yggdrasil Plug-and-Play Linux CD-ROM and the Linux Bible

Distributor

Yggdrasil Computing, Incorporated
4880 Stevens Creek Blvd., Suite 205
San Jose, CA 95129-1034

Tel: (408) 261-6630
Toll free: (800) 261-6630
Fax: (408) 261-6631info@yggdrasil.com

Description

Yggdrasil Plug-and-Play Linux is a complete CD-ROM distribution of the Linux operating system. It includes a great deal of software—nearly every package that you would expect to find on a complete Unix system is available. A complete file list is available via ftp from yggdrasil.com.

The Linux Bible is a compendium of Linux documentation, including three books from the Linux Documentation Project, the Yggdrasil installation manual, and the complete set of Linux HOWTO guides.

Programmers who want to explore or add the occasional feature know that Yggdrasil is at the top of the sophistication hierarchy—it's the Linux distribution with a fully buildable source tree and the ability to automatically trace installed files back to their sources.

Users who want maximum performance will appreciate that the major system components have been recompiled with -06 optimization, and the SCSI clustering reduces the build time on the source tree from 28 to 22 hours (over 20%) on 486DX2-66. Using IDE? Activate the multisector IDE code!

Everybody, especially new users, will appreciate the Plug-and-Play operation for which Yggdrasil's product is named. Put the media in a computer with supported hardware, turn the computer on, and it runs everything straight from the CD-ROM.

The login screen lists a number of preconfigured user names, including "install," which installs the system, giving paragraphs of explanation about every question that it asks the user. The install script even searches for a modem, and upon finding it, configures mail and UUCP so that mail sent to an internet address is transparently delivered through a bulletin board system at Yggdrasil.

X Window configuration is automated too, prompting the user for configuration information the first time `xinit` is run.

From X Window, a graphical control panel allows simple "fill in the blanks" configuration of networking, SLIP, outgoing UUCP, the printer, NNTP, and many other features that previously required the knowledge of a system administrator to configure.

For more information, send mail to `info@yggdrasil.com`, ftp to `yggdrasil.com`, or contact us by any convenient method.

Ordering

Plug-and-Play Linux costs $39.95 and is available directly from Yggdrasil or from your local computer, software, or technical bookstore. If Plug-and-Play Linux is not available from your favorite reseller, help promote Linux by making it your mission to change that. Give your reseller our phone number and demand that they carry Plug-and-Play Linux.

Yggdrasil offers a $10 discount for upgrades or crossgrades. Send us your old Yggdrasil release and a check for $29.95 plus $5 shipping and handling to upgrade. Or do the same, but send us a competing distribution such as any version of SCO, Esix, Minix, or one of the CDs with the slackware floppy images, and tell us where you got it, so that we can make sure your favorite reseller carries our products, too.

Miscellaneous

Yggdrasil also sells OSF/Motif and *The Linux Bible*, a compilation of works from the Linux Documentation Project. In addition to a copy of the Plug-and-Play Linux manual, *The Linux Bible* includes *Linux Installation and Getting Started, Network Administrator's Guide, Kernel Hacker's Guide*, and HOWTO guides on hardware compatibility, distributions, DOS emulation, Ethernet, floppy tape, installation, mail, networking version 2, MGR (an alternative to X Window), X Window, Usenet news, printing, SCSI, serial communications, sound, and UUCP. *The Linux Bible* costs $39.95 and is printed on recycled paper. $1 from every copy sold is donated to the Linux Documentation Project. OSF/Motif costs $149.95, $5 of which is donated to the development of a free Motif clone.

Entry Last Modified

May 16, 1994

Linux from Nascent CD-ROM

Distributor

Nascent Technology

Description

The Linux from Nascent CD-ROM is a new distribution of the Linux operating system that includes over 400 MB of source code, binaries, and documentation for Linux and applications. It features automated root, swap, package, network, and user account installation from CD-ROM. Linux can be run directly from the CD-ROM and a floppy. The Nascent CD-ROM features X Window, Openlook, TEX, GNU compiler and utilities, Magic and Spice electronic design tools, and over 100 high-resolution images translated from Kodak PhotoCD™. Each source archive is distributed with an associated notes file to allow you to browse and install applications using a consistent interface.

A listing of the contents of the Nascent CD-ROM as well as a current copy of the CD-ROM announcement and order form may be obtained via anonymous ftp at `netcom.com:/pub/nascent`.

Ordering

The Linux from Nascent CD-ROM, Version 1.0, is only $39.95 plus shipping and handling. Nascent also offers the Linux from Nascent Plus package for only $89.95, which includes six months of e-mail support and a 30% discount off a future release of the CD-ROM with your CD-ROM purchase. Nascent accepts Mastercard, Visa, checks, and money orders as payment.

To order your Linux from Nascent CD-ROM, mail, e-mail, or fax a completed order form to:

Nascent Technology
Linux from Nascent CD-ROM
P.O. Box 60669

Sunnyvale, CA 94088-0669

Tel: (408) 737-9500
Fax: (408) 241-9390
E-mail: nascent@netcom.com

Entry Last Modified

November 28, 1993.

Unifix 1.02 CD-ROM

Distributor

Unifix Software GmbH, Braunschweig, Germany

Description

This is a Linux CD-ROM distribution with emphasis on easy and fast installation. Though it is possible to install everything on the hard disk, we do not recommend doing so, because it runs fast enough directly from CD. For example, starting emacs the first time (in text mode) takes:

From single speed Mitsumi: 24 s

From double speed Mitsumi: 11 s

From Toshiba 3401: 7 s

Linux's dynamic buffer cache takes care of the second and subsequent times a program is started, which takes less than one second.

Our system requires about 5 MB on the hard disk for configuration files and system management tools. Additionally, we recommend a 16 MB swap partition. The distribution contains most of the standard programs in current versions (e.g. Linux 0.99.15e, XFree 2.0, emacs 19.22 and gcc 2.5.7). Full preconfigured source for everything is included.

Because Unifix is a European distribution, it provides full support for iso8859-1 character sets. From the shells and emacs through ls, TEX, and the print system, everything supports 8-bit characters.

Printing is supported through System V-compatible printer drivers, which can be controlled through lp's -o options. Printer drivers are included for dumb text mode printers, for postscript- or ghostscript- compatible printers, and for networked printing. These drivers know how to guess the type of file so, for example, compressed manual pages or DVI files can be printed directly.

Ordering

Unifix is available only on CD. It comes in a Unifix/Linux binder with two boot floppies and about 70 pages of installation instructions in German. An English version will be available April 19, 1994. The price is DM 159 (about $100) and includes taxes and shipping; Eurocard/MasterCard/Visa are accepted.

> Unifix Software GmbH
> Postfach 4918
> D-38039 Braunschweig
> Germany
>
> Tel: +49 (0)531 515161
> Fax: +49 (0)531 515162

Entry Last Modified

February 18, 1994.

Redistributors and Miscellany

This section lists resellers or redistributors of the Linux distributions listed above. In other words, the people selling the software below more than likely do *not* maintain or support the software itself.

This section also lists distributors selling commercial software for Linux, such as Motif, and miscellany, such as documentation.

Clark Internet Services

Distributor

Clark Internet Services, c/o Stephen Balbach

Description

The latest version of Linux on disk and tape direct from the net at affordable prices. 120 MB installed on 3½" disks. 90 MB installed on 5¼" disks.

Ordering

Slackware on 32 3½" disks costs $50 (USPS 2nd day). SLS on 32 5¼" disks costs $40 (USPS 2nd day).

Linux Installation and Getting Started © Copyright Matt Welsh is a 150+ page laser printed, professionally bound manual. It's everything you need to get Linux installed and running in one easy book. The set costs $15 (at cost price!); the book alone, $20.

Availability

For more complete information, including a multipage description of Linux, a hardware compatibility sheet, and more detailed package descriptions, send mail to linux-all@clark.net for auto-reply information (30 K of text).

Ordering

Send check or money order to:

    Stephen Balbach
    5437 Enberend Terrace
    Columbia, MD 21045

To order by credit card, call (410) 740-1157 (Visa, MasterCard, and American Express accepted).

Entry Last Modified

October 31, 1993.

Extent Verlag, LDP Distribution

Distributor

Extent Verlag Berlin, Berlin, Germany

Description

Extent has published the *Linux Installation and Getting Started* manual, Version 2.0 by Matt Welsh in order to make it available to Linux users within Germany and Europe. In spite of being noncommercial, the manual was printed with 2540 dpi and bound in soft cover. Its handy paperback format is 148 x 210 mm. Other Linux Documentation Project manuals are being prepared as soon as possible.

Extent also tries to make Slackware available to anybody within Germany and Europe for the ordinary diskette price. This means you pay only for the diskettes and get the newest Slackware distribution for free, just in the sense of Free Software. The 3.5″ diskettes are fully error-checked, of course.

Availability

For information on availability, contact:

Extent Verlag Berlin
Postfach 12 66 48
D-10594 Berlin, Germany

Tel: +49 30 3244021
Fax: +49 30 3249685

Ordering

Send a check to the address above, or a money order to:

Extent Verlag Berlin
Germany Postbank Berlin
BLZ 10010010
bank account 1769-104

(Don't forget to include your address!)

Linux Installation and Getting Started, 192 pages. ISBN 3-926671-12-2. Cost is DM 15.80 (tax and shipping included) within Germany, DM 16.50 (shipping included) within Europe.

Full Slackware (latest version) on 50 diskettes. Cost is DM 100 plus DM 10 for shipping within Germany, DM 100 plus DM 20 for shipping within Europe.

Entry Last Modified

March 25, 1994.

Fintronic Linux Systems

Distributor

Fintronic Linux Systems

Description

We sell fully installed, custom configured Linux systems for about the price you'd pay for the hardware alone. We also offer desktop and notebook machines. We ship worldwide and accept payment by check and credit cards. If you have any questions or would like to be added to our mailing list, send mail to `linux@fintronic.com`.

Availability

For our latest pricelist, finger `linux@fintronic.com` or web to `http://www.fintronic.com/linux/catalog.html`. Prices change frequently, as we are constantly looking for the best deals for our customers.

Ordering

Fintronic USA, Inc.
1360 Willow Rd., Suite 205
Menlo Park, CA 94025
USA

E-mail: `linux@fintronic.com`
Fax: (415) 325-4908
Voice-mail: (415) 325-4474

Entry Last Modified

March 24, 1994.

InfoMagic Developer's Resource CD-ROM Kit

Distributor

InfoMagic, Inc.

Description

The InfoMagic Linux Developer's Resource is a complete snapshot of the `sunsite.unc.edu` and `tsx-11.mit.edu` archives. It also includes the complete GNU software collection (in source form). The following Linux "distributions" are included on the disks: Slackware, Debian, SLS, TAMU, MCC, and JE (Japanese Extensions).

The Slackware distribution has been completely unpacked, allowing many packages to be run directly from the disk. Sources for all the packages in Slackware are also included.

The Linux HOWTO documents have been formatted for use with the Microsoft Multimedia Viewer (which is included) to allow browsing and full-text search under Microsoft Windows.

Availability

InfoMagic, Inc.
PO Box 30370
Flagstaff, AZ 86003-0370

Tel: 800-800-6613 (within the US)/602-526-9565
Fax: 602-526-9573
E-mail: `Orders@InfoMagic.com`

Ordering

The 2-CD set is $20/copy. Shipping within the U.S. is $5 (USPS Priority Mail), outside the U.S. $10 (International Airmail). FedEx and UPS on request. Orders may be placed via phone, fax, or e-mail (a PGP key is available: finger `orders@Info Magic.com`).

We accept Visa, MasterCard, and American Express. One-year subscriptions are available for $125 within the U.S., and $135 outside the U.S., including shipping. A one year subscription consists of six releases, one every two months.

Miscellaneous

The contents of the CDs may be found at either: `InfoMagic.com:/pub/Linux` or `ftp.uu.net:/vendor/InfoMagic/cd-roms/linux`.

This 2-CD set is updated every two months. Please call for the latest information on contents, availability, and pricing.

Entry Last Modified

July 10, 1994.

Lasermoon Ltd.

Distributor

Lasermoon Ltd., `info@lasermoon.co.uk`, `support@lasermoon.co.uk`.

Description

The following Linux products are distributed and supported, (although there are many more of interest).

- The Yggdrasil LGX CD-ROM
- The Infomagic Linux Developer Resource CD-ROM
- The *Linux Journal* (Monthly Mag), European Distributors

Availability

Lasermoon Ltd,
2a Beaconsfield Road,
Fareham,
Hants,
England,

PO16 0QB
Voice: +44 (0) 329 826444
Fax: +44 (0) 329 825936

E-mail: info@lasermoon.co.uk (general inquiries), support@laser moon.co.uk (support desk), lj@lasermoon.co.uk (Linux Journal desk).

Ordering

LGX currently £44.95, LDR currently £12.95.

All prices exclude postage and VAT at the UK rate (17.5%). Discounts available—please call. Visa, MasterCard, Access, and EuroCard accepted.

Miscellaneous

We provide snapshots of any part of any product on (almost) any media. Call us for details.

Free catalogue of many other CD-ROM freeware products for Unix, DOS and Novell available on request (either by e-mail or post). Books by SSC and O'Reilly Associates.

Entry Last Modified

Feb 16, 1994.

Linux Journal

Publisher

Linux Journal
P.O. Box 85867
Seattle, WA 98145-1867

Tel: (206) 527-3385 (subscriptions) or (206) 524-8338 (advertising).
Fax: (206) 527-2806 (subscriptions) or (206) 526-0803 (advertising).

Description

Linux Journal is a monthly publication covering the Linux Community. Most material in *LJ* is new (not reprinted from Usenet). Each issue includes columns and articles on

Linux programming, Free Software Foundation issues, systems administration, Questions and Answers, interviews, and more. *LJ* is a professional-quality magazine for the Linux community.

Availability

Subscriptions are $19/year (U.S.), $24/year (Canada/Mexico), $29/year (elsewhere).

Ordering

Payment can be made by VISA, MasterCard or American Express (make sure you include the credit card number, expiration date and signature). We can also accept checks in native currency. If you have a question concerning appropriate method of payment, phone or fax our subscription numbers or send e-mail to `subs@ssc.com`. For security reasons, we discourage sending credit card numbers via e-mail.

Miscellaneous

If you are interested in advertising in *LJ*, contact Joanne Wagner by phone or e-mail at `joanne@fylz.com`. Article queries, new product announcements and other editorial material should be sent to our address above or e-mailed to `liedtor@sunsite.unc.edu`. Generic questions can be sent to `linux@fylz.com`.

Entry Last Modified

May 26, 1994.

The Linux Quarterly CD-ROM

Distributor

Morse Telecommunication, Inc.

Description

The Linux Quarterly CD-ROM contains the complete contents of `tsx-11.mit.edu`, one of the most popular Internet Linux sites. It provides both source and binaries of major Linux distributions, utilities, source code, and documentation. This includes

Slackware, SLS, MCC, and Debian releases of Linux. Additionally, beginning with the Spring 1994 edition, the complete contents of `prep.ai.mit.edu`, the repository of the FSF's GNU source archives, is included. For first-time users, this CD-ROM contains a Microsoft Windows™ front-end to assist the user in creating boot disks that can be used to install Linux directly from The Linux Quarterly CD-ROM. Support for the UMS DOS filesystem is now also available. This gives the user the ability to install Linux directly to an MS-DOS system without having to repartition their hard drive. 90 days of technical support is provided with each disc at no additional charge.

Availability

Morse Telecommunication, Inc.
26 East Park Avenue, Suite 240
Long Beach, NY 11561

Tel orders: (800) 60-MORSE

Tech support: (516) 889-8610 Fax: (516) 889-8665

E-mail Orders: `Order@morse.net`

E-mail information: `Linux@morse.net`

Hours: 9 AM to 5 PM EST, Monday through Friday. Fax available 24 hours.

Ordering

Orders may be placed via phone, fax, or e-mail as listed above. The Linux Quarterly CD-ROM is priced at $29.95 plus $5 shipping and handling per order. Existing customers may upgrade for $22.95 plus shipping and handling. All orders generally ship the same day if received by 4 PM EST.

Miscellaneous

The contents of the CD-ROM, the cover artwork in JPEG format, and the text of the Usenet announcement can be found on the following ftp sites:

```
tsx-11.mit.edu:/pub/linux/advertisements/TLQ-Spring94.tar.z
sunsite.unc.edu:/pub/Linux/distributions/cdrom/TLQ-Spring94.tar.z
```

Entry Last Modified

May 23, 1994

Linux Systems Labs

Distributor

Linux Systems Labs, `dirvin@vela.acs.oakland.edu`.

Description

We sell Slackware (all 50 disks and I&GS) for $69.95(updated weekly), and resell the Yggdrasil CD-ROM. Motif by Metrolink is available for $175.00, and you may bundle any version of Linux with Motif (version 1.2.4) for $215.00. We currently print Linux Documentation Project documents on a 600 DPI Duplexed on a laser printer.

We have begun publishing *The Linux Bible: The GNU Testament*, Spring Quarterly Edition, which includes *Linux Installation and Getting Started*, the *Yggdrasil Plug-and-Play Linux Manual: Summer 1994*, *The Linux Network Administrators' Guide* by Olaf Kirch, *The Kernel Hackers' Guide* by Michael K. Johnson, and the following HOW-TOS: distribution, DOSEMU, Ethernet, ftape, installation, mail, mgr, net-2, news, printing, SCSI, serial, sound, UUCP, and XFree86.

We also just started selling a commercial database called `/rdb` for Linux by Revolutionary Software for $149.00. (It's quite impressive.) Contact us for more information.

Availability

Linux Systems Labs
18300 Tara Drive
Clinton Township MI 48036

Tel: (313) 954-2829,
Toll Free: (800) 432-0556
Fax: (313) 954-2806

Ordering

See prices above. We take MasterCard and Visa and will discount all products (except `/rdb`) 20% for internet customers.

Entry Last Modified

May 11, 1994.

Mark Horton Linux
Documentation Hardcopy Service

Distributor

Mark Horton Associates, mah@ka4ybr.atl.ga.us.

Description

The Linux Hardcopy Service provides printed, punched, and bound copies of the various Linux Documentation Project manuals, FAQs, HOWTOs and other related publications. The goal is to provide both new and experienced Linux users with laser printed, high quality documentation. This is particularly useful to new users without access to ftp or the facilities required to print .dvi format, TEX, or PostScript files.

Availability

Mark Horton Associates
P.O. Box 747
Decatur, GA 30031

Tel: (404) 371-0291
E-mail: mah@ka4ybr.atl.ga.us

Ordering

Please e-mail mah@ka4ybr.atl.ga.us for complete information; only prices are given here.

Linux Installation and Getting Started, 150 pages, $20.00

Linux Network Administrators' Guide, 250 pages, $30.00

Linux Kernel Hackers' Guide, 120 pages, $20.00

Das LinuxXHandBuch, 250 pages, $30.00

LILO Technical Overview and User's Guide, 35 pages, $10.00

FAQs and HOWTOS, 250 pages, $30.00

Shells, shells, shells (man pages), 100 pages, $15.00

If you want any other documentation printed, make a request, I'll print a copy, look it over, and provide a price. If it's of general interest I'll offer additional copies. (Somehow I feel like I just committed to ending up with a *lot* of printed documentation on my shelves!) I can't take credit cards (you wouldn't believe what the bank wants to process those things!) Personal checks, money orders, and cash are all okay. I'll accept purchase orders from very large businesses and educational sites. Please add $2.00 per manual for UPS ground shipping. Add an additional $10.00 for UPS blue label. Special overnight shipping can be arranged upon request. Call for quantity discount pricing.

$1.00 per manual sale goes to the Free Software Foundation. $1.00 per manual sale goes to Linus and the Linux Documentation Project's virtual beer fund.

Please make checks payable to Mark Horton Associates at the address above.

Miscellaneous

Custom t-shirts available on request—send e-mail.

Entry Last Modified

January 15, 1994

Sequoia International Motif Development Package

Distributor

Sequoia International, Inc.
600 West Hillsboro Blvd, Suite 300
Deerfield Beach, FL 33441

Tel: (305) 480-6118,
Fax: (305) 480-6198
E-mail: info@seq.com

Description

Sequoia International, Inc. has a complete Motif 1.2.3 run-time and development package called SWiM 1.2.3 available for $149.95. In addition to providing shared library versions of libXm and libMrm, the following is included in each package: The Window Manager (mwm), shared libraries (libXm, libMrm), static libraries (libXm, libMrm, libUil), UIL compiler, header and include files, complete on-line manual pages, source code to OSF/Motif demo programs, and complete *OSF/Motif Users Guide*.

Requirements

Linux 0.99pl13 or higher, libc 4.4.4, XFree 2.0, 12 MB free disk, 8-12 MB RAM suggested.

Ordering

USA: Sequoia International, Inc. (305) 480-6118, info@seq.com.
Japan: Fortune Co., Ltd. (03-5481-8974).
England: Lasermoon Ltd. (+44-0-329-826444).
Australia: Space Age Import-Export Proprietary (61-7-266-3418).

Entry Last Modified

March 24, 1994.

SSC Linux Documentation Project Manuals

Distributor

SSC, Inc., sales@ssc.com.

Availability

SSC has printed the *Linux Installation and Getting Started* manual, Version 2.1, to make it available for those who do not have the capability to print it themselves, and to support our customers who buy Linux (Yggdrasil) from us. It is printed double-sided, perfect-bound, and with a cover. SSC also intends to make comb-bound versions of the other Linux Documentation Project manuals available.

Ordering

Linux Installation and Getting Started, Version 2.1, is available for $12.95 plus shipping ($3 in the U.S.). We can accept credit card orders (Visa, MasterCard or American Express). Mail, phone, or fax your order to:

SSC
P.O. Box 55549
Seattle, WA 98155

Tel: (206)-FOR-Unix/(206) 527-3385
Fax: (206) 527-2806

Miscellaneous

SSC also publishes a series of reference cards on Unix and Unix-related programs such as emacs, VI, Korn Shell, C language, etc. SSC also sells the Yggdrasil, Trans-Ameritech, and Morse Linux distributions, Free Software Foundation books, and a complete Linux package consisting of *Linux Installation and Getting Started*, a printed copy of the Linux HOWTOS, four SSC Pocket References, and a one-year subscription to *Linux Journal* for $88.95. Call or e-mail sales@ssc.com for a free catalog.

Entry Last Modified

June 26, 1994.

SW Technology Linux Systems

Distributor

SW Technology

Description

SW Technology has been selling Linux workstations locally with high customer satisfaction. Our installation of Linux follows the style of the Slackware distribution, with system specific kernel image and configuration files to ensure optimal performance. The installation is a fairly complete distribution of available Linux utilities, including gcc, X, Interviews, Xview, Tcl/Tk, emacs, TeX/LaTeX, Groff, etc.

We custom configure systems: our clients will get the hardware components and software configuration per their specification.

Availability

For up-to-date prices and information, contact:

SW Technology
251 West Renner, Suite 229
Richardson, TX 75080

Tel: (214) 907-0871
E-mail/finger: swt@netcom.com
Anonymous ftp: netcom8.netcom.com:/pub/swt/info

Entry Last Modified

January 15, 1994.

Takelap Systems Ltd.

Distributor

Takelap Systems Ltd., info@ddrive.demon.co.uk.

Description

We offer:

The SLS 1.04 distribution on diskettes. twenty-five 3½" or thirty 5¼" diskettes including 0.99.13 kernel, X11R5, TEX, doc(WYSIWYG), GNU software development tools and more.

The SLS 1.04 Linux Distribution on CD-ROM: 0.99.13 kernel, X11R5, TEX, Andrew, GNU software development tools. May be installed and optionally run from CD-ROM mounted remotely. Many installation and operational options.

The Yggdrasil LGX Fall 1993 Linux distribution on CD-ROM: 0.99.13 kernel, X11R5, TEX, Andrew 5.1, Postgres 4.1, GNU software development tools.

Availability

Takelap Systems Ltd.,
The Reddings,
Court Robin Lane,

Llangwm,
Usk,
Gwent,
NP5 1ET United Kingdom,

Tel: +44 (0)291 650357
Fax: +44 (0)291 650500
E-mail: info@ddrive.demon.co.uk.

Ordering

SLS on diskettes costs £42 plus £1.50 p&p plus VAT.
SLS CD-ROM costs £66 plus £1.50 p&p plus VAT.
Yggdrasil LGX CD-ROM costs £40 plus £1.50 p&p plus VAT.

Visa and MasterCard accepted.

Miscellaneous

Free catalogue of CD-ROMs and books (mostly Unix related) on request.

Entry Last Modified

October 31, 1993.

Trans-Ameritech Linux plus BSD CD-ROM

Distributor

Trans-Ameritech Corporation.

Description

CD-ROM based on the Slackware distribution of Linux with all the sources, full un-compressed filesystem, and NetBSD source and binary distribution. The current release is "Spring 94." The two previous releases cover Linux from 0.99 p.9 on the SLS release to 0.99 p.14 and have FreeBSD and the original 386BSD.

The installation is highly automated by the Slackware scripts fine-tuned to this CD-ROM, but leaves a lot of room for customization. In addition to standard device drivers in the Linux kernel, BIOS-less aha1522 SCSI is supported (it covers Sound Blaster 16 SCSI , too). To minimize the possibility of hardware conflicts, many extra kernels are provided for different configurations. They are usable for installation and normal use.

Many on-line documents are provided for quick reference, including the Linux Documentation Project files in source, dvi and ps formats.

A lot of applications are included:

- The C/C++ compiler GNU GCC 2.5.8
- GNU and international versions of the `ispell` spell-checker
- The communications apps: `term` 1.1.4, mini com, Seyon (X-Window based)
- Editors: elvis (`vi` clone), joe, jove
- PostScript clone ghostscript 2.6.1
- Network package with news and e-mail
- TCP/IP (net2debugged), UUCP, SLIP, CSLIP
- Object oriented GNU Smalltalk 1.1.1, and the Smalltalk Interface to X(STIX).
- Tcl/Tk (Powerful scripting language with Motif-like X interface)
- SPICE for electric engineering
- Several window managers—`openwin`, `twm`, `gwm`, `fvwm`.
- Easy X-Window configuration with many real-life examples
- Many X applications
- Interview libraries, include files, and the docword processor and `idraw` drawing program
- Typesetting: TeX, LaTeX, `xdvi`, `dvips`, Metafont, `groff`
- Ingress and Postgress databases

- Multimedia: mpeg video and sound applications. Mosaic 2.2
  `xgopher.1.3.2, tracker, adagio04, speak-1.0`
- GIF pictures and sounds in various formats
- Andrew multimedia word processor with hyperlinks
- FlexFax send and receive fax on either class 1 or class 2 fax modems
- A lot more

To help the first time Linux user, many documentation files are provided that are readable from DOS even before installing Linux.

All the sources are available on the CD-ROM. The most often needed sources are uncompressed and can be used directly from CD-ROM.

An uncompressed Linux filesystem is available for reference and disk space conservation. You can run programs directly from CD-ROM! There is a large `info` directory for on line reference and many manual pages.

For hackers' reference, an uncompressed FreeBSD source tree is provided.

Availability and Ordering

You can order by e-mail, phone, or fax. If you prefer to send a check, our address is:

Trans-Ameritech Enterprises, Inc.
2342A Walsh Ave
Santa Clara, CA 95051 USA
Tel: (408)727-3883

Fax: (408)727-3882
E-mail: `Roman@Trans-Ameritech.com`

If you order with a credit card (Visa, MasterCard, American Express), please indicate the card number, expiration date, and your mailing address. The order will be processed and the CD shipped the same day.

The price for a single CD-ROM is $30 if you are an Internet user and found the information on the Net (you must have an e-mail address). Shipping and handling in the U.S. is $5; overseas is $8. COD is available in the U.S. for $4.50. California residents please add sales tax.

Annual subscriptions are available for $80 plus shipping and handling. There are four shipments in a subscription, so a subscription in the U.S. is: $80 + ($5 x 4) = $100; a subscription in Europe, Japan, etc. is: $80 + ($8 x 4) = $112.

Miscellaneous

We answer technical questions about our distribution by e-mail sent to roman@trans-ameritech.com within 24 hours! Trans-Ameritech is a well established, efficient organization. We guarantee timely printing and shipping of this product. If you have a 3½" boot floppy and have ftp access, please look on sun site.unc.edu in pub/Linux/distributions/TransAmer for a new boot floppy image with support for many CD-ROM drives.

Entry Last Modified

April 19, 1994.

Unifix Custom Linux CD-ROM Mastering

Distributor

Unifix Software GmbH, Braunschweig, Germany

Description

We use our own Linux-based premastering system to make custom CDs that include the customer's programs in addition to our Linux distribution. This enables our customers to sell their Unix-based applications together with the operating system tested and ready to run. Our CD recorder makes it possible to create prototypes and very small series at interesting prices.

Availability

For more information or prices, contact:

Unifix Software GmbH
Postfach 4918 D-38039
Braunschweig, Germany

Tel: +49 (0)531 515161
Fax: +49 (0)531 515162

UPython SLS and Slackware Diskette Labels

Distributor

UPython Computer and Network Services

Description

Labels for Softlanding and Slackware disks

Availability

The labels that we print for you are available in several formats at `sunsite.unc.edu:/pub/linux/distributions/SLSlabels`.

Ordering

For ordering information, send mail to `DGray@uh.edu`. Cost is $6.50 per set including domestic shipping. Overseas orders must send payment in U.S. funds and add $1 for shipping. Texas residents add 6% sales tax.

Entry Last Modified

November 11, 1993.

Wizvax Communications

Distributor

Richard Shetron, `multics@acm.rpi.edu` or `multics@wizvax.wizvax.com`, and Stephanie Gilgut, `stephie@acm.rpi.edu` or `stephie@wizvax.wizvax.com`.

Description

We sell modem and terminal cables for multi port serial boards, mainly the Boca Research BB2016, BB1008, BB1004, and IOAT66. We also sell multi port serial boards.

We can supply other products and services, so please ask. We are looking into writing drives for one or more of the intelligent serial boards—probably COMTROL first, and perhaps others.

Availability

Wizvax Communications\
1508 Tibbits Ave.
Troy, NY 12180 USA

Tel: (518) 271-6005 (9AM–9PM Monday-Saturday).
Fax: available soon
E-mail: orders@wizvax.wizvax.com (orders only, please)
catalog@wizvax.wizvax.com (automatic response robot)
multics@acm.rpi.edu or multics@wizvax.wizvax.com
stephie@acm.rpi.edu or stephie@wizvax.wizvax.com

Ordering

Send orders and requests for catalogs to the address above. Personal/company checks, U.S. Postal money orders, money orders, and bank checks accepted. Orders will not be sent until payment clears. Inquire about purchase orders.

Miscellaneous

wizvax.wizvax.com does a nightly uucp mail exchange.

APPENDIX

C

ftp Tutorial and Site List

C

ftp ("File Transfer Protocol") is the set of programs that are used for transferring files between systems on the Internet. Most Unix, VMS, and MS-DOS systems on the Internet have a program called `ftp`, which you use to transfer these files, and if you have Internet access, the best way to download the Linux software is by using `ftp`. This appendix covers basic `ftp` usage—of course, there are many more functions and uses of `ftp` than are given here.

At the end of this appendix there is a listing of ftp sites where Linux software can be found. Also, if you don't have direct Internet access but are able to exchange electronic mail with the Internet, information on using the `ftpmail` service is included below.

If you're using an MS-DOS, Unix, or VMS system to download files from the Internet, then `ftp` is a command-driven program. However, there are other implementations of `ftp` out there, such as the Macintosh version (called `Fetch`) that has a nice menu-driven interface, and is quite self-explanatory. Even if you're not using the command-driven version of `ftp`, the information given here should help.

`ftp` can be used to both upload (send) or download (receive) files from other Internet sites. In most situations, you're going to be downloading software. On the Internet, there are a large number of publicly-available *ftp archive sites*, which are machines that allow anyone to `ftp` to them and download free software. One such archive site is `sunsite.unc.edu`, which has a lot of Sun Microsystems software, and acts as one of the main Linux sites. In addition, ftp archive sites *mirror* software to each other—that is, software uploaded to one site will be automatically copied over to a number of other sites. So don't be surprised if you see the exact same files on many different archive sites.

Starting ftp

Note that in the example "screens" printed below I'm showing only the most important information, and what you see may differ. Also, commands in *italic* represent commands that you type; everything else is screen output.

To start `ftp` and connect to a site, simply use the command

```
ftp <hostname>
```

where *<hostname>* is the name of the site you are connecting to. For example, to connect to the mythical site `shoop.vpizza.com` we can use the command

```
ftp shoop.vpizza.com
```

Logging In

When `ftp` starts up we should see something like

```
Connected to shoop.vpizza.com.
220 Shoop.vpizza.com ftpD ready at 15 Dec 1992 08:20:42 EDT
Name (shoop.vpizza.com:mdw):
```

Here, `ftp` is asking us to give the username that we want to login as on `shoop.vpizza.com`. The default here is `mdw`, which is my username on the system I'm using `ftp` from. Since we don't have an account on `shoop.vpizza.com`, we can't login as ourselves. Instead, to access publicly-available software on an `ftp` site you login as `anonymous`, and give your Internet e-mail address (if you have one) as the password. So, we would type

```
Name (shoop.vpizza.com:mdw): anonymous
331-Guest login ok, send e-mail address as password.
Password: mdw@sunsite.unc.edu
230- Welcome to shoop.vpizza.com.
230- Virtual Pizza Delivery[tm]: Download pizza in 30 cycles or less
230- or you get it FREE!
ftp>
```

Of course, you should give your e-mail address instead of mine, and it won't echo to the screen as you're typing it (since it's technically a "password"). `ftp` should allow us to login and we'll be ready to download software.

Poking Around

Okay, we're in. `ftp>` is our prompt, and the `ftp` program is waiting for commands. There are a few basic commands you need to know about. First, the commands ls *<file>*

and

dir *<file>*

both give file listings (where *<file>* is an optional argument specifying a particular filename to list). The difference is that ls usually gives a short listing and dir gives a longer listing (that is, with more information on the sizes of the files, dates of modification, and so on).

The command

cd *<directory>*

will move to the given directory (just like the cd command on Unix or MS-DOS systems). You can use the command

cdup

to change to the parent directory (the directory above the current one).

The command

help *<command>*

will give help on the given ftp *<command>* (such as ls or cd). If no command is specified, ftp will list all of the available commands.

If we type dir at this point we'll see an initial directory listing of where we are.

```
ftp> dir
200 PORT command successful.
150 Opening ASCII mode data connection for /bin/ls.
total 1337


dr-xr-xr-x   2 root      wheel          512 Aug 13 13:55 bin
drwxr-xr-x   2 root      wheel          512 Aug 13 13:58 dev
drwxr-xr-x   2 root      wheel          512 Jan 25 17:35 etc
drwxr-xr-x  19 root      wheel         1024 Jan 27 21:39 pub
drwxrwx-wx   4 root      ftp-admi      1024 Feb  6 22:10 uploads
drwxr-xr-x   3 root      wheel          512 Mar 11 1992 usr

226 Transfer complete.
921 bytes received in 0.24 seconds (3.7 Kbytes/s)
ftp>
```

Each of these entries is a directory, not an individual file that we can download (specified by the d in the first column of the listing). On most ftp archive sites, the publicly available software is under the directory /pub, so let's go there.

```
ftp> cd pub
ftp> dir
200 PORT command successful.
150 ASCII data connection for /bin/ls (128.84.181.1,4525) (0 bytes).
total 846
```

```
-rw-r--r--   1 root       staff         1433 Jul 12 1988  README
-r--r--r--   1 3807       staff        15586 May 13 1991  US-DOMAIN.TXT.2
-rw-r--r--   1 539        staff        52664 Feb 20 1991  altenergy.avail
-r--r--r--   1 65534      65534        56456 Dec 17 1990  ataxx.tar.Z
-rw-r--r--   1 root       other      2013041 Jul  3 1991  gesyps.tar.Z
-rw-r--r--   1 432        staff        41831 Jan 30 1989  gnexe.arc
-rw-rw-rw-   1 615        staff        50315 Apr 16 1992  linpack.tar.Z
-r--r--r--   1 root       wheel        12168 Dec 25 1990  localtime.o
-rw-r--r--   1 root       staff         7035 Aug 27 1986  manualslist.tblms
drwxr-xr-x   2 2195       staff          512 Mar 10 00:48  mdw
-rw-r--r--   1 root       staff         5593 Jul 19 1988  t.out.h
```

```
226 ASCII Transfer complete.
2443 bytes received in 0.35 seconds (6.8 Kbytes/s)
ftp>
```

Here we can see a number of files, one of which is called README, that we should download (most ftp sites have a README file in the /pub directory).

Downloading Files

Before downloading files, there are a few things that you need to take care of.

- **Turn on hash mark printing**. *Hash marks* are printed to the screen as files are being transferred; they let you know how far along the transfer is, and that your connection hasn't hung up (so you don't sit for 20 minutes, thinking that you're still downloading a file). In general, a hash mark appears as a pound sign (#), and one is printed for every 1024 or 8192 bytes transferred, depending on your system.

To turn on hash mark printing, give the command `hash`.

```
ftp> hash
Hash mark printing on (8192 bytes/hash mark).
ftp>
```

- **Determine the type of file that you are downloading**. As far as `ftp` is concerned, files come in two flavors: *binary* and *text*. Most of the files that you'll be downloading are binary files: that is, programs, compressed files, archive files, and so on. However, many files (such as READMEs) are text files. Why does the file type matter? Only because on some systems (such as MS-DOS systems), certain characters in a text file, such as carriage returns, need to be converted so that the file will be readable. While transferring in binary mode, no conversion is done—the file is simply transferred byte after byte.

  The commands `bin` and `ascii` set the transfer mode to binary and text, respectively. *When in doubt, always use binary mode to transfer files.* If you try to transfer a binary file in text mode, you'll corrupt the file and it will be unusable. (This is one of the most common mistakes made when using `ftp`.) However, you can use text mode for plain text files (whose filenames often end in .txt). For our example, we're downloading the file README, which is most likely a text file, so we use the command

  ```
  ftp> ascii
  200 Type set to A.
  ftp>
  ```

- **Set your local directory**. Your *local directory* is the directory on your system where you want the downloaded files to end up. Whereas the `cd` command changes the remote directory (on the remote machine that you're ftping to), the `lcd` command changes the local directory. For example, to set the local directory to /home/db/mdw/tmp, use the command

  ```
  ftp> lcd /home/db/mdw/tmp
  Local directory now /home/db/mdw/tmp
  ftp>
  ```

Now you're ready to actually download the file. The command

```
get <remote-name> <local-name>
```

is used for this, where *<remote-name>* is the name of the file on the remote machine, and *<local-name>* is the name that you wish to give the file on your local machine. The *<local-name>* argument is optional; by default, the local filename is the same as the remote one. However, if for example you're downloading the file README, and you already have a README in your local directory, you'll want to give a different *<local-filename>* so that the first one isn't overwritten.

For our example, to download the file README, we simply use

```
ftp> get README
200 PORT command successful.
150 ASCII data connection for README (128.84.181.1,4527) (1433 bytes).
#
226 ASCII Transfer complete.
local: README remote: README
1493 bytes received in 0.03 seconds (49 Kbytes/s)
ftp>
```

Quitting ftp

To end your ftp session, simply use the command

```
quit
```

The command

```
close
```

can be used to close the connection with the current remote ftp site; the open command can then be used to start a session with another site (without quitting the ftp program altogether).

```
ftp> close
221 Goodbye.
ftp> quit
```

Using ftpmail

ftpmail is a service that allows you to obtain files from ftp archive sites via Internet electronic mail. If you don't have direct Internet access, but are able to send mail to the Internet (from a service such as CompuServe, for example), ftpmail is a good way to get files from ftp archive sites. Unfortunately, ftpmail can be slow, especially when sending large jobs. Before attempting to download large amounts of software using ftpmail, be sure that your mail spool will be able to handle the incoming traffic. Many systems keep quotas on incoming electronic mail, and may delete your account if your mail exceeds this quota. Just use common sense.

sunsite.unc.edu, one of the major Linux ftp archive sites, is home to an ftpmail server. To use this service, send electronic mail to

ftpmail@sunsite.unc.edu

with a message body containing only the word:

help

This will send you back a list of ftpmail commands and a brief tutorial on using the system.

For example, to get a listing of Linux files found on sunsite.unc.edu, send mail to the above address containing the text

```
open sunsite.unc.edu
cd /pub/Linux
dir
quit
```

You may use the ftpmail service to connect to any ftp archive site; you are not limited to sunsite.unc.edu. The next section lists a number of Linux ftp archives.

Linux ftp Site List

Table C.1 is a listing of the most well-known ftp archive sites that carry the Linux software. Keep in mind that many other sites mirror these, and you'll more than likely run into Linux on a number of sites not on this list.

TABLE C.1: Linux ftp Sites

Site Name	IP Address	Directory
tsx-11.mit.edu	18.172.1.2	/pub/linux
sunsite.unc.edu	152.2.22.81	/pub/Linux
nic.funet.fi	128.214.6.100	/pub/OS/Linux
ftp.mcc.ac.uk	130.88.200.7	/pub/linux
fgb1.fgb.mw.tu-muenchen.de	129.187.200.1	/pub/linux
ftp.informatik.tu-muenchen.de	131.159.0.110	/pub/Linux
ftp.dfv.rwth-aachen.de	137.226.4.105	/pub/linux
ftp.informatik.rwth-aachen.de	137.226.112.172	/pub/Linux
ftp.ibp.fr	132.227.60.2	/pub/linux
kirk.bu.oz.au	131.244.1.1	/pub/OS/Linux
ftp.uu.net	137.39.1.9	/systems/unix/linux
wuarchive.wustl.edu	128.252.135.4	/systems/linux
ftp.win.tue.nl	131.155.70.100	/pub/linux
ftp.stack.urc.tue.nl	131.155.2.71	/pub/linux
ftp.ibr.cs.tu-bs.de	134.169.34.15	/pub/os/linux
ftp.denet.dk	129.142.6.74	/pub/OS/linux

`tsx-11.mit.edu`, `sunsite.unc.edu`, and `nic.funet.fi` are the "home sites" for Linux software, where most of the new software is uploaded. Most of the other sites on the list mirror some combination of these three. To reduce network traffic, choose a site that is geographically closest to you.

APPENDIX

D

Linux BBS List

The following is a list of bulletin board systems (BBSs) that carry Linux software. Zane Healy, `healyzh@holonet.net`, maintains this list. If you know of or run a BBS that provides Linux software and isn't on this list, you should get in touch with him.

The Linux community is no longer an Internet-only society. In fact, it is now estimated that the majority of Linux users don't have Internet access. Therefore, it is especially important that BBSs continue to provide Linux and support to users worldwide.

United States

Citrus Grove Public Access, (916) 381-5822. ZyXEL 16.8/14.4k Sacramento, CA. Internet: `citrus.sac.ca.us`.

Higher Powered BBS, (408) 737-7040. CA. RIME ->HIGHER.

hip-hop, (408) 773-0768. 19.2k Sunnyvale, CA. Usenet.

hip-hop, (408) 773-0768. 38.4k Sunnyvale, CA.

Unix Online, (707) 765-4631. 9600 Petaluma, CA. Usenet.

The Outer Rim, (805) 252-6342. Santa Clarita, CA.

Programmer's Exchange, (818) 444-3507. El Monte, CA. Fidonet.

Programmer's Exchange, (818) 579-9711. El Monte, CA.

Micro Oasis, (510) 895-5985. 14.4k San Leandro, CA.

Test Engineering, (916) 928-0504. Sacramento, CA.

Slut Club, (813) 975-2603. USR/DS 16.8k HST/14.4k Tampa, FL. Fidonet 1:377/42.

Lost City Atlantis, (904) 727-9334. 14.4k Jacksonville, FL. FidoNet.

Acquired Knowledge, (305) 720-3669. 14.4k v.32bis Ft. Lauderdale, FL. Internet, UUCP.

The Computer Mechanic, (813) 544-9345. 14.4k v.32bis St. Petersburg, FL. Fidonet, Sailnet, MXBB Snet.

AVSync, (404) 320-6202. Atlanta, GA.

Information Overload, (404) 471-1549. 19.2k ZyXEL Atlanta, GA. Fidonet 1:133/308.

Atlanta Radio Club, (404) 850-0546. 9600 Atlanta, GA.

Rebel BBS, (208) 887-3937. 9600 Boise, ID.

Rocky Mountain HUB, (208) 232-3405. 38.4k Pocatello, ID. Fionet, SLNet, CinemaNet.

EchoMania, (618) 233-1659. 14.4k HST Belleville, IL. Fidonet 1:2250/1, f'req LINUX.

UNIX USER, (708) 879-8633. 14.4k Batavia, IL. Usenet, Internet mail.

PBS BBS, (309) 663-7675. 2400 Bloomington, IL.

Third World, (217) 356-9512. 9600 v.32bis IL.

Digital Underground, (812) 941-9427. 14.4k v.32bis IN. Usenet.

The OA Southern Star, (504) 885-5928. New Orleans, LA. Fidonet 1:396/1.

Channel One, (617) 354-8873. Boston, MA. RIME ->CHANNEL.

VWIS Linux Support BBS, (508) 793-1570. 9600 Worcester, MA.

WayStar BBS, (508) 481-7147. 14.4k V.32bis USR/HST Marlborough, MA. Fidonet 1:333/14.

WayStar BBS, (508) 481-7293. 14.4k v.32bis USR/HST Marlborough, MA. Fidonet 1:333/15.

WayStar BBS, (508) 480-8371. 9600 v.32bis or 14.4k USR/HST Marlborough, MA. Fidonet 1:333/16.

Programmer's Center, (301) 596-1180. 9600 Columbia, MD. RIME.

Brodmann's Place, (301) 843-5732. 14.4k Waldorf, MD. RIME ->BROD MANN, Fidonet.

Main Frame, (301) 654-2554. 9600 Gaithersburg, MD. RIME ->MAINFRAME.

1 Zero Cybernet BBS, (301) 589-4064. MD.

WaterDeep BBS, (410) 614-2190. 9600 v.32bis Baltimore, MD.

Harbor Heights BBS, (207) 663-0391. 14.4k Boothbay Harbor, ME.

Part-Time BBS, (612) 544-5552. 14.4k v.32bis Plymouth, MN.

The Sole Survivor, (314) 846-2702. 14.4k v.32bis St. Louis, MO. WWIVnet, WWIVlink, etc.

MAC's Place, (919) 891-1111. 16.8k, DS modem Dunn, NC. RIME ->MAC.

Digital Designs, (919) 423-4216. 14.4k, 2400 Hope Mills, NC.

Flite Line, (402) 421-2434. Lincoln, NE. RIME ->FLITE, DS modem.

Legend, (402) 438-2433. Lincoln, NE. DS modem.

MegaByte Mansion, (402) 551-8681. 14.4k v.32bis Omaha, NE.

Mycroft QNX, (201) 858-3429. 14.4k NJ.

Steve Leon's, (201) 886-8041. 14.4k Cliffside Park, NJ.

Dwight-Englewood BBS, (201) 569-3543. 9600 v.42bis Englewood, NJ. Usenet.

The Laboratory, (212) 927-4980. 16.8k HST, 14.4k v.32bis NY. FidoNet 1:278/707.

Valhalla, (516) 321-6819. 14.4k HST v.32bis Babylon, NY. Fidonet (1:107/255), Usenet (`die.linet.org`).

Intermittent Connection, (503) 344-9838. 14.4k HST v.32bis Eugene, OR. 1:152/35.

Horizon Systems, (216) 899-1086. USR v.32bis Westlake, OH.

Horizon Systems, (216) 899-1293. 2400 Westlake, OH.

Centre Programmers Unit, (814) 353-0566. 14.4k v.32bis/HST Bellefonte, PA.

Allentown Technical, (215) 432-5699. 9600 v.32bis/v.42bis Allentown, PA. WWIVNet 2578.

Tactical-Operations, (814) 861-7637. 14.4k v.32bis/v.42bis State College, PA. Fidonet 1:129/226, `tac ops.UUCP`.

North Shore BBS, (713) 251-9757. Houston, TX.

The Annex, (512) 575-1188. 9600 Houston, TX. Fidonet 1:3802/217.

The Annex, (512) 575-0667. 2400 TX. Fidonet 1:3802/216.

Walt Fairs, (713) 947-9866. Houston, TX. FidoNet 1:106/18.

CyberVille, (817) 249-6261. 9600 TX. FidoNet 1:130/78.

splat-ooh, (512) 578-2720. 14.4k Victoria, TX.

splat-ooh, (512) 578-5436. 14.4k Victoria, TX.

alaree, (512) 575-5554. 14.4k Victoria, TX.

Ronin BBS, (214) 938-2840. 14.4k HST/DS Waxahachie (Dallas), TX. RIME, Intelec, Smartnet, etc.

VTBBS, (703) 231-7498. Blacksburg, VA.

MBT, (703) 953-0640. Blacksburg, VA.

NOVA, (703) 323-3321. 9600 Annandale, VA. Fidonet 1:109/305.

Rem-Jem, (703) 503-9410. 9600 Fairfax, VA.

Enlightend, (703) 370-9528. 14.4k Alexandria, VA. Fidonet 1:109/615.

My UnKnown BBS, (703) 690-0669. 14.4k v.32bis VA. Fidonet 1:109/370.

Georgia Peach BBS, (804) 727-0399. 14.4k Newport News, VA.

S'Qually Holler, (206) 235-0270. 14.4k USR D/S Renton, WA. FidoNet: 1:343/34, `squally.halcyon.com`, UUCP.

Top Hat BBS, (206) 244-9661. 14.4k WA. Fidonet 1:343/40.

victrola.sea.wa.us, (206) 838-7456. 19.2k Federal Way, WA. Usenet.

Outside of the United States

Galaktische Archive, 0043-2228303804. 16.8 ZYX Wien, Austria. Fidonet 2:310/77 (19:00-7:00).

Linux-Support-Oz, +61-2-418-8750. v.32bis 14.4k Sydney, NSW, Australia. Internet/Usenet, E-Mail/News.

500cc Formula 1 BBS, +61-2-550-4317. v.32bis Sydney, NSW, Australia.

Magic BBS, (403) 569-2882. 14.4k HST/Telebit/MNP Calgary, AB, Canada. Internet/Usenet.

Logical Solutions, (403) 299-9900 through 9911. 2400 AB, Canada.

Logical Solutions, (403) 299-9912, 299-9913. 14.4k Canada.

Logical Solutions, (403) 299-9914 through 9917. 16.8k v.32bis Canada.

V.A.L.I.S., (403) 478-1281. 14.4k v.32bis Edmonton, AB, Canada. Usenet.

The Windsor Download, (519)-973-9330. v.32bis 14.4 ON, Canada.

r-node, (416) 249-5366. 2400 Toronto, ON, Canada. Usenet.

Synapse, (819) 246-2344, (819) 561-5268. Gatineau, QC, Canada. RIME->SYN-APSE.

Radio Free Nyongwa, (514) 524-0829. v.32bis ZyXEL Montreal, QC, Canada. Usenet, Fidonet.

DataComm1, +49.531.132-16. 14.4 HST Braunschweig, NDS, Germany. Fido 2:240/550, LinuxNet.

DataComm2, +49.531.132-17. 14.4 HST Braunschweig, NDS, Germany. Fido 2:240/551, LinuxNet.

Linux Server /Braukmann, +49.441.592-963. 16.8 ZYX Oldenburg, NDS, Germany. Fido 2:241/2012, LinuxNet.

MM's Spielebox, +49.5323.3515. 14.4 ZYX Clausthal-Zfd., NDS, Germany. Fido 2:241/3420.

MM's Spielebox, +49.5323.3516. 16.8 ZYX Clausthal-Zfd., NDS, Germany. Fido 2:241/3421.

MM's Spielebox, +49.5323.3540. 9600 Clausthal-Zfd., NDS, Germany. Fido 2:241/3422.

Bit-Company/J. Bartz, +49.5323.2539. 16.8 ZYX MO Clausthal-Zfd., NDS, Germany. Fido 2:241/3430.

Fractal Zone BBS/Maass, +49.721.863-066. 16.8 ZYX Karlsruhe, BW, Germany. Fido 2:241/7462.

Hipposoft/M. Junius, +49.241.875-090. 14.4 HST Aachen, NRW, Germany. Fido 2:242/6, (4:30–7:00, 8:00–23:30).

UB-HOFF/A. Hoffmann, +49.203.584-155. 19.2 ZYX+ Duisburg, Germany. Fido 2:242/37.

FORMEL-Box, +49.4191.2846. 16.8 ZYX Kaltenkirchen, SHL, Germany. Fido 2:242/329, LinuxNet (6:00–20:00).

BOX/2, +49.89.601-96-77. 16.8 ZYX Muenchen, BAY, Germany. Fido 2:246/147, info magic: LINUX (22:00–24:00, 00:30–2:00, 5:00–8:00).

Die Box Passau 2+1, +49.851.555-96. 14.4 v.32b Passau, BAY, Germany. Fido 2:246/200 (8:00–3:30).

Die Box Passau Line 1, +49.851.753-789. 16.8 ZYX Passau, BAY, Germany. Fido 2:246/2000 (8:00–3:30).

Die Box Passau Line 3, +49.851.732-73. 14.4 HST Passau, BAY, Germany. Fido 2:246/202 (5:00–3:30).

Die Box Passau ISDN, +49.851.950-464. 38.4/64k V.110/X.75 Passau, BAY, Germany. Fido 2:246/201 (8:00–24:00, 1:00–3:30).

Public Domain Kiste, +49.30.686-62-50. 16.8 ZYX BLN, Germany. Fido 2:2403/17.

CS-Port/C. Schmidt, +49.30.491-34-18. 19.2 Z19 Berlin, BLN, Germany. Fido 2:2403/13.

BigBrother/R. Gmelch, +49.30.335-63-28. 16.8 Z16 Berlin, BLN, Germany. Fido 2:2403/36.4 (16:00–23:00).

CRYSTAL BBS, +49.7152.240-86. 14.4 HST Leonberg, BW, Germany. Fido 2:2407/3, LinuxNet.

Echoblaster BBS #1, +49.7142.213-92. HST/v.32b Bietigheim, BW, Germany. Fido 2:2407/4, LinuxNet (7:00–19:00, 23:00–1:00).

Echoblaster BBS #2, +49.7142.212-35. v.32b Bietigheim, BW, Germany. Fido 2:2407/40, LinuxNet (20:00–6:00).

LinuxServer/P. Berger, +49.711.756-275. 16.8 HST Stuttgart, BW, Germany. Fido 2:2407/34, LinuxNet (8:30–17:50, 19:00–2:00).

Rising Sun BBS, +49.7147.3845. 16.8 ZYX Sachsenheim, BW, Germany. Fido 2:2407/41, LinuxNet.(5:30–2:30).

bakunin.north.de, +49.421.870-532. 14.4 D 2800 Bremen, HB, Germany. `kraehe@bakunin.north.de`.

oytix.north.de, +49.421.396-57-62. ZYX HB, Germany. `mike@oytix.north.de`, login as `gast`.

Fiffis Inn BBS, +49-89-5701353. 14.4-19.2 Munich, Germany. FidoNet 2:246/69, Internet, Usenet, LinuxNet.

The Field of Inverse Chaos, +358 0 506 1836. 14.4k v.32bis/HST Helsinki, Finland. Usenet `ichaos.nullnet.fi`.

Modula BBS, +33-1 4043 0124. HST 14.4 v.32bis Paris, France.

Modula BBS, +33-1 4530 1248. HST 14.4 v.32bis Paris, France.

STDIN BBS, +33-72375139. v.32bis Lyon, Laurent Cas, France. FidoNet 2:323/8.

Le Lien, +33-72089879. HST 14.4/v.32bis Lyon, Pascal Valette, France. FidoNet 2:323/5.

Basil, +33-1-44670844. v.32bis Paris, Laurent Chemla, France.

Cafard Naum, +33-51701632. v.32bis Nantes, Yann Dupont, France.

DUBBS, +353-1-6789000. 19.2 ZyXEL Dublin, Ireland. Fidonet 2:263/167.

Galway Online, +353-91-27454. 14.4k v.32b Galway, Ireland. RIME, `@iol.ie`.

Nemesis' Dungeon, +353-1-324755 or 326900. 14.4k v.32bis Dublin, Ireland. Fidonet 2:263/150.

nonsolosoftware, +39 51 6140772. v.32bis, v.42bis Italy. Fidonet 2:332/407.

nonsolosoftware, +39 51 432904. ZyXEL 19.2k Italy. Fidonet 2:332/417.

Advanced Systems, +64-9-379-3365. ZyXEL 16.8k Auckland, New Zealand. Singet, INTLnet, Fidonet.

Thunderball Cave, 472567018. Norway. RIME ->CAVE.

DownTown BBS Lelystad, +31-3200-48852. 14.4k Lelystad, Netherlands. Fido 2:512/155, UUCP.

MUGNET Intl-Cistron BBS, +31-1720-42580. 38.4k Alphen a/d Rijn, Netherlands. UUCP.

The Controversy, (65) 560-6040. 14.4k v.32bis/HST Singapore. Fidonet 6:600/201.

Pats System, +27-12-333-2049. 14.4k v.32bis/HST Pretoria, South Africa. Fidonet 5:71-1/36.

Gunship BBS, +46-31-693306. 14.4k HST DS Gothenburg, Sweden.

Baboon BBS, +41-62-511726. 19.2k Switzerland. Fido 2:301/580 and /581.

The Purple Tentacle, +44-734-590990. HST/v.32bis Reading, UK. Fidonet 2:252/305.

A6 BBS, +44-582-460273. 14.4k Herts, UK. Fidonet 2:440/111.

On the Beach, +444-273-600996. 14.4k/16.8k Brighton, UK. Fidonet 2:441/122.

APPENDIX

E

The GNU General Public License

Printed below is the GNU General Public License (the *GPL* or *copyleft*), under which Linux is licensed. It is reproduced here to clear up some of the confusion about Linux's copyright status—Linux is *not* shareware, and it is *not* in the public domain. The bulk of the Linux kernel is copyright ©1993 by Linus Torvalds, and other software and parts of the kernel are copyrighted by their authors. Thus, Linux *is* copyrighted, however, you may redistribute it under the terms of the GPL printed below.

GNU GENERAL PUBLIC LICENSE

Version 2, June 1991

Copyright ©1989, 1991 Free Software Foundation, Inc. 675 Mass Ave, Cambridge, MA 02139, U.S.A. Everyone is permitted to copy and distribute verbatim copies of this license document, but changing it is not allowed.

Preamble

The licenses for most software are designed to take away your freedom to share and change it. By contrast, the GNU General Public License is intended to guarantee your freedom to share and change free software—to make sure the software is free for all its users. This General Public License applies to most of the Free Software Foundation's software and to any other program whose authors commit to using it. (Some other Free Software Foundation software is covered by the GNU Library General Public License instead.) You can apply it to your programs, too.

When we speak of free software, we are referring to freedom, not price. Our General Public Licenses are designed to make sure that you have the freedom to distribute copies of free software (and charge for this service if you wish), that you receive source code or can get it if you want it, that you can change the software or use pieces of it in new free programs; and that you know you can do these things.

To protect your rights, we need to make restrictions that forbid anyone to deny you these rights or to ask you to surrender the rights. These restrictions translate to certain responsibilities for you if you distribute copies of the software, or if you modify it.

For example, if you distribute copies of such a program, whether gratis or for a fee, you must give the recipients all the rights that you have. You must make sure that they, too, receive or can get the source code. And you must show them these terms so they know their rights.

We protect your rights with two steps: (1) copyright the software, and (2) offer you this license which gives you legal permission to copy, distribute and/or modify the software.

Also, for each author's protection and ours, we want to make certain that everyone understands that there is no warranty for this free software. If the software is modified by someone else and passed on, we want its recipients to know that what they have is not the original, so that any problems introduced by others will not reflect on the original authors' reputations.

Finally, any free program is threatened constantly by software patents. We wish to avoid the danger that redistributors of a free program will individually obtain patent licenses, in effect making the program proprietary. To prevent this, we have made it clear that any patent must be licensed for everyone's free use or not licensed at all.

The precise terms and conditions for copying, distribution and modification follow.

Terms and Conditions for Copying, Distribution, and Modification

0. This License applies to any program or other work which contains a notice placed by the copyright holder saying it may be distributed under the terms of this General Public License. The "Program", below, refers to any such program or work, and a "work based on the Program" means either the Program or any derivative work under copyright law: that is to say, a work containing the Program or a portion of it, either verbatim or with modifications and/or translated into another language. (Hereinafter, translation is included without limitation in the term "modification".) Each licensee is addressed as "you".

    Activities other than copying, distribution and modification are not covered by this License; they are outside its scope. The act of running the Program is not restricted, and the output from the Program is covered only if its contents constitute a work based on the Program (independent of having been made by running the Program). Whether that is true depends on what the Program does.

1. You may copy and distribute verbatim copies of the Program's source code as you receive it, in any medium, provided that you conspicuously and appropriately publish on each copy an appropriate copyright notice and disclaimer of warranty; keep intact all the notices that refer to this License and to the absence of any warranty; and give any other recipients of the Program a copy of this License along with the Program.

   You may charge a fee for the physical act of transferring a copy, and you may at your option offer warranty protection in exchange for a fee.

2. You may modify your copy or copies of the Program or any portion of it, thus forming a work based on the Program, and copy and distribute such modifications or work under the terms of Section 1 above, provided that you also meet all of these conditions:

   a. You must cause the modified files to carry prominent notices stating that you changed the files and the date of any change.

   b. You must cause any work that you distribute or publish, that in whole or in part contains or is derived from the Program or any part thereof, to be licensed as a whole at no charge to all third parties under the terms of this License.

   c. If the modified program normally reads commands interactively when run, you must cause it, when started running for such interactive use in the most ordinary way, to print or display an announcement including an appropriate copyright notice and a notice that there is no warranty (or else, saying that you provide a warranty) and that users may redistribute the program under these conditions, and telling the user how to view a copy of this License. (Exception: if the Program itself is interactive but does not normally print such an announcement, your work based on the Program is not required to print an announcement.)

These requirements apply to the modified work as a whole. If identifiable sections of that work are not derived from the program, and can be reasonably considered independent and separate works in themselves, then this License, and its terms, do not apply to those sections when you distribute them as separate works. But when you distribute the same sections as part of a whole which is a work based on the Program, the distribution of the whole must be on the terms of this License, whose permissions for other licensees extend to the entire whole, and thus to each and every part regardless of who wrote it.

Thus, it is not the intent of this section to claim rights or contest your rights to work written entirely by you; rather, the intent is to exercise the right to control the distribution of derivative or collective works based on the Program.

In addition, mere aggregation of another work not based on the Program with the Program (or with a work based on the Program) on a volume of a storage or distribution medium does not bring the other work under the scope of this License.

3. You may copy and distribute the Program (or a work based on it, under Section 2) in object code or executable form under the terms of Sections 1 and 2 above provided that you also do one of the following:

   a. Accompany it with the complete corresponding machine-readable source code, which must be distributed under the terms of Sections 1 and 2 above on a medium customarily used for software interchange; or,

   b. Accompany it with a written offer, valid for at least three years, to give any third party, for a charge no more than your cost of physically performing source distribution, a complete machine-readable copy of the corresponding source code, to be distributed under the terms of Sections 1 and 2 above on a medium customarily used for software interchange; or,

   c. Accompany it with the information you received as to the offer to distribute corresponding source code. (This alter native is allowed only for noncommercial distribution and only if you received the program in object code or executable form with such an offer, in accord with Subsection b above.)

The source code for a work means the preferred form of the work for making modifications to it. For an executable work, complete source code means all the source code for all modules it contains, plus any associated interface definition files, plus the scripts used to control compilation and installation of the executable. However, as a special exception, the source code distributed need not include anything that is normally distributed (in either source or binary form) with the major components (compiler, kernel, and so on) of the operating system on which the executable runs, unless that component itself accompanies the executable.

If distribution of executable or object code is made by offering access to copy from a designated place, then offering equivalent access to copy the source code from the same place counts as distribution of the source code, even though third parties are not compelled to copy the source along with the object code.

4. You may not copy, modify, sublicense, or distribute the Program except as expressly provided under this License. Any attempt otherwise to copy, modify, sublicense or distribute the Program is void, and will automatically terminate your rights under this License. However, parties who have received copies, or rights, from you under this License will not have their licenses terminated so long as such parties remain in full compliance.

5. You are not required to accept this License, since you have not signed it. However, nothing else grants you permission to modify or distribute the Program or its derivative works. These actions are prohibited by law if you do not accept this License. Therefore, by modifying or distributing the Program (or any work based on the Program), you indicate your acceptance of this License to do so, and all its terms and conditions for copying, distributing or modifying the Program or works based on it.

6. Each time you redistribute the Program (or any work based on the Program), the recipient automatically receives a license from the original licensor to copy, distribute or modify the Program subject to these terms and conditions. You may not impose any further restrictions on the recipients' exercise of the rights granted herein. You are not responsible for enforcing compliance by third parties to this License.

7. If, as a consequence of a court judgment or allegation of patent infringement or for any other reason (not limited to patent issues), conditions are imposed on you (whether by court order, agreement or otherwise) that contradict the conditions of this License, they do not excuse you from the conditions of this License. If you cannot distribute so as to satisfy simultaneously your obligations under this License and any other pertinent obligations, then as a consequence you may not distribute the Program at all. For example, if a patent license would not permit royalty-free redistribution of the Program by all those who receive copies directly or indirectly through you, then the only way you could satisfy both it and this License would be to refrain entirely from distribution of the Program.

If any portion of this section is held invalid or unenforceable under any particular circumstance, the balance of the section is intended to apply and the section as a whole is intended to apply in other circumstances.

It is not the purpose of this section to induce you to infringe any patents or other property right claims or to contest validity of any such claims; this section has the sole purpose of protecting the integrity of the free software distribution system, which is implemented by public license practices. Many people have made generous contributions to the wide range of software distributed through that system in reliance on consistent application of that system; it is up to the author/donor to decide if he or she is willing to distribute software through any other system and a licensee cannot impose that choice.

This section is intended to make thoroughly clear what is believed to be a consequence of the rest of this License.

8. If the distribution and/or use of the Program is restricted in certain countries either by patents or by copyrighted interfaces, the original copyright holder who places the Program under this License may add an explicit geographical distribution limitation excluding those countries, so that distribution is permitted only in or among countries not thus excluded. In such case, this License incorporates the limitation as if written in the body of this License.

9. The Free Software Foundation may publish revised and/or new versions of the General Public License from time to time. Such new versions will be similar in spirit to the present version, but may differ in detail to address new problems or concerns.

Each version is given a distinguishing version number. If the Program specifies a version number of this License which applies to it and "any later version," you have the option of following the terms and conditions either of that version or of any later version published by the Free Software Foundation. If the Program does not specify a version number of this License, you may choose any version ever published by the Free Software Foundation.

10. If you wish to incorporate parts of the Program into other free programs whose distribution conditions are different, write to the author to ask for permission. For software which is copyrighted by the Free Software Foundation, write to the Free Software Foundation; we sometimes make exceptions for this. Our decision will be guided by the two goals of preserving the free status of all derivatives of our free software and of promoting the sharing and reuse of software generally.

NO WARRANTY

11. BECAUSE THE PROGRAM IS LICENSED FREE OF CHARGE, THERE IS NO WARRANTY FOR THE PROGRAM, TO THE EXTENT PERMITTED BY APPLICABLE LAW. EXCEPT WHEN OTHERWISE STATED IN WRITING THE COPYRIGHT HOLDERS AND/OR OTHER PARTIES PROVIDE THE PROGRAM "AS IS" WITHOUT WARRANTY OF ANY KIND, EITHER EXPRESSED OR IMPLIED, INCLUDING, BUT NOT LIMITED TO, THE IMPLIED WARRANTIES OF MERCHANTABILITY AND FITNESS FOR A PARTICULAR PURPOSE. THE ENTIRE RISK AS TO THE QUALITY AND PERFORMANCE OF THE PROGRAM IS WITH YOU. SHOULD THE PROGRAM PROVE DEFECTIVE, YOU ASSUME THE COST OF ALL NECESSARY SERVICING, REPAIR OR CORRECTION.

12. IN NO EVENT UNLESS REQUIRED BY APPLICABLE LAW OR AGREED TO IN WRITING WILL ANY COPYRIGHT HOLDER, OR ANY OTHER PARTY WHO MAY MODIFY AND/OR REDISTRIBUTE THE PROGRAM AS PERMITTED ABOVE, BE LIABLE TO YOU FOR DAMAGES, INCLUDING ANY GENERAL, SPECIAL, INCIDENTAL OR CONSEQUENTIAL DAMAGES ARISING OUT OF THE USE OR INABILITY TO USE THE PROGRAM (INCLUDING BUT NOT LIMITED TO LOSS OF DATA OR DATA BEING RENDERED INACCURATE OR LOSSES SUSTAINED BY YOU OR THIRD PARTIES OR A FAILURE OF THE PROGRAM TO OPERATE WITH ANY OTHER PROGRAMS), EVEN IF SUCH HOLDER OR OTHER PARTY HAS BEEN ADVISED OF THE POSSIBILITY OF SUCH DAMAGES.

END OF TERMS AND CONDITIONS

Appendix: How to Apply These Terms to Your New Programs

If you develop a new program, and you want it to be of the greatest possible use to the public, the best way to achieve this is to make it free software which everyone can redistribute and change under these terms.

To do so, attach the following notices to the program. It is safest to attach them to the start of each source file to most effectively convey the exclusion of warranty; and each file should have at least the "copyright" line and a pointer to where the full notice is found.

> *<one line to give the program's name and a brief idea of what it does.>* Copyright ©19yy *<name of author>*
>
> This program is free software; you can redistribute it and/or modify it under the terms of the GNU General Public License as published by the Free Software Foundation; either version 2 of the License, or (at your option) any later version.
>
> This program is distributed in the hope that it will be useful, but WITHOUT ANY WARRANTY; without even the implied warranty of MERCHANTABILITY or FITNESS FOR A PARTICULAR PURPOSE. See the GNU General Public License for more details.
>
> You should have received a copy of the GNU General Public License along with this program; if not, write to the Free Software Foundation, Inc., 675 Mass Ave, Cambridge, MA 02139, USA.

Also add information on how to contact you by electronic and paper mail.

If the program is interactive, make it output a short notice like this when it starts in an interactive mode:

> Gnomovision version 69, Copyright ©19yy name of author
>
> Gnomovision comes with ABSOLUTELY NO WARRANTY; for details type `show w`. This is free software, and you are welcome to redistribute it under certain conditions; type `show c` for details.

The hypothetical commands `show w` and `show c` should show the appropriate parts of the General Public License. Of course, the commands you use may be called something other than `show w` and `show c`; they could even be mouse-clicks or menu items—whatever suits your program.

You should also get your employer (if you work as a programmer) or your school, if any, to sign a "copyright disclaimer" for the program, if necessary. Here is a sample; alter the names:

> Yoyodyne, Inc., hereby disclaims all copyright interest in the program 'Gnomovision' (which makes passes at compilers) written by James Hacker.
>
> *<signature of Ty Coon>*, 1 April 1989 Ty Coon, President of Vice

This General Public License does not permit incorporating your program into proprietary programs. If your program is a subroutine library, you may consider it more useful to permit linking proprietary applications with the library. If this is what you want to do, use the GNU Library General Public License instead of this License.

INDEX

Note to the Reader: Throughout this index **boldfaced** pagenumbers indicate primary discussions of a topic. *Italicized* page numbers indicate illustrations.

M

FOR EVERY COMPUTER QUESTION,
THERE IS A SYBEX BOOK THAT HAS THE ANSWER

Each computer user learns in a different way. Some need thorough, methodical explanations, while others are too busy for details. At Sybex we bring nearly 20 years of experience to developing the book that's right for you. Whatever your needs, we can help you get the most from your software and hardware, at a pace that's comfortable for you.

We start beginners out right. You will learn by seeing and doing with our **Quick & Easy** series: friendly, colorful guidebooks with screen-by-screen illustrations. For hardware novices, the **Your First** series offers valuable purchasing advice and installation support.

Often recognized for excellence in national book reviews, our **Mastering** titles are designed for the intermediate to advanced user, without leaving the beginner behind. A **Mastering** book provides the most detailed reference available. Add our pocket-sized **Instant Reference** titles for a complete guidance system. Programmers will find that the new **Developer's Handbook** series provides a more advanced perspective on developing innovative and original code.

With the breathtaking advances common in computing today comes an ever increasing demand to remain technologically up-to-date. In many of our books, we provide the added value of software, on disks or CDs. Sybex remains your source for information on software development, operating systems, networking, and every kind of desktop application. We even have books for kids. Sybex can help smooth your travels on the **Internet** and provide **Strategies and Secrets** to your favorite computer games.

As you read this book, take note of its quality. Sybex publishes books written by experts—authors chosen for their extensive topical knowledge. In fact, many are professionals working in the computer software field. In addition, each manuscript is thoroughly reviewed by our technical, editorial, and production personnel for accuracy and ease-of-use before you ever see it—our guarantee that you'll buy a quality Sybex book every time.

To manage your hardware headaches and optimize your software potential, ask for a Sybex book.

FOR MORE INFORMATION, PLEASE CONTACT:

Sybex Inc.
2021 Challenger Drive
Alameda, CA 94501
Tel: (510) 523-8233 • (800) 227-2346
Fax: (510) 523-2373

SYBEX

GET A FREE CATALOG JUST FOR EXPRESSING YOUR OPINION.

Help us improve our books and get a *FREE* full-color catalog in the bargain. Please complete this form, pull out this page and send it in today. The address is on the reverse side.

Name _____   Company _____

Address _____   City _____ State _____ Zip _____

Phone (___) _____

1. How would you rate the overall quality of this book?

❑ Excellent
❑ Very Good
❑ Good
❑ Fair
❑ Below Average
❑ Poor

2. What were the things you liked most about the book? (Check all that apply)

❑ Pace
❑ Format
❑ Writing Style
❑ Examples
❑ Table of Contents
❑ Index
❑ Price
❑ Illustrations
❑ Type Style
❑ Cover
❑ Depth of Coverage
❑ Fast Track Notes

3. What were the things you liked *least* about the book? (Check all that apply)

❑ Pace
❑ Format
❑ Writing Style
❑ Examples
❑ Table of Contents
❑ Index
❑ Price
❑ Illustrations
❑ Type Style
❑ Cover
❑ Depth of Coverage
❑ Fast Track Notes

4. Where did you buy this book?

❑ Bookstore chain
❑ Small independent bookstore
❑ Computer store
❑ Wholesale club
❑ College bookstore
❑ Technical bookstore
❑ Other _____

5. How did you decide to buy this particular book?

❑ Recommended by friend
❑ Recommended by store personnel
❑ Author's reputation
❑ Sybex's reputation
❑ Read book review in _____
❑ Other _____

6. How did you pay for this book?

❑ Used own funds
❑ Reimbursed by company
❑ Received book as a gift

7. What is your level of experience with the subject covered in this book?

❑ Beginner
❑ Intermediate
❑ Advanced

8. How long have you been using a computer?

years _____
months _____

9. Where do you most often use your computer?

❑ Home
❑ Work

❑ Both
❑ Other _____

10. What kind of computer equipment do you have? (Check all that apply)

❑ PC Compatible Desktop Computer
❑ PC Compatible Laptop Computer
❑ Apple/Mac Computer
❑ Apple/Mac Laptop Computer
❑ CD ROM
❑ Fax Modem
❑ Data Modem
❑ Scanner
❑ Sound Card
❑ Other _____

11. What other kinds of software packages do you ordinarily use?

❑ Accounting
❑ Databases
❑ Networks
❑ Apple/Mac
❑ Desktop Publishing
❑ Spreadsheets
❑ CAD
❑ Games
❑ Word Processing
❑ Communications
❑ Money Management
❑ Other _____

12. What operating systems do you ordinarily use?

❑ DOS
❑ OS/2
❑ Windows
❑ Apple/Mac
❑ Windows NT
❑ Other _____

13. On what computer-related subject(s) would you like to see more books?

_____

_____

_____

_____

14. Do you have any other comments about this book? (Please feel free to use a separate piece of paper if you need more room)

_____

_____

_____

_____

– – – – – – – – – – – PLEASE FOLD, SEAL, AND MAIL TO SYBEX – – – – – – – – – – –

SYBEX INC.
Department M
2021 Challenger Drive
Alameda, CA
94501